THE HYPOCRISY TRAP

The MIT Press's publishing mission benefits from the generosity of our donors, including Lindsay Androski.

THE HYPOCRISY TRAP

How Changing What We Criticize Can Improve Our Lives

MICHAEL HALLSWORTH

The MIT Press
Cambridge, Massachusetts
London, England

The MIT Press
Massachusetts Institute of Technology
77 Massachusetts Avenue, Cambridge, MA 02139
mitpress.mit.edu

The MIT Press would like to thank the anonymous peer reviewers who provided comments on drafts of this book. The generous work of academic experts is essential for establishing the authority and quality of our publications. We acknowledge with gratitude the contributions of these otherwise uncredited readers.

This book was set in Adobe Garamond Pro by New Best-set Typesetters Ltd. Printed and bound in the United States of America.

Library of Congress Cataloging-in-Publication Data is available.

ISBN: 978-0-262-05094-4

10 9 8 7 6 5 4 3 2 1

EU Authorised Representative: Easy Access System Europe, Mustamäe tee 50, 10621 Tallinn, Estonia | Email: gpsr.requests@easproject.com

To Alice

Contents

INTRODUCTION

New York, late December 2021. Plates piled up in the kitchen.

"Can we have dessert, Mummy?"

"No, Alice—we've had too many sweet things lately."

Our daughter retreats to her room. We clear up. She comes to the kitchen ten minutes later and . . . catches my wife eating Christmas pudding from the fridge.

Outrage. And then something clicks in her brain.

"You're like the prime minister having the party when he had told people not to have parties."

At seven years old, my daughter instantly saw the connection between my wife's pudding eating and the major scandal on our minds—when hypocrisy brought down the leader of the United Kingdom.

* * *

The Christmas sweater is lurid, as they all are, and the man who wears it is awkward. The video shows him dancing with a woman in a red dress; in the foreground, colleagues mingle, holding beers. It's a scene repeated at countless office parties around the country.

But not when the video was shot. The country was in lockdown, and parties were illegal. Normally this kind of video might have prompted a wry smile of recognition; instead, it triggered furious accusations of hypocrisy. You see, this was a party held by employees of the United Kingdom's governing Conservative Party, which had created the restrictions in the first place.

Their opponents seized gleefully on the obvious attack: they think "it's one rule for them and one rule for everyone else."[1]

This wasn't some second-tier scandal. The hypocrisy went right to the top. The man who addressed the nation and gravely urged them to follow the rules, the man who pushed a message of "tougher enforcement and BIGGER FINES," was breaking those rules himself.[2] Away from the cameras, Prime Minister Boris Johnson stood in front of a boozy gathering in Number 10 Downing Street, joking that it was "the most unsocially distanced party in the UK right now."[3] Johnson ended up getting one of the fines that he had pushed for.

When it came out that leaders had repeatedly broken the rules they set, the fury was unstoppable. People thought of the painful sacrifices they had made at the government's insistence: birthdays missed, loved ones dying alone, babies born with one parent banished. Queen Elizabeth had to sit alone at Prince Phillip's funeral; the night before, staff at Downing Street had been drinking until four in the morning.[4]

The scandal entered the history books as "Partygate." And within months of Partygate breaking, Johnson was gone as prime minister. Hypocrisy poisoned his relationship with the public. A big part of his appeal had been his readiness to break rules—but breaking his *own* rules finished him. As one journalist put it, "He is a magician whose trick won't work any more. The spell has been broken. Hypocrisy has broken it."[5]

How? Why did these lapses fuel such fury? For one thing, the people making the rules gave the impression that they kept to them. They got credit for consistency that they didn't deserve. Second, the public felt cheated by the injustice of paying a price that others didn't. And third, if those in power knew the rules, then they must have believed those rules simply didn't apply to them. The double standards reeked of contempt.

* * *

As Partygate shows, hypocrisy can rip away trust that may never be restored. Blatant double standards can drive divisions deep into society. And accusations of hypocrisy can leave people humiliated, even ruined.

Given what's at stake, it seems natural to seek out hypocrisy relentlessly and condemn it furiously. We see hypocrisy in others every day—it's intuitive, as my daughter showed. Not only does calling out hypocrites make us feel good, it also seems like a way of striking a blow against injustice and deception.

I get that. Calling out hypocrisy can motivate people to do the right thing; it promotes trust, reliability, and stability in society. But the problem is that we're taking our accusations too far—the cure becomes poisonous at too large a dose.

The truth, which we know at some level, is that societies work better if we can tolerate some forms of hypocrisy. Sometimes our hypocrisies are just an expression of our humanity, of flawed yet decent attempts to navigate a complex world. Sometimes they're the only way of coping with inescapable conflicts that would otherwise tear us apart. And often they allow the compromises that get us to a better place overall, even though we'd prefer not to admit that fact.

Instead, our drive to seek and destroy *all* hypocrisy has created a trap—and it's closing around us rapidly. There are two main ways that the trap works.

First, our drive to kill hypocrisy breeds more hypocrisy.

When calling out hypocrisy, at least part of our desire is to feel good about ourselves. The accusations make us feel superior, and that's satisfying. But often we *tell* ourselves—and others—that we are motivated purely by principles, by a quest to crush injustice.

In other words, a gap emerges between our pristine self-image and our mixed motives. We feel better about ourselves than we deserve to. We fall into a self-satisfied certainty that pushes for rigid, inhuman standards of consistency for others that we don't—and can't—live up to ourselves. Our criticism of hypocrisy bends back into hypocrisy itself.

You can see traces of this risk even in clearcut cases like Partygate. The people who gathered outside the house of Johnson's main adviser to shout "Hypocrite!" were not following social distancing rules themselves.[6] The leader of the opposition, Johnson's main accuser, found his own beer drinking under scrutiny.[7] While eight in ten people said that they were following COVID regulations "all" or "nearly all" of the time, only one in ten thought that *others* were.[8] It seems likely that they were being lenient when judging their own actions, but harsh when it came to others.

The other danger is that we exhaust the concept of hypocrisy by overusing accusations, so they start to lose their power.

When people see the label *hypocrisy* applied to the slightest inconsistencies, they start to think that it's just another term of abuse.[9] Accusations are no longer about uncovering truth and maintaining trust—they've become endless and therefore meaningless. And if we empty hypocrisy of meaning, we empty our principles of meaning as well. That takes us closer to a bleak and cynical world where no one cares about being called a hypocrite because they can get what they want regardless.

This is the hypocrisy trap. Taking accusations too far can actually create more hypocrisy—or exhaust the force of accusations altogether. Our desire to crush hypocrisy completely can only backfire.[10]

I'm not excusing or encouraging hypocrisy in general. Being consistent with our principles matters, and this book offers new ways of achieving that goal. But to avoid the trap, we also need to be more selective about what kinds of hypocrisy we go after. We need a guide for which kinds we target and which we tolerate (as hard as that can be). That way, we can suck the poisonous parts of hypocrisy out of our societies without making accusations toxic through overuse.

We need to act—we're not just dealing with some quirk of human nature. The hypocrisy trap threatens some of the things we care about most, including democracy itself.

* * *

People in the United States generally say they are strong supporters of democracy. A recent survey asked how much they support core democratic tenets like "All adult citizens enjoy the same legal and political rights." On a scale of 0 to 100, the average rating was 90. There was no difference between Democrats and Republicans. However, the survey also asked about support for antidemocratic practices—such as altering electoral districts or closing opposing media stations—*if they helped your party*. That change had an impact. People were more willing to weaken democracy if it helped their team and hurt the opposition.[11]

This tendency to vary your support for democracy based on whether your side benefits is called "democratic hypocrisy."[12] You might think it's just blatant bad faith, but it comes from the concern that *your opponents are hypocrites*. That's how people end up bending their stated principles and feeling OK about it. That's the trap at work.

Increasingly, people in the United States see their political opponents as a threat to democracy.[13] By 2020, Republicans thought that the average Republican valued the principles and practices of democracy *80–90 percent* more than the average Democrat; the reverse gap was nearly as high for Democrats.[14] This distrust means that when you hear members of the opposition praising democracy, you think they must have bad motivations behind their fine words. Their principles must be cover for maneuvers to crush their opponents.[15] In other words, you think they must be hypocrites.

The trap opens: if you think the other side are hypocrites, while you are the true defenders of democracy, then it's OK to use double standards to stop them. Indeed, the evidence shows that the people who most fear the opposition's intentions are the most willing to break democracy to "save" it.[16] It's a sad irony that the ones who praise democracy the loudest may also be the ones who undermine it the most.[17]

* * *

Our shared principles don't need to get crushed in the hypocrisy trap. Everyone will benefit if we can temper our drive to see hypocrisy everywhere and focus instead on punishing the worst cases.

For example, it turns out that people strongly overestimate how much their political opponents support antidemocratic practices. Their opponents are less hypocritical than they thought. If you tell each side that fact, they reduce their own support for those tactics in turn. They start to step back from the trap.[18] This book draws the latest insights from a new wave of research to show how we all can step back like this—and why we need to.

In part I, "Building the Trap," I show hypocrisy's unique power to enrage us. I explain how inconsistency is woven into society and uncover the surprising cases where we see hypocrisy as benign or even helpful. Then I show the effects of the hypocrisy trap. I create four model "worlds" where our criticisms of hypocrisy have shaped societies in completely different ways—some good and comfortable, some bleak and terrifying. They show us what to aim for and what to avoid.

In part II, "Understanding the Trap," I explore the science of how hypocrisy works; it's a much more widespread and fluid force than we've tended to realize. Hypocrisy is best understood as the process of judging that someone's inconsistency has brought them unjust benefits. Put more simply: it's the name we give to an inconsistency we dislike. This part of the book will help you see which kinds of hypocrisy really get to us, why the reasons for that hate lie deep in our evolutionary past, and how those old drives play out in fascinating ways in the modern world. It reveals

- why hypocrisy is more like being funny than being a spy;
- what Marge Simpson's views on art reveal about how we judge others;
- why when you don't practice what you preach, it matters which one came first;
- how hypocrisy is different from lying;
- why we think we're looking at our phones for good reasons, while other people are just being rude.

Part III, "Escaping the Trap," shows a way forward. I offer three main ways we can help our politics, businesses, and relationships. Some of these ways will feel counterintuitive, some controversial—but I hope to persuade you.

The first path is to use new ways of increasing our own consistency. They are practical fixes, such as redesigning our workplaces or changing how we make commitments. We can make ourselves more likely to stick to our claims and principles; we can reduce our hypocrisy.

The second path is to reduce the risk of *accusations*. Maybe the first route fails, and we can't find a way to be more consistent. In that case, we can still use our new insights to anticipate and avoid the things that will make people angry. Politicians can show how they are making reasonable compromises; companies can spark minimal irritation when discussing their good deeds. If accusations are out of control, we need at least some defensive options.

The third path is to change our views about hypocrisy. This is where I offer a guide for when to call out hypocrisy and when to tolerate it. I explain why we need to ease off on accusations where a person or company is genuinely aiming for something better but failing to live up to their goals. And why we need to let some harmless strutting go by, even if it makes us feel sick.

However, some kinds of hypocrisy *are* poisonous. I'll show how we can spot and target the ones that are heavy with injustice that causes us harm. I call out the particular danger of "double-standards hypocrisy": where we judge ourselves or members of groups we are in differently from others, while still paying lip service to the idea that everyone should be treated the same. Like the way politicians who thought COVID-19 restrictions were for other people, not them.

Double standards can become patterns of thought that self-reinforce and intensify. As they spread throughout society, they start to shut off the paths for tolerance and reconciliation. It is a short journey from denying common ground with another group to denying their humanity altogether.

You'll see that the societies I have in mind are Western democracies. That's deliberate. They prize the ideal of the individual, consistent self, placed on an equal footing with others under the rule of law, which means they are particularly bothered by hypocrisy. Other cultures are more accepting of the need to vary one's views from social context to social context. Maybe we shouldn't expect so much consistency from ourselves; maybe rethinking hypocrisy can also help us reassess our ideas of the self.

* * *

Writing a book about hypocrisy is risky. By seeming to judge others, you invite them to judge you. So I want to be clear: I'm hypocritical like everyone else. In 2022, I flew from New York to London around seven times. Doing that released twice the yearly carbon emissions of the average person in the United Kingdom and three times more than someone in Thailand.[19]

Yet I will easily judge parents at my daughter's school when they announce they are flying to a faraway location (and we're staying home). If people are discussing climate change, I will express concern and signal that I think we all need to take it seriously (in some way). I will try to feel better about myself by holding onto articles I've read saying that my neighborhood has some of the lowest emissions in the United States, while quietly shuffling my boarding passes into a memory hole.[20] These mental tactics show the various ways that we try to look and feel good despite our inconsistencies.

So this book certainly applies to me as well. But after recognizing that complete consistency is unrealistic, what matters is the reaction. How do we reject cynicism, hold onto ideals, and continue striving to narrow the gap between aspirations and reality? How do we avoid self-righteously setting others up for failure? And how can we do this while also nailing the hypocrisy that harms us all?

This book tries to solve these core questions by putting the latest psychological research alongside older insights from history, literature, and philosophy. I want us to move us beyond a simplistic idea of hypocrisy that traps us in spirals of outrage, no matter how good they feel in the moment.

I think we can do it. I think we can find better ways of navigating the messy realities of human nature and discover new spaces for better selves and societies to grow. I believe we can avoid the hypocrisy trap—if we start thinking differently.

I BUILDING THE TRAP: WHAT WE GET WRONG ABOUT HYPOCRISY AND WHY IT MATTERS

1 THE DRIVE TO CRITICIZE

WE HATE HYPOCRISY

Let's start with a test of your reactions:

> You *hypocrite.*

These words hit people hard. They sting. Your pulse may quicken on seeing them.

This aversion has deep roots. For many people, disgust of hypocrisy is part of the cultural fabric that weaves together their beliefs, judgments, and decisions. Religion provides an obvious starting point. In the Bible, Jesus rails repeatedly against the hypocritical Pharisees.[1] Dante's *Inferno* shows vividly what hypocrites' fate could be: they are banished to the second-lowest circle of hell, together with "everything that fits / The definition of sheer filth."[2] There they are forced to trudge around wearing cloaks that have dazzling gold on the outside but are lined with crushing lead within—making them as deceptive as their wearers.

Philosophers have also given hypocrisy a hard time, from Plato onward. His *Republic* defines the "perfectly unjust man" as someone who has "secured for himself the greatest reputation for justice . . . while committing the greatest wrongs."[3] The eighteenth-century philosopher Jean-Jacques Rousseau hated hypocrisy with an unnerving intensity, writing, "The vile and groveling soul of the hypocrite is like a corpse, without fire, or warmth, or vitality left. I appeal to experience. Great villains have been known to return into themselves, end their life wholesomely, and die saved. But no one has ever known a hypocrite becoming a good man."[4]

Surprisingly, modern philosophers are not much more restrained. Hannah Arendt admits that "only crime and the criminal, it is true, confront us with the perplexity of radical evil; but only the hypocrite is really rotten to the core." Judith Shklar thinks that we see hypocrisy as "the only unforgivable sin" remaining today, while others have concluded that hypocrisy undermines "the whole of morality" itself.[5]

Maybe they're exaggerating, but studies show that people are disgusted by hypocrisy and try to punish it severely. We want greater penalties for drunk driving or domestic assault if the culprit has advocated against those crimes in the past. We even judge hypocrites more harshly than liars. If I download music illegally after condemning others for doing so, you will see me as worse than if I'd simply lied and said I never download illegally.[6] In the words of Tennessee Williams, "The only thing worse than a liar is a liar that's also a hypocrite!"[7]

The slightest whiff of hypocrisy can harm your career prospects, potentially permanently. Imagine that you are hiring an assistant for a junior position. One of the three candidates has a better academic record and more relevant qualifications. He has work experience as an intern at a marketing firm, where he helped with a campaign to reduce underage drinking. However, he also has a citation for hitting a stop sign because he was texting while driving. Would this affect your judgment of him?

How about if, instead of careless driving, he had been caught drinking while underage? After all, he worked on a campaign against precisely this behavior . . .

When this question was tested, even the *suggestion* of hypocrisy meant people were less likely to hire the candidate, saw him as less moral and less competent, and offered a lower starting salary—compared to if his offense was unrelated to his internship.[8] That judgment was despite the internship being years in the past, at a junior level, and taken solely for work experience rather than from any antidrinking conviction. What made the difference was not the offense itself but the sense that the candidate had expressed a position on it beforehand.

Hypocrisy can also harm your business. In one instance, when people read about a company that polluted a lake with toxic waste, they recommended more damages and more jail time for executives if they thought the company had made insincere commitments about the environment. The perceived corporate hypocrisy made them angry and more willing to issue punishments.[9]

In politics, being exposed as a hypocrite can be a death blow. The decline of Boris Johnson after the lockdown parties is not an isolated case. Whether a politician survives a sex scandal or not depends a lot on how hypocritical they seem. For example, the Italian public largely tolerated Silvio Berlusconi's hedonism and womanizing because those behaviors were consistent with (and part of) his public image. Whatever you thought of his behavior, at least he wasn't a hypocrite.[10]

This example highlights that the hypocrisy involved is often seen as *worse* than the politician's scandalous behavior. In 1993, Prime Minister John Major of the United Kingdom launched a high-profile "Back to Basics" campaign to champion traditional values like "respect for the family." It later came out that Major had had a four-year affair with a colleague just a few years earlier. In response to that revelation, the *Daily Mirror* newspaper thundered, "The major scandal is hypocrisy." In its view, although politicians can't be expected to live blameless lives, "the one sin they need never be guilty of is hypocrisy—telling us how to lead our lives while doing the opposite themselves."[11]

WE SEE HYPOCRISY EVERYWHERE

Our hatred of hypocrisy seems almost compulsive—and slightly out of control. (Is hypocrisy really the "major scandal," more so than the deed itself?) It's no exaggeration to say that we see hypocrisy everywhere. We're finely tuned for seeking it out in everyday life, and our judgments form quickly and intuitively.[12] Giving any opinion, even a very tentative one, can put you at risk. Even if someone just says that they think eating meat *might* be wrong but aren't sure how they really feel, and then they later devour a burger, people still see this as "moderate" hypocrisy.[13]

You don't even need to have given an opinion yourself to be accused of hypocrisy. In 2019, an insurance company put out a warning about the risks of Britain leaving the European Union. But because one of the directors of the company was also in the UK government, which supported Brexit, this connection was enough to prompt a newspaper article all about his "astonishing hypocrisy."[14] In fact, you don't need to give an opinion *at all* to be seen as hypocritical. Others can see it in your actions. For example, nearly half of respondents in one study thought it was hypocritical for a man to rent an adult film and then, later the same day, help at a church bake sale.[15]

What if you actively refuse to give an opinion? People will still judge you. This is particularly likely if you are asked about an issue in front of people who you know have a strong stance on the topic. Say you are at a barbecue where the hosts and most of the guests have conservative views. If you're asked what you think about protests against the police, and you respond, "Truthfully, I'd rather not get into it right now," people will infer that you support the protestors—but are concealing that view by being noncommittal.[16]

To prove this point, people were shown a short video clip of AJ McLean from the Backstreet Boys being interviewed in an airport. He is asked what he and the band think about politics and responds, "We are neutral. I'm not taking either side. It's just uncomfortable." Study participants were told that the reporter was from either a conservative (right-wing) news channel or a liberal (left-wing) channel. Then they were asked what they thought AJ's real political views were. As you might have guessed, people thought that his real political beliefs were the opposite of whatever stance the channel took—and that he was just trying to conceal them by being evasive.[17] We don't like people who do this: we would rather someone express an opinion we don't like than strategically sidestep the question. It looks like they're trying to gain favor by not saying what they mean—it looks hypocritical.

It seems like there's no escape from the web of accusations. But why do we make them so often? Well, it *feels good.*

WE ENJOY TAKING DOWN HYPOCRITES

A hypocrite's downfall is something to be savored. In fact, it's one of the main triggers for schadenfreude—the enjoyment of other people's misfortune.

Experiments show that we feel more pleasure at a cheat being exposed if they had previously railed against cheating.[18] Exposing hypocrites elates us because it revokes what we think they take unjustly. A core driver of our anger at hypocrisy is the sense that someone is getting an *unjustified* benefit to their social status or their self-image. Exposure feels like revenge for this injustice, and it's satisfying for two main reasons.

First, there's the sense that the punishment is *deserved*—justice has been done, and the world is working as it should. When a person is condemned for the exact thing they condemned in others, it creates a kind of symmetry and balance that people find innately pleasant. We call it "poetic justice."[19] Judge, prosecutor, and defendant are all wrapped up together in one neat package.

Experiments reveal how much we enjoy this kind of poetic justice. In one study, researchers compared reactions to two students: one who simply belonged to the French club, and another who served on a "Student Court" that punished plagiarism and often moralized about it. Participants read about these students getting caught in wrongdoing—either plagiarizing or stealing. If people simply enjoyed seeing self-righteous individuals get caught doing anything wrong, both offenses should have provoked similar reactions toward the Student Court member. But that's not what happened. People felt much greater pleasure when the antiplagiarism crusader was caught plagiarizing than when they were caught stealing.[20] The match matters.

The glee we feel in these situations reveals something else: often, they're *funny* (for the observer). Stories about hypocrisy are structured like jokes: the preaching is the setup, while the revelation is the punchline.[21] Repetition, symmetry, and backfires make us laugh. Imagine if the Student Court student had written an article about plagiarism *that turned out to be plagiarized*. In fact, you don't have to imagine—this exact thing happened in 2015: an academic journal had to retract an antiplagiarism article because it had, yes, been copied from someone else's work.[22] In cases like this, it's hard not to laugh.

There may be another reason why we laugh. The "superiority theory of humor" argues that we laugh when we look down on someone else. The sixteenth-century political philosopher Thomas Hobbes said that laughter is caused by the "sudden glory" that we feel when we see the flaws of others.[23] This insight introduces the other main reason that the fall of hypocrites feels good: we gain when they lose.

We constantly scan our social environment to gauge where we stand in the pecking order. Our self-image emerges largely from comparisons with others—in judging others, we also judge ourselves.[24] Claims to social status by others make us feel inferior, spawning unpleasant, painful emotions like envy that can even harm our health. For example, meat eaters can feel inferior and resentful just by thinking about vegetarians because they suspect that members of that group look down on them.[25]

And then it all changes. The tables are turned, and painful envy is replaced by "sudden glory" instead. The person who had been on top tumbles down the social rankings, revealed as a hypocrite, and the inferior observers rise to become justified accusers. The social comparison now works in our favor; we feel good about ourselves.[26]

All this means that we have powerful incentives to search for hypocrisy: calling it out is a way we can gain status, relieve bad feelings, and punish perceived injustice. And if we cast our eyes around, we see plenty of material to work with.

HYPOCRISY IS WOVEN INTO SOCIETY

Inconsistency is a core building block of hypocrisy, so let's start there. One thing is clear: people's political views do not hang together in a completely consistent way. In fact, the political scientist Timothy Collins has used US national survey data to show that less than 1 percent of respondents had completely consistent political opinions. Conservatives say that government activity should be limited, except when it comes to spending on the military and restricting activities such as abortion. Liberals say the reverse: government should take an active role, except when it tries to limit things that they approve of. Hypocrisy like this is not a partisan issue. As Collins puts it, "Virtually every American, it turns out, has logically inconsistent, hypocritical attitudes. Virtually every American is a political hypocrite."[27]

What about inconsistency between words and deeds? One way this type of hypocrisy has been measured is by giving people the chance to express some principle (such as fairness) and then observing whether they also violate this principle with their actions (as in unfairly awarding themselves money). If they do, that can be evidence of hypocrisy.

Imagine being presented with two tasks, one far superior to the other: perhaps a chance to win money versus tedious chores. You are asked to allocate the tasks between yourself and an unseen partner, using whatever method you like—though you are given a coin to flip if you choose. You are then left alone to make your decision.

Around half the people in the study chose to use the coin to decide who got the better task. Those people rated the morality of their decision much higher than people who just decided who would get which task. But here's the interesting thing. Around 75–90 percent of those who flipped the coin still gave themselves the favorable task. Consistently, across studies, people who take the apparently fair option end up getting the better deal.[28]

So either the coin is very biased, or there's a substantial group of people who want to look and feel good—while still getting the goods. What makes this worse is that people who believe themselves to be particularly moral are more likely to use the coin (to appear good) but are just as likely to cheat when they use it.[29]

Can we use these studies as a measure of how much hypocrisy is "out there"? One of the biggest recent tests found that 62 percent of all participants in such studies chose to use a randomizer, yet gave themselves the better option anyway.[30] But there are reasons to be cautious about drawing wider conclusions from these results. People were doing stylized tasks that stripped away the real-world stakes that influence us so much.

Alternatively, we could ask people how much hypocrisy they think exists. In a survey I ran with 6,100 adults in the United Kingdom, around one in five people said that they had done or thought something hypocritical *in the past week*. Many critics who think deeply about the world also consider hypocrisy to be widespread. In 1764, the philosopher David Hume argued that "the common duties of society usually require [hypocrisy]," saying that it is "impossible to pass through the world" without it. Two hundred and fifty years later, David Runciman argued that hypocrisy is "more or less inevitable in most political settings, and in liberal democratic societies it is practically ubiquitous."[31]

Yet it's Sigmund Freud who offers the most haunting explanation for why hypocrisy may be woven into the very fabric of society. It comes in his essay "Thoughts for the Times on War and Death." Not a cheery title, but then it was written in response to the horrors of World War I. Looking at the sea of slaughter made Freud wonder how such violence could explode so quickly and how these impulses were contained in peacetime.

He starts by reflecting that human nature consists of "instinctual impulses" that fulfill certain needs. They may be cruel and violent ones that involve us taking what we want when we want it. But these impulses are "neither good or bad" *in themselves*—we just end up labeling them as such based on the needs and demands of society.

Civilization suppresses these instincts by instilling principles. We want to kill someone who humiliates us, but religious teaching or the fear of punishment holds us back. In Freud's view, society keeps tightening moral standards and taking us away from our primal impulses. But we can't suppress them entirely; they are ready to "break through to satisfaction at any suitable opportunity."

Society makes acting against our "true" impulses the price of harmony and (relative) safety. This is the hypocrisy at the core of civilization. Here's how Freud puts it all together: "Anyone thus compelled to act continually in accordance with precepts which are not the expression of his instinctual inclinations, is living, psychologically speaking, beyond his means, and may objectively be described as a hypocrite, whether he is clearly aware of the incongruity or not. It is undeniable that our contemporary civilization favors the production of this form of hypocrisy to an extraordinary extent. One might venture to say that it is built up on such hypocrisy."[32]

For Freud, war shows what happens if some of the checks on our instincts are removed. In this view, hypocrisy is not just a necessary by-product of civilization: it is what makes civilization possible in the first place. Maybe our drive to criticize hypocrisy comes from this very tension—we can't live with it, but we can't live without it.

If you accept the basic idea that some level of hypocrisy is endemic, then you may wonder if that level has changed over time. Maybe we're driven to see hypocrisy everywhere because there's more of it around?

This claim is certainly popular. Hypocrisy has been called "the central term of condemnation for our age."[33] Yet recent research has shown that we're prone to "illusions of decline": we tend to think that things have become worse over time even though they haven't.[34] So we need to tread carefully.

There do seem to be good data that social trust has declined in many Western countries. The US General Social Survey asks people whether "most people can be trusted or you can't be too careful when dealing with others." In 1973, 46 percent of respondents said that most people can be trusted; by 2018, only 32 percent did.[35]

Trust in most US institutions—from Congress to churches, from the presidency to public education—has also declined. Compared with the 1970s, people in the 2010s had lower confidence in fourteen institutions, higher confidence in one (the military), and similar levels for another (science).[36] In the European Union, many countries have seen a "dramatic drop" in citizens' trust of political institutions since 2009.[37]

Distrust breeds hypocrisy. If we are distrustful, we may fear or suspect that others intend to exploit us. We will feel justified in trying to protect our self-interest against the anticipated bad intentions of others. That justifying tendency means we judge our actions more leniently than those of others—we adopt hypocritical double standards.[38] Remember how fear that the other side will destroy democracy makes you feel OK about getting there first.

Experiments reveal how distrust drives hypocrisy. In one study, some participants were asked to write about a time in their life when they had *distrusted* a person; another group wrote about when they *trusted* someone. All participants then read about six everyday moral transgressions, such as keeping excess change from a grocery store, speeding on a quiet road, or keeping a found wallet.[39]

The twist was that some participants saw a version of the scenarios where *they* were doing the actions ("you think about keeping the wallet"), while some read about *others* doing them ("the person thinks about keeping the wallet"). They were then asked to rate how acceptable the actions were on a seven-point scale. Participants who had been asked to think about distrust rated the actions as less acceptable if they were done by someone else. Double standards emerged. But that was not true for people who had thought about trust—if anything, they excused others more than themselves.

Distrust can develop into a state of "victim sensitivity," where you are always on the lookout for being exploited. Being victim sensitive also means you adopt self-serving double standards.[40] So rising distrust may be making us chronically more sensitive to being exploited by others, which in turn makes us more hypocritical.

The picture painted so far is that we hate hypocrisy, we always want to punish it, and the tide may be rising. But, looking closer, this picture doesn't seem quite right: sometimes we aren't so bothered by hypocrisy. Understanding why will bring us one step closer to seeing its true impact.

THE HYPOCRITES WE LIKE

And no one's to blame
it's just hypocrisy.
—Portishead, "Elysium"

Sometimes accusations of hypocrisy fail to hit home: people don't seem too bothered by them.[41] Here are four cases that start to unpick the view that we simply hate hypocrisy and instead show that there's something else going on.

The Virtuous Hypocrite

Noel Biderman founded Ashley Madison, a website designed to enable affairs. What if he were faithful in his private life, despite publicly promoting infidelity? Such a scenario contains what many consider the main ingredients of hypocrisy: failing to practice privately what one preaches publicly.

A study tested whether people would agree.[42] It showed one group of people an article about Biderman that simply mentioned he had promoted adultery; a separate group saw the article with additional information that it had been discovered that Biderman was personally faithful in private.

As expected, this second group rated Biderman as much more hypocritical, but they *also* saw him in a much more positive and praiseworthy light. Discovering hypocrisy doesn't always move judgments in a negative direction. You can benefit from an action that creates hypocrisy if people think it is admirable on its own terms.

This may seem like a contrived example. Surely people go around concealing their vices, not their virtues? But, as I explain later, hypocrisy is not just about morality—it's about claims to self-image or status of various kinds. Say you build your personal or corporate brand as a freethinking maverick. If it turns out that you have always played by the rules, that will mark you as an inauthentic hypocrite who nonetheless does the right thing.

The Relatable Hypocrite

Not practicing what you preach may make that preaching more effective. For example, some doctors emphasize their commitment to exercising and being healthy. It turns out that doing this goes down badly with overweight people who are concerned about their weight. They are more likely to avoid fitness-focused doctors because they worry that such doctors will be disapproving and judgmental.[43] Sedentary doctors may be hypocrites, but that's OK if you think it makes them more relatable or insightful about the struggle to be healthy—or if your main fear is being looked down on.

It's unfortunate that overweight and obese doctors are the least likely to discuss weight loss with patients and feel less confident in doing so.[44] They may not realize that they can be the most effective advocates for those in greatest need. Instead, fear of appearing hypocritical may be holding them back. Important things are left unsaid.

This dislike of the virtuous reflects a tendency called "do-gooder derogation."[45] As I noted earlier, we can feel resentful when others get social credit, since their rise lowers our relative standing. If that person is then exposed as a hypocrite, our fury intensifies. Yet this same tendency can lead us to prefer fallible hypocrites over unyielding zealots—if they are upfront about their flaws.

Take climate activists. Imagine that you are talking to someone who claims that they are in the top 1 percent for efficiency of household energy consumption, doesn't eat meat or cheese, and avoids flying. How credible would you find them as an advocate for making changes in your own behavior?

It turns out that this person isn't more effective than someone whose energy consumption is only in the top 50 percent for efficiency, who has cut down but not stopped eating meat, and who just avoids flying whenever possible. In fact, the ultra-sustainable person is slightly *less* persuasive. They are seen as extreme and unrelatable, even though they are living up to their principles fully.[46]

The Principled Hypocrite

Big claims can bring benefits. Leaders who make moral arguments seem more authentic and inspire more commitment in their followers. Caring about issues makes you seem like you have integrity and can be trusted.[47] Do all these benefits just evaporate when hypocrisy comes to light?

New evidence suggests not. In fact, if someone states their principles strongly and then falls short, they may end up looking better than someone who gives more pragmatic messages from the start.

This finding emerges from a study where people were asked to judge a fictional politician from the party they supported. One group heard that he had taken a firm position that lying is never OK. The other group was told that he had stated a more flexible position that "it's sometimes OK to lie." Everyone then discovered that the politician had lied about the source of his campaign donations. When he had taken a strong stance on lying, he was (unsurprisingly) rated as more hypocritical. What's interesting, however, is that he was also seen as *more moral*—and people were more inclined to vote for him than his flexible incarnation![48] It seems that the benefits of having staked out a clear moral position were not completely lost when it was violated.

To be clear: the hypocritical politician did go down in people's estimation. There *was* a hypocrisy penalty. It's just that the pragmatic politician had already taken an even bigger hit by not committing to absolute moral principles upfront. People disliked someone saying "it's sometimes OK to lie" so much that even the exposure of the moral politician as a hypocrite didn't bring him down to the same level. What seems to be happening here is that people trust the person's original strong stance as a reliable signal that they will be honest in the future, even if their behavior doesn't show that. Even repeated lies don't seem to shift that perception. In contrast, a flexible stance seems to give the general impression that you are a slippery person.[49]

The Reasonable Hypocrite

Anyone who has run a business or a team will know the constant pressure to balance values, priorities, and commitments that conflict with each other. You may genuinely believe in a range of jostling principles; different parts of your life can bring varying demands.

Viewed this way, avoiding hypocrisy can be like asking us to be faithful to just one thing at the expense of all others. That expectation can seem unrealistic and unreasonable. Take the case of an ardent vegetarian who politely praises their grandmother's treasured meat stew when it appears in front of them. On the one hand, they believe in vegetarianism; on the other, they can't bear to insult and upset their grandmother. Only 30 percent of people think that this behavior is hypocritical, perhaps because they think the vegetarian has done the right thing.[50] We tell white lies all the time.

Indeed, making these trade-offs may be seen as the decent, human thing to do. The philosopher Peter Singer has been an advocate for acting according to rules that are counterintuitive and unemotional. For instance, he believed that euthanasia could be justified in some cases of dementia. Yet when his own mother became severely ill with Alzheimer's disease, he and his sister paid for a team of helpers to look after her at home. That decision seems more like a reason to praise Singer than to condemn him. As he said, "Perhaps it's more difficult than I thought before, because it's different when it's your mother."[51]

Given the shifting range of demands we face, what some people push as hypocrisy may start to look like a reasonable compromise. Many media stories consist solely of claims about someone's inconsistency, even if those claims are tenuous. An animal rights activist accepts a drug tested on animals to save her own life. A tech CEO strictly limits his children's access to the products he built. Working too hard to get outrage in this way may just lead people to shrug and think, "So what?"[52]

* * *

At this point, our judgments of hypocrisy may seem confusing or inconsistent. In fact, they're governed by a set of rules. I will explain them soon, but first we need to take these insights a final step. Not only do we decide if hypocrisy is acceptable, but we also decide if an inconsistency even counts as hypocrisy in the first place. That insight leads to the strange idea that accusations of hypocrisy are entangled with hypocrisy itself—and that's what creates the trap.

THE HYPOCRISY TRAP

> OK, let's save humanity, shall we? . . . Get me a chalkboard and a copy of Judith Shklar's *Ordinary Vices*. Oh, and maybe some warm pretzels.
> —Chidi Anagoyne, *The Good Place*, season 4, episode 10

The division seems simple enough. There are hypocrites, and there are those who criticize them. They seem to play distinct roles: one side does the bad thing, and the other one calls them out on it.

That's an illusion: the two sides are bound together. Hypocrisy and criticisms of hypocrisy are inextricably linked. Although they are different, they create and affect each other.

In fact, it's best to see hypocrisy as a process of judging. First, we notice inconsistency. Then we decide whether we think that inconsistency is hypocritical and how strongly we feel about it. We make that judgment based on the kind of inconsistency and how far someone benefited unjustly from it. In this view, *hypocrisy* is the name we give to an inconsistency that we dislike—because we think it's unjust. Hypocrisy always requires an audience, even if that audience is yourself.[53]

Here are some examples of how criticisms of hypocrisy are bound up with their target. Take social media. People can now capture their thoughts and actions as they happen and display them to countless others. In 2021, 1.9 billion people logged into Facebook daily. Five hundred hours of content are uploaded to YouTube every minute.[54] The digital traces of your views and behavior have exploded.

The very act of recording your life may increase the potential for inconsistency.[55] You may not have thought through your opinions beforehand, but they came out in a particular way at one time, and now they're public. You may have exaggerated your behavior or views for the camera for greater impact. The norms of social media may encourage you to create an idealized version of yourself for public display.[56]

But the other integral dynamic of social media is that they give people new platforms to create *accusations* of hypocrisy—to take these digital traces and try to ensure that they are noticed, exposed, and labeled as hypocrisy, to combine and interpret your climate handwringing on Facebook with your long-haul selfies on Instagram.[57] If those attempts succeed, then the amount of hypocrisy around seems to grow—simply because we see more of it. It's hard to separate out how much hypocrisy there "is" from how easily we can see it and name it.

Our ability and motivation to make the case for hypocrisy will vary from moment to moment. That means that inconsistency can sit benignly in the open until someone interprets and packages it as a case of outrageous hypocrisy.

Let's go back to Boris Johnson's lockdown parties. Partygate saw a furious investigation by the media and lawmakers into whether Downing Street had hosted birthday parties for staff during the lockdown. The search for evidence was intense. Had people gathered? How many? Had there been drinks? Had there been cake? The slightest clues were pounced on.[58]

Then someone noticed that a major newspaper article from June 2020 (the time in question) had opened like this: "Boris Johnson celebrated his 56th birthday yesterday with a small gathering in the cabinet room. Rishi Sunak, the chancellor, and a group of aides sang him Happy Birthday before they tucked into a Union Jack cake."[59]

The evidence that was so contested had been public at the time, but no one had noticed. No one had cried hypocrisy even though these actions were definitely against the rules in place at the time. Barely a murmur greeted the same facts that triggered an explosion the following year.

Why was there such intense interest and debate over the exact facts of the party? Because details like these weaken or strengthen the case for hypocrisy. If the gathering was truly an unplanned event, taking place as part of normal work activities, then it might be seen as not violating the rules. Johnson could claim there was no inconsistency, no hypocrisy. This is why his defenders claimed that he had been "ambushed with a cake" (instead of planning the party) or even tried to insist that there had been no cake at all.[60]

Understanding both hypocrisy and its criticism as part of the same process helps us make sense of some of the things we've seen. Hypocrisy is "everywhere" because we're driven to see it everywhere. We can always find enough inconsistency to work with.

I know this may seem strange. Surely some things are hypocrisy regardless of what we think? But taking this stance brings dangers. If you just focus on the hypocrisy you see and ignore your role in seeing it, you'll fall into the hypocrisy trap. We instead need to step back and see how that process of perception and judgment plays out.

This was the big insight of the philosopher Judith Shklar, whose book *Ordinary Vices* (1984) was seen as a blueprint for humanity by Chidi in *The Good Place*. Shklar's view was that "hypocrisy and antihypocrisy are joined to form a discrete system." The two sides engage so intensely because they are *similar*.[61]

What this means is that accusations of hypocrisy can be part of the problem rather than just being the solution. That's the hypocrisy trap: we risk creating more hypocrisy by calling it out.

Let's unpack this seemingly strange claim. People come along to tear down puffed-up, inauthentic hypocrites. They seem like the ones who have integrity, the guardians of the rules who stick to the principles. And they often feel that way about themselves: they believe they are acting for a justified, even noble cause.

Here's where the hypocrisy creeps back in. Even though the critics may claim or believe to be acting solely out of righteous anger, they may also be driven by the desire to feel good about themselves. They may seem to be humble people checking the claims of the powerful, but they are also motivated by a covert form of pride. They may be vain about their virtue, which they show off to their own internal audience.[62]

As Shklar puts it, this process can lead to "the spiraling escalation of hypocrisy, unwittingly set in motion by the very hatred of hypocrisy."[63] Accusations breed accusations, making us more willing to see hypocrisy everywhere—including in the people who seem to be against it. The result can be that the concept collapses, exhausted, and trust disintegrates.

So that's the problem. We are driven to criticize hypocrisy and seek it out everywhere. But our accusations don't just report on the hypocrisy we find: they decide what *is* "hypocrisy." We seem to intuit that some of those cases are actually benign. At the same time, those accusations can themselves produce more hypocrisy and, taken too far, create pervasive cynicism that stops societies from working.

You don't exit this trap by calling out more hypocrisy. Instead, you start by looking clearly at the harms and benefits that both hypocrisy and its critics produce.

2 THE REAL IMPACT OF HYPOCRISY

Mass extinction, darling, hypocrisy
These things are not good for me
—Nick Cave, "Abattoir Blues"

The impact of hypocrisy depends on if (and when) it is perceived, exposed, and criticized. Here's a simple example.

Suppose you say that hypocritical politicians harm society. Take the classic case of someone who preaches family values but has a secret affair. What if no one ever finds out? On the one hand, the preaching may inspire people and raise society. On the other hand, if the affair is revealed, it may breed cynicism and a loss of trust that harms society. Yet again, the politician may be emboldened by a successful deception to engage in other secret actions—maybe a bit of corruption as well.

Seeing the importance of criticism allows us to cut through our confusion about hypocrisy. The key insight is that *criticism of hypocrisy can produce good or bad outcomes by its presence or absence.*

We can use this insight to reveal how hypocrisy really works in society. The good or bad effects of hypocrisy are driven by how our criticisms work—or don't work. Sometimes it's the persecution of hypocrisy that can get out of hand and create a nightmare. Or the nightmare may come if accusations of hypocrisy have lost all power to influence people.

I have used this insight to create four distinct "worlds." These worlds show how the criticism of hypocrisy can drive us either toward societies that are stable and functioning or toward ones that are feverish and broken.

They act as models for evading the hypocrisy trap and warnings of what can happen if we get caught.

		Good outcomes	Bad outcomes
Criticism of hypocrisy drives outcomes	*Yes*	**Trust Machine** *People are kept in line by criticisms of hypocrisy.*	**Purity Regime** *Criticism of hypocrisy gets out of control.*
	No	**Everyday Compromises** *We learn to live productively with our inconsistencies.*	**Brazen Power Plays** *People openly serve their own interests if they have enough power to do so.*

In the trust machine, societies flourish by exposing and condemning hypocrisy. People see hypocrites being publicly castigated, and the threat of meeting the same fate motivates them to do the right thing. When we are shown that we are not living up to our ideals and commitments, we change our behavior accordingly. The result is trust, reliability, and stability in society. People know that others mean what they say and won't take advantage of them.

In the purity regime, the drive to tear down hypocrites has gone to an extreme. The critics of hypocrisy—let's call them *zealots*—feel good about themselves. They are acting for a just cause. Their inflexible, self-satisfied certainty licenses cruelty. If someone doesn't act completely in line with their own stated ideals, zealots will try to tear them down—even if that person is doing good overall. The result can be that people just don't bother with ideals out of fear of falling short. Or, if they must conform to ideals publicly, they are subjected to a relentless, endless hunt for any signs of hypocrisy.

In the world of everyday compromises, exposure of hypocrisy is met mostly with indifference or acceptance. It's a place of tolerance and understanding, where people have ruefully recognized their flaws and accepted them. The priorities are social cohesion, compromise, pragmatism, and peace. Hypocritical preaching is OK as long as it ends up having good consequences. Keeping up appearances is important in its own right because it sustains faith in the system and the good things that brings. Collective practices are prized over individual authenticity. The danger is that all this acceptance leads to complacency, cynicism, and the maintenance of power for its own sake.

In the world of brazen power plays, people do not fear being accused of hypocrisy. They feel free to exercise power to serve their interests without the dressings of principle. You can be blatantly inconsistent—as long as you are stronger than the people who want to enforce consistency. You can look them in the eye and dare them to do something about it. Power is the only currency. If you mention principles, it is with a sneer, mockery, or flagrant bad faith. This world is marked by deep cynicism about human behavior and motivations. There's no real point in calling people hypocrites because *of course* they are—that's part of the game.

None of these worlds really exists on its own; they are stylized visions of how things could be. But they show how the trap can make us fall from a world in which our criticisms are helpful into one where they are harmful. Criticizing hypocrisy can produce a functioning, trusting society (the trust machine). But if those criticisms go too far, they start creating an intolerant, rigid one (the purity regime). If people don't think hypocrisy is such a big deal, that can result in a tolerant place of pragmatism, where people accept that they are imperfect (the world of everyday compromises). But if this *lack* of criticism goes too far, it starts to create complacency and cynicism, and we enter the dark world of brazen power plays.

Our goal is to find the right criticisms—and the right amount—that allow us to stay in the stable space of the trust machine or everyday compromises. But first let's explore how these worlds differ. To make them real, I bring each one to life with a story.

THE TRUST MACHINE

> A certain degree of moral consistency is essential to a well-functioning society.
>
> —Daniel Effron and Beth Helgason, "Moral Inconsistency"

Samir put down his phone and looked at the wall. His lips still formed a smile, but his eyes had narrowed. Well. Mark Lillow. Why did someone run these risks? Mark Lillow, featured in *Forbes* as the face of a more enlightened corporate age. The CEO who highlighted his all-female board at every opportunity. Two million TED Talk views for his fiery plea that diversity is both good and good for business.

The same Mark Lillow who, he had just read, was a serial bully of women in the workplace, demeaning and undermining them from hiring to resignation. Dozens of people across the years, with NDAs ensuring silence. Until now.

Samir had never liked Lillow and had read the online reaction with relish. Echo chambers rang with the accusation of rank hypocrisy. Lillow had quickly been fired by the board and removed from charitable roles. But even this did not appease the anger at all that he had gained unjustly.

Rain came against the window.

A few years ago, Samir had signed a pledge that he wouldn't take part in all-male panels. The pledge was up on his personal website. It said he would turn down the offer and suggest someone else.

He'd kept to the pledge, even when it had hurt him professionally. But as he sat and thought of the vitriol thrown at Lillow, he began to wonder. Had holding to the pledge been more about fear of being called out than the strength of his belief?

He stood up and walked across the room, phone in hand. He needed to send this to Josh.

[Seen this?]

[. . . Yes.]

[You never can tell can you]

[. . . Said he was too good to be true]

[And he was posting stuff online]

[Not under his name obviously. about women—not nice things]

[. . . Unbelievable]

[. . . I mean, who acts that way]

Who acts that way? Josh sat staring at the words he had just typed. Him, five years ago. He had acted that way. Not the bullying or the unpleasantness, but the hypocrisy.

The startup had begun with big ambitions, like all the other ones. Josh had been clear and vocal. All interview slots filled by rating anonymized answers to standard questions. No résumés, no done deals. No more cementing privilege through winks and nods.

It worked; they grew. Businesses really did want an online platform to design and order sustainable packaging for their products. Success only strengthened Josh's rhetoric.

Then they needed a chief marketing officer to let Josh focus on the next stage of product development. It was a crucial hire, and he was nervous about letting go.

This was when Tony reemerged. He had been Josh's first boss, some fifteen years before. A text message, a drink, and Josh remembered that Tony had been inspirational. Someone who would make things happen. Someone looking for a new challenge.

It was not so difficult to spot Tony's answers and give them full marks. His interview was solid. But Angela Raihani blew them away with her mix of acumen and ambition. Josh felt bad for the work she'd put in.

Tony flopped in the role. Angela went on to take a middling mental health app to enormous success. The startup folded, but its hiring practices were lauded and copied by others. Josh got more recognition.

He thought of all the things he'd said in public. He remembered the look of bitter yet amused recognition on Angela's face. And, with a shudder, he thought of Mark Lillow's ruin. Now he would live up to his commitments, always.

The phone flew onto the sofa, and he went to get a drink.

Let me show you the workings of a machine, a machine that strongly shapes how we see hypocrisy—even if it never quite works the way we imagine.

The trust machine operates by exposing and condemning hypocrisy. In doing so, it helps societies flourish. The hypocrisy of the powerful is brought into the light; exposure forces them to stop their deceit. When others see hypocrites held up as an example, the threat of being treated the same way motivates them to behave consistently as well. Or it prompts them to reflect on whether they are living up to their principles.

Inside the trust machine, the traditional view of how hypocrisy should be handled rules. Hypocrites try to gain benefits unjustly, and so they should be exposed.[1] Hypocrisy can cover up horrible cruelty, and so it should be stopped.[2] If we know which companies have integrity, we can avoid exploitation and put our money toward principles we care about.

And what does the machine produce when it's working well? Trust, reliability, stability. We know that others mean what they say and won't take advantage of us.[3] We are always trying to work out what's going on with other people. Why did my business partner flinch in that meeting? Are they going to walk away, despite everything they've said? And, perhaps most obviously: Let me look at this politician. Is this someone whose words I can trust? Do I dare risk getting my hopes up again?

As the psychologist Jeff Stone told me, "We don't like inconsistent people because they're hard to predict."[4] That inconsistency can lead to spirals of distrust. But inside the trust machine, people have strong incentives to follow through on what they say and keep their claims and actions in line. They know that otherwise abuse may follow.

The benefits of the trust machine are clearest in politics—at least, in the politics of democracies. After all, the ideal is that politicians say what they believe, and we vote for them to turn those principles into action. Since we do not know them personally, we depend on being able to predict their future deeds from their words.[5] We need to know what we are voting for; enforced consistency can make that happen.

A free press is an important part of this process because it can expose political hypocrisy. People generally agree with this function when asked. A survey found that 40 percent of people thought that "exposure of corruption and hypocrisy" should get maximum media coverage, with 38 percent opting for quite a lot of coverage.[6] To put this in context, the figures were not much higher—42 percent (maximum) and 43 percent (a lot)—when considering how much coverage serious crimes should get.[7]

The trust machine also protects and maintains shared values. In this world, people basically agree and affirm what is right. That includes hypocrites, since they know what it means to look good—even if they don't follow through in practice. Exposing hypocrisy is like flushing impurities from our collective system and affirming what binds us together. If we don't do this, then hypocrites will exploit those values, sabotage the system, and erode our trust from within. That's why people have often seen hypocrisy as a parasite that grows fat by sucking out society's strength.[8]

In fact, calling out hypocrisy may not just be about protecting shared values—in a diverse society, it may *itself* become one of the few values that are shared. You can disagree over whether taking cocaine is right or wrong but agree on the fact that you shouldn't condemn it while being a user. Condemning hypocrisy may act as a common language for groups that otherwise talk past each other. It can be one of the few things that cut across communities and bind them together.[9] You can see this when a particularly hypocritical scandal unites the public in disgust.

The trust machine gets results in two main ways. The first is by making appeals for us to be consistent. Pope Francis made a very clear appeal like this just as the coronavirus was tearing across the globe. He said: "This coronavirus crisis is affecting us all, rich and poor alike, and putting a spotlight on hypocrisy. I am worried by the hypocrisy of certain political personalities who speak of facing up to the crisis, of the problem of hunger in the world, but who in the meantime manufacture weapons. This is a time to be converted from this kind of functional hypocrisy. It's a time for integrity. Either we are coherent with our beliefs or we lose everything."[10]

This kind of appeal starts with our good points—with the times when we try to do the right thing. For Pope Francis, the concern that leaders showed for the pandemic was praiseworthy. But he also wanted to use that concern to create wider change. Why don't they apply this concern elsewhere as well? What about their weapons, which could kill as many people as the pandemic?

This part of the trust machine is about making the case for a principled, coherent, and integrated approach to life as a means for improvement. In fact, the pope's message is similar to a known psychological technique for changing behavior—"induced hypocrisy."[11] Here's how it works.

First, you ask someone to advocate for a cause. This could be something like the need to take action to slow climate change, or a more general principle about treating others with respect. Perhaps they sign a petition or record a video message for use in a campaign. Then you get them to think of times when they didn't do what they just advocated for. Maybe they drive a fuel-inefficient car; maybe they were rude to a cashier while feeling stressed.

You're making people aware of a conflict between their beliefs and their behavior. Their self-image is threatened. We want to think that we are competent and consistent people who do the right thing. If we encounter a thought that conflicts with our positive self-image, this creates an unpleasant feeling.[12] We want to get rid of this painful "cognitive dissonance" quickly.[13]

And how do we do that? When induced hypocrisy works, we change our behavior to bring it in line with our beliefs and attitudes. We eliminate hypocrisy by living up to our principles.

Take cyberbullying—the sending of aggressive, harmful, or discomforting messages in online environments.[14] Misery and suicide can ensue. Most people are probably against cyberbullying in principle; others have done it themselves; many more have stood by and let it happen. Induced hypocrisy could work here.

To test this idea, people were shown an online campaign against cyberbullying, spread across three webpages. The first page talked about the consequences: "Cyberbullying leaves deep emotional scars on victims." The second page asked the viewers to engage: "Please leave some kind words for victims of cyberbullying." They were told that their messages would be used in a video clip to help victims feel better.[15]

Then came the test. Half the people also saw a third screen, where they were asked four questions: whether they had ever tried to help someone being bullied online; if they had paid attention to victims; if they had donated to victims; and if they had "stood by" victims. If someone answered "yes" to all of these, they were excluded—they were living up to their principles! For the other participants, these questions may have triggered unpleasant feelings of conflict.

The study then measured how strongly people said they supported the campaign and how much they were willing to donate to the campaign. The people who had seen the third "hypocrisy" screen were more likely to both support and donate to the campaign. In a follow-up study, the researchers isolated that much of this change happens because the hypocrisy screen makes people feel guilty.

Induced hypocrisy can bring many kinds of behavior into line with our principles: students buy more condoms after thinking they are hypocritical about safer sex; people use less household energy if told that their consumption conflicts with their responses to a recent survey. Children who draw a poster showing what "they would not do" in a playground change it to feature less risky activities after advocating for safe play.[16]

It's also what happens with Josh. His revulsion for Mark Lillow clashes with his realization that he denied Angela the job unjustly. The sense that he's a hypocrite like Mark stings and brings change.

But induced hypocrisy doesn't always work. You may relieve your discomfort in a different way. Rather than bringing your behavior into line with your beliefs, you may just adjust your beliefs. You may try to justify your existing behavior, downplay the evidence of inconsistency, decide you didn't really care about the issue anyway: "Maybe I've never helped a victim of cyberbullying because it's really not such a big deal!"[17]

Take the example of someone who is in favor of supporting homeless people but who walks past several homeless people in the street without helping them. They can use several tactics to deal with their discomfort. They can

- **Adjust.** "Actually, maybe I don't care so much about helping homeless people—or maybe I think you should only support them through official charities and nonprofits."
- **Minimize.** "I am basically a good person—just think of all the worthy things I've done. Not supporting homeless people is only a small thing when you put it in context."
- **Deny responsibility.** "I only had large notes on me, it was dark, and I didn't really see the person."

- **Justify.** "Actually, I remember reading an article that giving money to homeless people in the street is ineffective and maybe even harmful. Let's search online for some more stuff like that."[18]

All these ways of thinking reduce the tension and make us feel better. They can act like airbags that stop us from feeling any discomfort when our thoughts and perceptions crash into each other. This is why induced hypocrisy works best when the principle at stake is one strongly supported by society. When it's a principle that is widely reinforced—such as treating others with respect—it's harder to change your mind about it. Some core elements of your self-image may be at stake.[19] And so the trust machine operates well when it appeals to us to live up to shared goals.

As well as appeals, the other way that the trust machine works is through fear. Hypocrisy is a betrayal of the collective good, so it must be punished when it's revealed—otherwise, it's a signal that defecting pays off. People are kept in line by the threat of exposure, punishment, and public ridicule.[20] That's why Samir never dared to break his pledge about serving on all-male panels.

In the world of the trust machine, this threat would generally work. But what does it mean to say it "works"? After all, if people are just complying out of fear, they may be doing the right thing without truly believing in it. Most people would see that discrepancy as hypocrisy: their actions are deceiving people about their true motivations.[21]

But the trust machine has a clever solution.

Let's lay out the situation again: you do what society says is the right thing, while claiming that you're doing it for the right reasons, but in fact you're motivated by the desire to look good and the fear of disapproval.[22] So it's hypocrisy, just with a good outcome. That's why this setup has been called the "civilizing force of hypocrisy."[23] That's the situation Samir was in with his pledge.

Then things get interesting. Over time, you may start to believe the performance, the story you're telling others about your noble motives.[24] You forget that you were motivated by fear and begin to embrace the principle sincerely. As George Orwell puts it, "He wears a mask, and his face grows to fit it."[25] Imagine it's two years later, and Samir has found that stepping aside for others has actually been rewarding. His professional network has expanded; he has a new perspective on his work. He forgets that he was just trying to look good at the start.

This situation is the opposite of induced hypocrisy. Rather than believing something and not doing it, you're doing something but not believing in it. After all, there's pressure to comply. So, instead of changing your behavior, the easiest option may be to embrace the performance and bring your beliefs into line with your actions. It's a different way of making the unpleasant tension go away.[26]

The result is that the trust machine does kill hypocrisy, but not by making us step back and realize the error of our ways. Instead, it forces us to play a role hypocritically. Then, over time, we start to live that role for real.

Some people really don't like things working this way. They prize the idea of a true and authentic self. Playacting might be OK; we all must wear masks in society. But they think that the real danger comes when we forget it's a performance, when the role and the actor collapse into each other. The mask becomes all there is; the real self is lost.[27]

This danger really bothered the philosopher Hannah Arendt. In her view, "the hypocrite is too ambitious; not only does he want to appear virtuous before others, he wants to convince himself," which means he destroys his own integrity. That's why she thought hypocrites were "rotten to the core."[28]

She may have a point. But I think the trust machine raises a bigger moral question: What is it driving us toward? How do we judge what is the "right thing" or a "good" outcome? From Freud's perspective, what we see as "right" or "good" is whatever society decides—impulses aren't good or bad in themselves.

The issue is that societies vary in what they value. If you have a machine that is geared toward making people's behavior consistent with their society's principles, it isn't hard to see how this could have bad outcomes. We may think that people complying through fear of being exposed as hypocrites is OK if it means they stop being cruel or start being generous. But if you installed this trust machine in Nazi Germany, it would force people to comply with abhorrent ideals just to survive. Think of a Jewish person who must conceal their identity, and express antisemitic beliefs they do not hold, just to avoid persecution. This kind of situation has been called "victim hypocrisy," where hypocrisy emerges as a necessary response to an unjust, inescapable situation.[29] All the same elements of the trust machine are there—trust, predictability, shared values—but we see the outcomes very differently.

With this realization, we start to slip closer to our second world, in which the criticism of hypocrisy creates harm and suffering. Let's go there now.

THE PURITY REGIME

They are proud in humility, proud in that they are not proud . . . they brag inwardly, and feed themselves fat with a self-conceit of sanctity, which is no better than hypocrisy.
—Robert Burton, *The Anatomy of Melancholy*

"The meeting has begun."

They were crowded into Sonia's basement. The Group had no official leader, but they all knew who was in charge.

A few glances at Madeline, expecting her to continue, but she had paused. Why? Her eyes were wide, and one finger was tapping against an arm. Then, voice tight: "There's been an accusation. Someone has broken their word."

No movement. No noise except floorboards creaking overhead.

"This person has been talking to a member of the Other Group at school."

No one was quite sure how the two societies had come about. Probably just some small slight at first. But over time principles had bubbled up to fill the growing gap between the two, like lava cooling into new land.

Madeline was up and picking around the Group in the dust.

"You all know the rules. We have them for a reason. If you talk to the Others at school, we expel you from the Group."

What went unsaid: we don't just expel you. We can't talk to you anymore. We treat you like one of the Others.

She had stopped with her hand on a shoulder.

"You should know that, Grace."

Now there were sounds, feet moving. So this was happening. Grace was popular, helped people, made them feel good in all the ways that Madeline did not. They all knew that Grace's sister Zoe was a member of the Other Group, the only time that the groups had crossed family lines. And Zoe had been spinning out since their mother died, often publicly in the corridors. They knew all this and had understood that no one would mention the times that Grace had calmed her down. There were rules, but surely they weren't the only rules.

Ripples of unease. Maybe swells of discontent.

But Madeline hadn't finished. She waited for a beat: "You should know that better than anyone."

They saw what this meant as well. Last year Grace had whispered to Madeline that another girl, Jasmine, had broken the rules. Jasmine was expelled from the Group and ended up leaving for a different school. Although Madeline had been the face of condemnation, everyone knew where the accusation had come from.

The feeling in the basement shifted as people processed. Grace had denounced Jasmine for the same thing she'd just done. Grace's humanity versus the rules and the accusations.

Madeline needed only a couple of them to speak for others to follow. "Hypocrite." Maybe they felt bad, but why turn down the opportunity to look good in the Group? Grace was already out anyway. Later, when they saw Zoe, they tried to remember this line of thinking.

Madeline stood there, knowing that the power of the rules had never been greater.

Eyes full, Grace ran up the steps, out of the yard, down the street, and did not stop until she was looking straight at the river in the center of town. In the basement, Madeline sat under a circle of light, eyes still and unblinking as the room emptied behind her.

The purity regime is what happens when criticisms of hypocrisy get out of control and start creating harm. It's a cruel and constricted place. But its origins lie in the same good intentions as those in the trust machine. Jesus criticized the hypocrisy of the Pharisees to get people to focus on achieving virtue rather than just its appearance. Otherwise, sin just festers within us: "You are like whitewashed tombs, which look beautiful on the outside but on the inside are full of the bones of the dead and everything unclean. In the same way, on the outside you appear to people as righteous but on the inside you are full of hypocrisy and wickedness."[30]

In contrast to making a big show of piety, Jesus recommended the opposite. If you are doing good, don't let people know. When praying, for example, "do not be like the hypocrites, for they love to pray standing in the synagogues and on the street corners to be seen by others." Instead, go into your room; close the door; pray in private. Only God needs to see what you are doing, and he will reward you accordingly.[31]

Although this advice may seem to encourage integrity, it may lead to a hypocritical self-satisfaction that you are being better than others, which undermines the purpose of the act itself. You get a warm glow of superiority just as you think you're better than people who want that warm glow.

This risk is tough to avoid: we all need some kind of psychological reward. But if we are claiming to ourselves that we're above all that, we have fallen into the hypocrisy trap.[32] Here's a small instance where I did that.

About fifteen years ago, a lot of people would approach you on the street and ask for donations to charity. They were very persuasive. In fact, they often used induced hypocrisy as a ploy. They started out with a statement like, "Do you care about children?" And if you said, "Yes," then donating was pushed as the way to bring your behavior into line with your stated principles.

I used to end up paying money to causes that I didn't really care about supporting, just because it would have been awkward to walk away. Then I started to reflect. I wasn't giving money because I cared about the cause but rather because of social pressure.

Just like Samir in the earlier story, I was being a hypocrite by giving the impression that I donated because I cared about the cause, when in fact I was concerned only with how I looked.

Then I saw a way out of this hypocrisy. I knew about the principle that you should do things only because you think they are right—not because of other factors, such as social pressure or embarrassment. So I started responding to anyone's confident greeting with my own ready response: "I don't give money to charities when approached in the street because my principle is that I have to be sure that, on reflection, I really care about the cause."

On the face of it, I had brought everything into line: my beliefs, my public statement, and my public actions. I had thrown off the pretense and become authentic. I'd taken a stand against hypocrisy.

But here you can see the hypocrisy trap in action. I was now walking around feeling satisfied with myself because I felt that I was adhering consistently to a moral standard. I felt authentic and principled.

Of course, in reality I was covering up the fact that I was motivated mainly to avoid cost, delay, and discomfort. I had fallen into the covert form of pride I mentioned just now. Did I actually go home and research the causes that people mentioned to me, then make a donation if I agreed with them? Yes, sometimes that happened. But many times it didn't: my drive to be less hypocritical had just created a new form of hypocrisy.

Of course, you may not be having an internal dialog. In Jesus's terms, you may not be closing the door and praying on your own. You may be out there criticizing and crushing hypocrites publicly, like Madeleine does. The risks of becoming what you despise loom large here as well.

Suppose an online mob is currently piling on a footballer who joined a club in Saudi Arabia after strongly expressing support for LGBTQ+ rights.[33] Joining the mob is an easy way to look as if you care about the issue, even though maybe you never really thought about it much until now—and maybe you don't really care. You are making a deceptive claim to status, just like a hypocrite. Except in this case the status comes from criticizing hypocrisy. Think of the members of the Group who joined in criticizing Grace just to look good within the Group.

You may think the interplay between hypocrisy and critics of hypocrisy is interesting but hardly harmful. Let me explain how it leads to bad outcomes. Zealots want to smash inauthenticity and pretense and replace it with pure integrity and principle. This mission tends to breed an unquestioning belief in yourself and the purity of your motives. The result can be an inflexible lack of compromise, even fanaticism.

Imagine the principles of the trust machine—the need to root out hypocrisy to restore trust—taken to an extreme. That's the dream of some enemies of hypocrisy. When the zealot Jean-Jacques Rousseau was asked if he wanted all vice or bad behavior to be uncovered, he asserted: "Certainly I would. Confidence and esteem would be reborn among the good, men would learn to distrust the wicked, and society would be the more secure for it."[34]

But is this true? As I mentioned, the relentless *exposure* of hypocrisy can damage trust in society. Don Quixote might be right when he says that "the hypocrite who pretends to be good does less harm than the open sinner."[35] If someone is preaching the right thing, exposing the fact that they aren't living up to their principles may discredit those principles. Bitter and demoralized, people may start to think that all virtues are just a sham. From this perspective, zealots are also threats to society, even if their accusations are accurate. They are on a never-ending hunt that can only demoralize.[36]

You may think this argument is all back to front. If people just weren't hypocrites in the first place, there would be nothing to expose. That's true—and I offer various ways to reduce hypocrisy. But attempts to stop hypocrisy "in the first place" bring their own risks. More threats and stronger enforcement can mean we stop trying to take a position on any issue. A recent overview of the latest research concluded that when it comes to hypocrisy, "*any* moral engagement poses an inherent liability."[37] If we recognize this risk, we may simply not bother standing up for what we think is right.[38]

For example, in some places companies can get certified that they meet agreed environmental standards—say, becoming a member of the Dow Jones Sustainability Index. But many that are certified deliberately withhold that fact because they think that their green credentials might be called into question later.[39] Fear of the zealots stops companies from putting out signals that might push others in the right direction.

Even if your business does show off its good practices publicly, the smart move is to say that your underlying motives are financial. Don't claim that you are trying to do good for its own sake but rather because it boosts your bottom line. Businesses that take this pragmatic stance are judged better when they fall short compared to the ones that fall short after claiming to act out of principle.[40] Cynicism is like buying insurance against hypocrisy.

But this cynicism incurs wider costs. Those costs are particularly visible in politics, which often depends on us having shared goals and aspirations. These goals inspire us, give us hope, provide language to express our needs, and create clear standards for holding our leaders accountable.[41] They can remain true even if we do not always live up to them. You could even say that "a just and peaceful society depends on hypocrites who ultimately refuse to abandon the ideals they betray."[42]

Zealots despise this way of thinking. They want to tear down anyone who is inconsistent with their own ideals, even if the zealots themselves share those ideals—and even if the inconsistency is improving society overall.

That view seems a bit naive. It reflects a desire to believe reassuringly simple fictions that prize absolutism over ambiguity. And this stiff-necked lack of realism can backfire. In the play *The Misanthrope* (1666) by Molière, the main character, Alceste, is an extreme zealot. He loathes any kind of pretense and demands complete honesty always, saying that people should never conceal what they think and feel. This rigid stance doesn't work out well for him. He loses his friends, the woman he loves, and his place in society, ending up as an exiled recluse. Madeline, the inflexible leader of the Group, may not have many true friends.

Zealots may also be naive about what their crusading revelations will achieve. They might expect people to embrace their puncturing of hypocrisy with delight and encouragement, but people may just be irritated at the disruption. In 2010–2011, the organization WikiLeaks leaked a quarter of a million cables sent by diplomats. WikiLeaks showed the reality of power dynamics that exist beneath the hypocritical words of diplomats, who would flatter the French president but call him "thin-skinned and authoritarian" behind his back.[43]

The leaks certainly were embarrassing. But what's interesting is that they may not have had the impact expected. As the philosopher Slavoj Žižek saw them, "The only truly surprising thing about the revelations is that there was no surprise in them: didn't we learn exactly what we had expected to learn? All that was disturbed was the capacity to 'keep up appearances.' . . . Appearance, the public face, is never a simple hypocrisy whose truth resides in the scandalous hidden details."[44]

Maybe there is more value in keeping up appearances than zealots expect; maybe people know the truth, anyway, but find the pretense of not knowing productive. That is the world of everyday compromises, which we will explore next.

But perhaps the biggest concern with zealotry is not its naivety but its cruelty. Again, it was Judith Shklar who saw that "the revolt against hypocrisy [is] an affirmation of joy through cruelty."[45] If you see hypocrisy as the worst sin, cruelty will enter in. Indeed, recent psychology studies have shown a link between moral vigilantism and sadism.[46] There's an edge of cruelty in Madeline's enjoyment of destroying hypocrites.

The cruelty comes from two places. One is anger. Discovering unjust claims to status can unleash simmering resentment; betrayal bites deep; revenge can be ferocious. It didn't take much for members of the Group to join the attacks on Grace.

The other driver of cruelty is certainty. Zealots want to destroy pretense and enforce truth and integrity. They want to tear off masks and force people to look each other in the face. That's a clear mission, and its clarity can push everything else out of the way. It can lock in the self-righteous certainty that cruelty is OK if it smashes the rotten system. Nuance, context, and forgiveness are tossed to the side of the road as the march toward purity proceeds.

James Baldwin picked up on the danger when he wrote that "no one is more dangerous than he who imagines himself pure in heart: for his purity, by definition, is unassailable."[47] There's something hard and inhuman here. That becomes clear when the principles being enforced seem obviously fanatical. As one academic paper puts it, "If you are someone who believes that truly living your moral values entails becoming a suicide bomber, then those around you would likely prefer you remain a moral hypocrite."[48]

But the inhuman edge of zealotry can play out in more mundane situations as well. I know someone who refused to go to a friend's wedding because the bridegroom had previously said he didn't believe in the institution of marriage. Perhaps turning up would have condoned hypocrisy, but maybe you should put people above principles at least some of the time.

What kind of world emerges when zealotry grips society? It's the dark mirror image of the trust machine, with the good outcomes switched out for bad. Something like this happened in France 250 years ago. It was called the Reign of Terror.

In 1793, four years into the French Revolution, its leaders started an aggressive search for enemies within. The feared Committee of Public Safety accused thousands of people of being secret enemies of the revolution. Around 300,000 people were arrested; one in ten of them was killed. Seventeen thousand were beheaded in public.

Their supposed crime? Hypocrisy—false public support for the revolution. The revolution became a purge of insincerity, so that only those who displayed their true and pure motives would be left. But this war on hypocrisy escalated out of control because we can never be sure what someone is *really* thinking.[49]

In this inversion of the trust machine, everyone becomes suspect—even the purity regime's leaders. Most of the zealots running the Reign of Terror also ended up on the scaffold. As one of them, Camille Desmoulins, reflected mournfully, "As soon as comments became state crimes, from there it is but one step to turn simple looks, sadness, compassion, sighs, even silence, into crimes."[50]

The important thing is that the purity regime isn't just power exercised for its own sake. That happens in brazen power plays, the fourth and final world we will explore. As far as we can tell, the zealots of the revolution really believed in their cause. In Hannah Arendt's judgment, "The eighteenth-century terror was still enacted in good faith, and if it became boundless it did so only because the hunt for hypocrites is boundless by nature."[51]

When you have both devotion to a cause and relentless suspicion of hypocrisy, the result may be what has been called a "purity spiral."[52] This is where members of a movement increasingly try to assert they are the only true believers among hypocrites. The threshold for triggering an accusation falls; the standards for purity rise. The leaders turn their zealot purges on each other, as happened in the French Revolution.[53] Grace accused Jasmine and then was accused of being a hypocrite in turn.

The final irony is that this world of zealotry *produces* hypocrisy. In practice, the drive for purity requires people to suppress the very real doubts, ambiguities, and nuances of human existence.[54] You can see this happening as the members of the Group wrestled with their feeling that what Grace did was right at some level. The punishing of inconsistency leads to its being covered up hypocritically. Unlike in the trust machine, the result of these maneuvers in the purity regime is seething distrust of others.[55]

The spirit of zealotry rarely rules over society, however—perhaps because it's inherently unstable. Zealotry is "a splendid weapon of psychic warfare, but not a principle of government."[56] It's more likely to act as an insurgency challenging conventions, the forces of sincerity striking at complacency. So let's look at what they are attacking. Let's explore the zealots' nightmare: a world where criticism of hypocrisy is not such a big deal, people think that's OK, and things seem to work. Welcome to the world of everyday compromises.

EVERYDAY COMPROMISES

And now that you don't have to be perfect, you can be good.
—John Steinbeck, *East of Eden*

I can't do this, Diana thought. He's worse than I realized.

He was still talking. She was half-listening enough to know that Jeff Hatch was not really interested in the welfare of the kids in this city. He just saw them as a nuisance, and nonprofits like hers were a means of keeping them away from his properties. But, and she kept focusing on this fact, he did have half a billion dollars to spend, and this was the meeting that could move some of that money from him to them. Money that could do a lot in the northeast neighborhoods.

Of course, they knew the origin story of this money. The painkiller profits of the aughts had flowed to many different places. Meanwhile, the painkillers themselves had flowed into the northeast neighborhoods, where they remained. Maybe Jeff wanted to move on from all that. For others, moving on was harder.

The team had talked things over after the first approach from Hatch's people. Money made from the problems they were trying to solve. A funder who might have another agenda. How could they keep speaking out in the same way? The gut feeling was not good.

But then . . . it would be the biggest donation in their history. A year's relief from the treadmill of fundraising. The chance to focus on what they were really here to do. And who would sit in judgment of them? There but for the grace of God: every nonprofit in the city had taken money from hands that were dirty in some way. A film of pharma on the palms, tobacco-stained thumbs, fossil fuels lingering under the fingernails. When you come down to it, no one's money is clean in the way some people demand. Every dollar bill has the watermark of past compromises and betrayals. The main thing that Diana kept in mind, the question that drove her on, was: What good is the cash doing now?

And when it came to that question, she felt pretty confident. Of course, there had been times of doubt—times when, tired of the work, unsure they were getting anywhere, they felt ground down by the waves of need. But they knew that letting that exhaustion show would break the cycle of belief and purpose that sustains an organization like theirs. So they didn't. They kept saying the same lines. And slowly the belief began to come back again.

Jeff Hatch was flinging a hand from side to side as he spoke. Just like Cathy, their chief fundraising officer. Cathy also showed what could happen if you kept the appearance going. Cathy hadn't been the biggest believer in their mission to start with. Truth be told, they had hired her because she was Darren's niece, and they knew what impact his death had had on the family. But they saw strength in her inexperience, and before too long she saw it, too. Now no one could match her.

Maybe, she thought, while nodding at Hatch, it's about keeping track of your compromises and how they stack up. As long as

> you know where you are going, what it's worth, and what it's not. So let's keep the grin in place, let's nod even while he says things that make me want to scream, and, finally, when he's done, let's just say one thing: "Please sign here."

Slip into the cozy, battered chair of everyday compromises. Welcome to a world of tolerance and understanding, where people have ruefully recognized their flaws and made peace with them. Imperfection is inevitable; to compromise is to be human. Criticism of hypocrisy is not a driving force here because even if it were exposed, most people would respond with indifference or acceptance. The extreme effects of the ferocious drive for complete consistency have been averted. The mood is conservative rather than radical. Instead of relentless purges, the threat is one of internal decay, complacency, and cynicism.

In the film *In the Loop* (2009), events start spiraling out of control for the combative government press officer Malcolm Tucker. He needs a talk with colleague Linton Barwick. Wandering around the United Nations building, they end up diving into the Meditation Room. Tucker starts getting angry and dropping expletives, but Barwick brings him up short: "Don't raise your voice. This is a sacred place. Now, you may not believe it, and I may not believe it but, by God, it's a useful hypocrisy."[57]

Everyday compromises support social cohesion, the smoothing over of differences, peace. Linton and Malcolm may not *believe* that the Meditation Room is special, but the convention produces real results regardless. They don't get into a shouting match.

Politeness is widely thought to be hypocritical in this way.[58] Maybe I find your opinions offensive and your clothes crude, but my manners restrain me from saying so. And that means the situation does not escalate into confrontation, even violence. Maybe we end up liking each other more next time. The politeness is fake, but it works.

That's why an American visiting London in 1970 ended up calling for "a revival of hypocrisy" in the United States. Whereas New Yorkers came out swinging, Londoners concealed feelings and avoided confrontations. The result was a system that functioned, according to the American reporter, "because everyone is willing to indulge shamelessly in hypocrisy." Or, in the words of Honore de Balzac, "Manners are the hypocrisy of nations."[59]

This is a very sociable kind of hypocrisy, which cares what other people think.[60] It may also develop into compassion. Maybe you recognize that broadcasting your authentic opinions may not be worth the pain it causes others. From this perspective, the truth telling that zealots think is authentic just looks like being rude and cruel—perhaps for the sake of it, perhaps for your own vanity ("I tell it like it is").

But even if the politeness is false, so what? That's the whole point of politeness as a virtue: you are *meant* to be exerting self-restraint and concealing your impulses. You could even say that the more hypocrisy there is in your politeness, the more you deserve credit. Politeness is like bravery in this regard. We expect a brave action to sit on top of a roiling, unstable mix of fear and doubt, not on top of consistent resolve. The behavior alone is what matters: if someone acts despite their feelings, that makes it more impressive, not less.[61] In the words of Lord Byron, "Each hath some fear, and he who least betrays [is] / The only hypocrite deserving praise."[62]

The act of politeness or bravery has an outsize impact for another reason. The playwright Jean Kerr put it this way: "Man is the only animal that learns by being hypocritical. He pretends to be polite and then, eventually, he becomes polite."[63] Even the famously upright moral philosopher Immanuel Kant, so keen on doing the right things for the right reasons, thought that pretending to be good could make us truly good.[64] The conflicted playacting of virtue becomes sincere. By seeming to be friendly you become friendly. You fake it until you make it.

The world of everyday compromises is not bothered by this process, seeing it as natural and constructive. It leaves room for people to grow into a role, just like Cathy did in the story at the beginning of this section. Frederich Nietzsche saw how much this change matters when he wrote: "The hypocrite who always plays one and the same role finally ceases to be a hypocrite. . . . If someone wants to *seem* to be something, stubbornly and for a long time, he eventually finds it hard to *be* anything else. The profession of almost every man, even the artist, begins with hypocrisy, as he imitates from the outside, copies what is effective."[65]

You may remember that a similar process happens in the trust machine. But in that world the behavior was compliance enforced through fear of exposure. Here, as Nietzsche indicates, criticism is not the driver. Instead, the behavior is motivated by a goal or desire to make the appearance a reality. It's deliberately faking it until you make it, not suppressing your flaws through fear.

This world accepts that there is a complex relationship between appearance and reality, falsity and truth. It understands the idea that we must play varying roles that do not betray some real inner self. Instead, they construct the self through every performance.[66] There is something redemptive here—every interaction in society is a chance to bring ourselves closer to our desired self. But at the same time there is a bittersweet understanding that we remain imperfect, that complete consistency will always elude us.

You may recognize that this is a more mature and compassionate view of human nature. It praises the efforts of beginners; it tolerates differences; it urges us to hold back and be the bigger person. And it may see hypocrisy as a reasonable response to unreasonable expectations of consistency.[67] Falling short of our ambitions is just a part of being human that we need to live with, as long as we can keep striving for something better.

Yet this world is not just about slipping into comfortable mediocrity. Tolerating hypocrisy can help to realize the values that society cares about. A starting point is the insight that simply preaching can bring benefits, even if it's hypocritical. Most people would prefer that police officers who are thieves do not refuse to arrest any thieves they encounter. We want politicians to publicly support the law even if we suspect they may have broken it in the past.

This way of thinking is called *consequentialism*: the end results are what matters. Even though hypocrites are doing something "wrong" on its own terms (e.g., deceptive preaching), that can be OK if the act then produces some good.

This is the way that Diana approached her work at the nonprofit. It was OK to take Jeff Hatch's tainted money in order to get results. Or imagine a lawyer who, despite secretly thinking that poor people should work harder and don't need any special help, volunteers at a clinic giving legal aid and does her duties well—because she wants to get a reputation for service that will help her career.[68]

Whereas the trust machine would focus on creating consistency in these lawyers, politicians, and police, the world of everyday compromises, well, compromises. It sets its sights lower and concentrates on not throwing the baby out with the bathwater. After all, why would you ignore things that are good and true in themselves just because someone imperfect is saying them?[69]

Indeed, this way of thinking is often dismissed as a logical fallacy. You can see it in everyday conversations:

> **You:** "Stop going over the speed limit!"
> **Me:** "Yeah but *you* speed all the time!"

I'm basically invalidating your right to criticize me by saying you're a hypocrite. But note that I'm not rejecting *your point* on its own terms. It just feels as if I've canceled your right to criticize. My accusation of hypocrisy, while satisfying, may stop me from doing the right thing. It follows that preaching may be more effective in a world less obsessed with hypocrisy. Accusations will come less often and inflict less damage when they do.[70]

This stance means that the world of everyday compromises welcomes those who want to support society's values, even if they have suspect motives. Maintaining collective practices is placed above achieving individual authenticity. When Diana and her team had doubts, they concealed them rather than being their authentic selves.

You can see this trade-off whenever we tolerate a known atheist getting married in a place of worship or having their baby baptized. A zealot priest might refuse to play along; his counterpart may just be happy to see people in the church. Of course, some aspects of religion encourage this kind of compliance. Rituals, for example, are all about conforming to a set pattern of behavior almost without thought: you don't need to have a reason other than "it's custom."[71]

George Orwell thought that this need to keep up appearances also acts as an important—and undervalued—check on our behavior. He saw hypocrisy running through Western societies like layers of rock. He pointed out that the United Kingdom's electoral system was rigged for the rich, making a mockery of the idea of "one person one vote." But he also noted that the system was not completely corrupt—there was no direct bribery, and people with guns did not stand at polling booths, telling others how to vote. Nor would this happen unless the people were to abandon their belief in certain core principles because "even hypocrisy is a powerful safeguard."[72]

Even if people know that ideals such as justice are compromised, these ideals can still have power. Belief in them shapes how we act. In Orwell's words, "the play-acting is taken seriously," and that preserves the system. That's why Orwell says that hypocrisy prevents tyranny: it creates "the strange mixture of reality and illusion . . . the subtle network of compromises, by which the nation keeps itself in its familiar shape."[73]

These everyday compromises may also produce a more realistic and perhaps more effective form of politics. I once saw an advocate for drug reform criticize the UK government on social media for providing funding to support local pubs. After quoting the prime minister condemning the use of recreational drugs, he pointed out that alcohol was a drug that killed thousands of people a year. This was #hypocrisy.[74]

I don't disagree that this is hypocrisy: there's a real inconsistency here. But the charge also ignores the fact that alcohol has played a major role in many human societies for thousands of years. Its role and history mean those societies have made a collective decision to treat it differently from other drugs.[75]

Now, you can argue about whether that arrangement is a good one. But the charge of hypocrisy may not be your best way of achieving change. Your accusation of inconsistency may lack bite because people are likely to understand that their society has decided to treat the two kinds of drugs inconsistently. It's one of the everyday compromises their society has made.

These compromises can lapse into abusive complacency, but a case can be made that politics in many countries works better when it allows some hypocrisy.[76] The idea is that both principles and pragmatism are essential. If you get rid of the principles, you have the corrosive cynicism of brazen power plays. If you get rid of the pragmatism, you have the inhuman, self-righteous conviction of the purity regime. Both of those scenarios are bad; everyday compromises can get the balance right and achieve good outcomes.

The trade-off is that this world tolerates hypocrisy and politicians talking out of both sides of their mouths.

In other words, politicians may be *doing their job* if they seem hypocritical because they are making necessary compromises without abandoning their principles. In the world of diplomacy and international relations, a kind of "organized hypocrisy" is the normal state of affairs.[77] Power imbalances, competing domestic demands, and the lack of an overall authority—they all mean that national leaders struggle to stick to a single set of principles.

Indeed, maybe the complexity of the modern world means that successful policies must be "clumsy."[78] Being "clumsy" means they contain elements that appeal to radically different worldviews. Policies that are logically inconsistent may also be flexible and resilient.

Imagine a low- or middle-income country that strongly argues at the United Nations for free global trade. At the same time, it has protectionist policies to shield some of its new and fast-growing industries. This position seems inconsistent and hypocritical, and it appeals to two different worldviews.[79] Yet it can also work well overall. The clumsiness may allow the country to join the global economy gradually—rather than having its industries overrun by established international competitors. The result may be that the country participates in global trade in a more resilient and successful way.

These compromises may be fine if the outcomes are good. After all, the end results are what matters. But compromises can curdle into complacency and cynicism. Behind the comfortable facade society has built up, cruelty may start seeping in.

The first point of weakness comes from complacency. Since no one is calling out hypocrisy, it's easy for people to think they are doing good just by going along with convention and keeping up appearances. Or they may decide, conveniently, that the thing they are doing happens to be the right one. They get a boost to their status and self-image without too much work or making too much of a sacrifice.[80] And getting that "free lunch" can make them complacent and disengaged from what's happening in society. "Who really cares? I'm doing good; things are good."

You can see the kernel of this attitude in George Orwell's argument that hypocrisy acts as a check on tyranny. It feels like a nice comforting story about how "it couldn't happen here." And it's a bit complacent. Yes, there may not be people with guns in polling stations. But, as noted earlier, people who erode democracy often think they are saving it—they think their actions are defending ideals. Someone who is seen as a danger to democracy may have their democratic rights suspended; perceptions of voter fraud may prevent many people from voting legally. If society complacently assumes that things are basically fine, no one may recognize such actions as signposts on a downward slope.[81]

Willful blindness plays a big role here. We often focus our attention on things that make us feel good and confirm our existing beliefs. If we can buy clothes or groceries cheaply, we often don't want to dig into the reasons why. Sometimes this is necessary protection: we cannot help everyone all the time. As George Eliot wrote in *Middlemarch*, "If we had a keen vision and feeling of all ordinary human life, it would be like hearing the grass grow and the squirrel's heart beat, and we should die of that roar which lies on the other side of silence."[82]

But that's not always the case. Sometimes the zealots hit home with their argument that every evil ignored is an evil endorsed.[83] Accepting hypocrisy to strengthen society may also mean accepting abuse and cruelty. You can see this danger in an opinion piece from the turn of the twenty-first century. "Forty years ago," it argued, "we more or less knew what we thought about hypocrisy—we accepted a certain amount of it as the price of having values." When proponents of these values violated them, "there was a rough societal consensus about how to handle these problems: Keep them quiet. . . . The less said about all this, it was felt, the better off everyone would be."[84]

It doesn't take much imagination to see that keeping quiet enabled a lot of toxic behavior. Executives could keep their jobs despite their violent alcoholic rages being known. Widespread corruption spread in the police forces of large cities.[85] Some Catholic priests were able to abuse children for decades because those in power feared the loss of confidence in the Catholic Church that exposure would bring.

Widespread tolerance of hypocrisy is more likely to benefit the powerful because the emphasis is on protecting convention and social harmony. Things can escalate: if you realize your power means you can be hypocritical with impunity, it can invite you to abuse power even more. Over time, everyday compromises can end up sustaining arrangements that are deeply unjust or harmful. I mentioned that many countries have decided to treat alcohol inconsistently, given the major role it plays for them. Hypocrisy is tolerated to support the current setup—the inconsistency is excused as "that's just how we do things." But what's to stop this same argument being used to excuse the worst acts imaginable?

If we bring all this together, we can see that the powerful may have a strong motive to think that what benefits them is also good for society and to ignore evidence to the contrary. Hypocrisy props up the existing power structure. And what starts to stir when people see that principles are just acting as a veil for selfishness? Anger. Instability. A deep and corrosive cynicism about human nature. We start to enter the bleak world of brazen power plays.

BRAZEN POWER PLAYS

There is a certain satisfaction in coming down to the lowest ground of politics, for we get rid of cant and hypocrisy.
—Ralph Waldo Emerson, "Napoleon: Man of the World"

March 15, 1974

I feel that the name "Elliot Spencer" had not so much been dismissed from my consciousness as it had been lying in wait, ready for when the trap would be sprung. That moment occurred some forty years later. I was reading the newspaper when my eye fixed on a side column in the obituaries page. "Elliot Spencer, Long-serving Headmaster." I was not surprised to see that his tenacious self-regard had propelled him to ninety-four years of age.

The jaws of the trap snapped, and I was returned to that unhappy half year I spent under Spencer's care or, should I say, under his control. For I experienced little of the former and a great deal of the latter. Any child at Braithwaites was acutely aware of Spencer's iron grip, particularly when it was closed around a ruler being swung at their calves.

His main motivation, it seemed, was to demonstrate that his power was complete. To this end, he established an intricate web of rules that constrained our lives. No one was allowed to raise their voice, to place their hands in their pockets, to lay a hand on anyone else. Once these strictures were announced, they were enforced harshly: his eye would forever scan the ranks of children, looking for the smallest infringement.

The most striking thing, though, was that he would flagrantly violate all these rules, sometimes even in the act of setting them. The rule about raised voices was shouted at us. The condemnation of violence preceded his throwing a clumsy pupil to the ground. He would eat with noise and mess.

I do not know whether this shearing of word and deed proceeded from some defect of mind. What I did know, along with all the other pupils, was that it rendered Spencer's principles pure pretense. We all spotted the causal scorn in his voice. These rules were mere accessories to his will; they had no value in themselves.

I'm afraid that this may have been the main lesson his pupils learned: that principles had little meaning and were not worthy of respect. He may have made me a cynic for life.

Regardless, we were entirely clear in our minds that there was no benefit to remarking on his hypocrisy. At Braithwaites, his control was total. Bitter resignation was the only prudent option. This fact was brought home to me forcibly the one time I chose otherwise.

It was a Saturday in March, just before my mother came to announce we were moving again. We were lining up in the dining hall, where Spencer sat at his raised table, watching us. I was looking at the high windows, mind elsewhere, when I heard his flat, barking voice.

"Richards!"

I yanked my hands out of my pockets instinctively. The whole hall went silent. He had moved between the lines of tables.

"Richards, no man must put his hands in his pockets. It marks you out instantly as a low-minded oaf. It's ungentlemanly."

> He was sauntering to and fro in front of me. His hands were in his pockets.
>
> A voice, which I realized was mine, then said: "But—sir . . . you have your hands in your pockets."
>
> He stopped and responded in a level, even neutral tone: "No, I do not." I looked helplessly at his hands stuffed into the legs of his charcoal suit.
>
> "Look at me." His voice had hardened. "And even if they had been . . . What. Of. It?"
>
> I looked at his hands again. They were now clasped tightly around the ruler.

Here we are, at the lowest ground. Hypocrisy is spent as a force: people do not fear it as a criticism. The result is a bleak place where people simply and openly exercise power to serve their interests. This world embodies the idea that you can sideline hypocrisy by not having any principles in the first place.[86]

The death of hypocrisy can play out in a few ways. The common factor running through all of them is the display of power without the dressings of principle.

One possible outcome is deep cynicism. Society may have familiar features, but the stabilizers no longer work. People with power may still refer to principles, but they blatantly contradict them. If others try to invoke hypocrisy in response, it has little effect.

A second scenario is autocracy. One group has achieved such a level of power that they don't need to pretend to have principles. Hypocrisy evaporates in a situation of total control.

And the final potential result is chaos. Here, the tension created by the hypocritical pressures of society breaks suddenly. People are no longer constrained by rules or values, so hypocrisy doesn't matter. Power is fragmented, and many people struggle for supremacy.

Given the stakes, we need to look at each of these outcomes—and see what must be avoided.

In deep cynicism, accusations of hypocrisy have become worn out. People have entered a spiral where they see politics merely as a game rather than as a contest of real principles.[87] In this view, politicians are just players trying to win the opponent's pieces. They may still make claims of principle, but only as actors try to sell a product—*and everyone knows that's what they're doing.*[88] People know that, really, the principles are cover for the exercise of power against opponents. That's the mood that prevailed at Braithwaites.

The result is scheming, disenchantment, and fatigue. If it's all a game, then nothing really is at stake, and it doesn't matter who wins. This is worse than simple cynicism where people are disgusted at the hypocrisy of politicians and say, "They're all the same." In the case of deep cynicism, there's no real point calling people hypocrites because *of course* they are—that's part of the game. And if politics is just an ironic joke, then it's easy to start allowing cruelty and lies to become part of the game. Whatever will rile and derail your opponents.

There are two opposing ways we can end up in this situation. One is by overusing hypocrisy. Politics can encourage a dynamic where every accusation of hypocrisy is met with a counter accusation. "You're a hypocrite!" "No, *you're* the hypocrite!" People see this unending cycle and begin to think that accusations of hypocrisy are merely a device, disconnected from meaning. They're not about uncovering the truth and maintaining trust. They're just part of the game of politics, and *hypocrite* is just another term of abuse.[89] The meaning of the concept begins to disintegrate. The spell is broken, and we enter a disenchanted world.

We can also enter that world by not making the effort to profess principles in the first place. Rather than killing hypocrisy through too much zeal, you kill it by indifference, by not claiming any consistent standards or moral high ground.[90] In this worldview, the worst thing is to be a fake who pretends that decisions are about more than power and dominance.

Of course, since this is a game, sometimes it may be useful for the player to deny they are engaged in power plays. Deniability is an advantage. But the assertion of principle, that they really care, will often be made with a wink or a smirk. In fact, it comes to look more like cynical lying than hypocrisy. You might think of the Putin government's stance that it would never engage in extrajudicial killings and that a lot of people are just careless around open windows or live grenades.

Sometimes there's no advantage in deniability. You may be secure enough in your power to admit the inconsistency. You get a flash of this when Elliot Spencer says, "So what if my hands had been in my pockets?" You may find that your supporters back you regardless—particularly in the realm of politics. The logic then becomes: Let's make my side as strong as possible, so we don't have to care about consistency. Let's make the game all about my side winning.

You can see this happening in the recent political rhetoric of the United States. For partisans, the other side winning seems apocalyptic, an existential threat to the country. The game has become all-out war, where the need for victory justifies almost anything. If someone on your side is a hypocrite, that's unimportant as long as they attack effectively. As one online post put it, "In an existential war, you do not remove an effective officer—much less cede his position to the enemy—because an affair or gambling problem comes to light."[91]

If groups are focused on building unchecked power, then continuing to focus on hypocrisy may be a dangerous *distraction*. While you are busy pointing out all of your opponents' hypocrisies, they may be busy building a power system where they can afford to be inconsistent and play by different rules. Focusing on hypocrisy may prevent you from seeing the underlying, coherent agenda.

This process of gathering power can end up with one group completely dominating. At the national level, this looks like autocracy or dictatorship. But in this world of brazen power plays, you can afford to be open and sincere about how you're exercising power. You don't need to be hypocritical.[92]

Of course, dictatorships do produce a rich seam of hypocrisy. The Soviet Communist Party claimed its mission was to advance the interests of the proletariat (working class), yet the interests that the party members advanced were mostly their own. While millions starved in the early 1930s, the elite had servants, second homes, and chauffeurs. They even produced children who "divided all those around them into categories according to the make of their cars. Lincolns and Buicks rated high, Fords low."[93] Ironically, this ranking of class according to car was also present in the United States, where it represented a less conflicted striving for status.[94]

The point, though, is that dictatorships make *accusations* of hypocrisy ineffective and thus irrelevant. In a world where the public thinks that "everything is possible and that nothing is true," they don't react to exposure of hypocrisy with feelings of rage and betrayal.[95] Instead, they shrug their shoulders and quickly switch to saying they knew it was a tactical lie all along.

No, the level of control required to eliminate hypocrisy fully has not yet been achieved. But it has been imagined. George Orwell's novel *Nineteen Eighty-Four* (1949) depicts the terrifying state of Oceania, ruled by The Party and its figurehead, Big Brother. It is a world where everything, even thought, is observed and controlled. And I think the novel should be understood as Orwell's warning about what happens when hypocrisy fails, when the everyday compromises he celebrated fall apart.

In *Nineteen Eighty-Four*, The Party has such a level of power that the idea of hypocrisy just stops making sense. All contradictions are both blatant and ignored. History is rewritten daily by a population that just ignores the sudden wrenching shifts in narrative. In the middle of a political speech, in the middle of a sentence, Oceania is suddenly at war with a different country, but there is "no admission that any change had taken place."[96] The absence of hypocrisy is starkest in The Party's ubiquitous slogans:

> WAR IS PEACE
> FREEDOM IS SLAVERY
> IGNORANCE IS STRENGTH

These statements are not hypocritical because they do not conceal anything. A hypocritical slogan would have been something more like WE GIVE YOU PEACE or EMBRACE YOUR FREEDOM. And they are not trying to create meaning, like a metaphor (e.g., as if "ignorance is strength" were another way of saying "not knowing things can help you be decisive"). Instead, they show that The Party can *collapse* meaning if it likes; the scale and boldness of the move make hypocrisy obsolete.[97]

Later in the novel, the official O'Brien makes The Party's intent clear: the point is to empty out principles in service of maintaining pure power. He makes the chilling claim that no dictatorship has ever gone this far before:

> The Party seeks power entirely for its own sake. We are not interested in the good of others; we are interested solely in power. . . . We are different from all the oligarchies of the past, in that we know what we are doing. All the others, even those who resembled ourselves, were cowards and hypocrites. The German Nazis and the Russian Communists came very close to us in their methods, but they never had the courage to recognize their own motives. They pretended, perhaps they even believed, that they had seized power unwillingly and for a limited time, and that just round the corner there lay a paradise where human beings would be free and equal. We are not like that. We know that no one ever seizes power with the intention of relinquishing it. Power is not a means; it is an end.

The hero of the novel, Winston Smith, listens to these words and agrees that O'Brien is "not pretending . . . he is not a hypocrite; he believes every word he says." Winston, however, *is* a hypocrite. Inside his head, he hates The Party and Big Brother. In fact, that's his whole goal in the novel—to not believe in the actions that he is forced to perform, to make his attitudes cut against his behavior. Hypocrisy is resistance in a world where "nothing was your own except the few cubic centimeters inside your skull."[98]

The novel shows how power can crush this resistance by making hypocrisy impossible. First, Winston has to take part in group activities that are difficult to fake, so the appearance becomes reality. One activity is the Two Minutes Hate, where a group works itself into a rage during a broadcast about the state's enemies. As Winston reflects, "The horrible thing about the Two Minutes Hate was not that one was obliged to act a part, but that it was impossible to avoid joining in. Within thirty seconds any pretense was always unnecessary."[99] The Party exerts control from the outside in.

The other way The Party wins is by torturing Winston until he is mentally broken and unable to maintain his hypocrisy: it breaches the few cubic centimeters inside his skull. The final sequence of the novel shows him fully believing the slogans he used to merely perform. It's the bleakest picture of the world where power has made hypocrisy not just irrelevant but impossible.

Of course, power may not get drawn together into a single place. Instead, the agreed order may collapse and fragment. The result can be a raw and chaotic struggle for control, unburdened by the need to adhere to principles.

How does this collapse come about? You may remember that Freud and others saw society as "an unceasing suppression of instinct" and "a gigantic effort in self-control."[100] People are not following their natures. Hypocrisy is baked into the gap between our impulses and the way we must appear towards others.

In this view, our impulses are always looking to "break through" and satisfy themselves.[101] And greater suppression—a widening of the gap—increases the chances that the break will occur. The result might be a sudden act of passion or violence. As the fictional detective Hercule Poirot explains, the hypocrisy of Christmastime may be a good example: "There is, at Christmas, a spirit of goodwill. . . . Now under these conditions, my friend, you must admit that there will occur a great amount of strain. People who do not feel amiable are putting great pressure on themselves to appear amiable! There is at Christmastime a great deal of hypocrisy! . . . If you dam the stream of natural behavior, *mon ami*, sooner or later the dam bursts and a cataclysm occurs!"[102]

As for individuals, so for society. Although things may seem stable, civilization is precarious and "constantly threatened with disintegration."[103] Rising perceptions of hypocrisy may be a symptom of underlying disease, like fever in a sick patient.[104] Workers may be frustrated about the economic prospects promised yet denied to them by a hypocritical system. Others may be appalled at the corruption endemic in elites who preach. In either case, a collapse may come when society's contradictions become too acute.

The bleakness here is important. This is not a case of zealots seizing power for principles in a revolution. Instead, it's a collapse of principles themselves.

This idea is tempting and troubling in ways that can fascinate us. The recent *Batman* movie adaptations, which have grossed more than $3 billion, make it their central theme. Here, Gotham City is filled with corruption and squalor, yet both the elite and ordinary citizens believe in their own virtues. Sickened by their self-satisfaction, the villain enters. Whether the Joker or the Riddler, they want to rip off the mask and expose "Gotham's true face. . . . Its corruption, its perversion masquerading under the guise of renewal."[105]

The Dark Knight (2008) shows this agenda most vividly. At one point, the Joker rigs two ferries with explosives. One ferry is filled with convicts, the other with civilians. He gives both groups the choice to blow up the other ferry before midnight, or he will blow up both. The goal is to trigger mass murder out in the harbor, so everyone sees the selfishness underlying the fine talk of principles. As the Joker says, "You see, their morals, their code, it's a bad joke. Dropped at the first sign of trouble. They're only as good as the world allows them to be. I'll show you. When the chips are down, these . . . these civilized people, they'll eat each other."[106]

The Joker is a damaged nihilist. What disgusts him is not the selfish *actions* of Gotham's citizens but the hypocritical principles they layer on top. Yes, he engineers this display to rip off the mask, destroy the social order, and unleash cruelty.[107] But, in doing so, he also wants to destroy the capacity for hypocrisy. The goal is to leave the citizens both demoralized and de-moralized. When people are eating each other, pretense is not possible.[108]

* * *

Although malcontents like the Joker welcome chaos, most people don't want to enter this world of brazen power plays. Yet such a world is easier to slip into than to escape from, making it crucial to recognize and act on early signals of its approach. As the four worlds have shown, that's not the same as trying to stamp out hypocrisy.

Instead, we need to understand hypocrisy properly and work out what kinds are constructive and what kinds are corrosive. But in our day-to-day lives we are far away from being able to do this. That's a problem because, as the four worlds have shown, the stakes are high.

The good news is that a new set of studies is starting to bring more clarity to the problem. In part II, I explain how hypocrisy really works.

II UNDERSTANDING THE TRAP: HOW HYPOCRISY REALLY WORKS

3 A BRIEF HISTORY OF THINKING ABOUT HYPOCRISY

The past fifteen years of thinking about hypocrisy have been very different from the preceding fifteen hundred.

Before 2010 or so, there was little scientific evidence on how people actually thought about hypocrisy.[1] Instead, philosophers were having a relatively narrow debate, focused on hypocrisy as deception that presents a virtuous face publicly and a vicious one privately. Hypocrisy was held to have a strong moral or religious dimension because it was about people pretending to be good.[2]

Many of these ideas are still present in people's impressions about hypocrisy. But recent evidence has challenged previous thinking and opened new ways of understanding and reducing hypocrisy.

Before digging into these new insights, we need to trace one big change that happened over a few thousand years. That was the move from seeing hypocrites as villainous, deceptive schemers to seeing that hypocrisy can also be a condition that emerges from common societal pressures, often outside our awareness.

The original hypocrites were literally actors. In the Ancient Greek language of Athens, the word *hypokritēs* meant "actor," and *hupokrinesthai* meant "to play a part on the stage."[3] These early meanings were morally neutral because they were about playing a part in a space where that's expected.[4]

But you can see how the negative connotations started to creep in. What if people are playing a part in real life, and you don't know about it?[5] Then they are deceiving you—potentially to harm you and benefit themselves.

When there's no way of knowing people are playing roles, it's harder to trust others in general. And so those playing a part need to be condemned.

This suspicion of deceptive playacting strongly shaped discussions of hypocrisy. You can see it in the *Oxford English Dictionary*'s definition of hypocrisy as "assuming of a false appearance of virtue or goodness . . . especially in respect of religious life or beliefs; hence in a general sense, dissimulation, pretense, sham."[6] But you can see that this modern definition also has a strong emphasis on morality and religion. So what drove this shift in meaning from the domain of playacting to that of morals?

When people began to suspect that some among them might be playacting about faith and fundamental truths: pretending to believe. Doing that not only is a sin but also raises the possibility of betrayal.

Judaism and Christianity played a big role here. In the third century BCE, the Old Testament was translated into Greek. The translators used *hypokritēs*, or "hypocrite," to represent the Hebrew word *hanef*," meaning "a deviator from faith" or "a godless person."[7] You can see how these negative connotations could combine with the theatrical ones to produce the idea of a bad person who deceives others into thinking they are good.[8]

It was Jesus, as set out in the New Testament, who really pushed this concept of hypocrisy as pious pretense for personal gain. As I mentioned earlier, he repeatedly criticized the religious authorities as playacting hypocrites. He thought that they were concerned only with the shows of faith that got them public credit. Their use of religion for personal gain incensed him.

The opportunities for personal gain only increased in Europe's medieval period as organized religion accrued power and wealth. And so one of the stereotypes of the age emerged: badly behaved monks, nuns, and priests who preached virtue but practiced greed and indulgence. The selling of spiritual pardons offered new ways for the clergy to enrich themselves. Sometimes there was little attempt to disguise this fact. In Geoffrey Chaucer's *Canterbury Tales*, the Pardoner openly admits that when he sells religious relics to gullible people, "my intent is only to win, / And not at all for correction of sin."[9]

But the unease about religious hypocrites who were *effective* deceivers continued to churn. The era was obsessively suspicious about "wolves under a sheep's skin," religious hypocrites who merely conformed for personal gain, without belief.[10] This suspicion led to much religious persecution. The Spanish Inquisition, which prosecuted some 150,000 people, was driven in part by concern that Jewish and Muslim converts to Christianity had not truly abandoned their previous beliefs and practices.[11]

The common thread here is the hypocrite as a deliberate deceiver who appears saintly yet does sin—in order to feather their nest. But this model saw two main additions over the centuries.

First, the nature of the sin expanded to become more secular. Hypocrites also became those who profess virtues such as honesty and kindness but then harm their fellow humans (rather than God). Skeptics and humanists began to reflect on the various ways we conceal our desire for social status from others. Writers of fiction fixed hypocrites in the popular imagination as dissemblers preying on our common values, such as Charles Dickens's Uriah Heep in *David Copperfield* (1850), whose claims to be humble are revealed as merely a mask for his "malice, insolence and hatred."[12]

This broader sense of betraying secular values was reflected in common use as well as in fiction. On February 14, 1865, Frank Parker from Brooklyn slipped and fell on ice on Mulberry Street in Manhattan. He was helped up by a stranger, David Clifton, whom he thanked with a drink at a nearby bar. It was then that Frank discovered that his watch and chain were missing. David was indignant at being accused, but after the police were called he confessed to being the thief. The *New York Times* headline? "Robbed by a Hypocrite."

Second, there was a growing recognition that hypocrites were not always deliberate schemers who formed clear intentions and then concealed them. A richer conception of how our minds work emerged. Here, we might have several motivations that are vague, changeable, and in conflict with each other. They fade or strengthen based on context and exchanges with others. Maybe I did start by aiming to rip you off, but the picture of your children on the wall of your shop swayed me.

That's assuming we are even fully aware of our motivations. People began to realize the truth of François de la Rochefoucauld's 119th maxim: "we are so used to disguising ourselves from others that, in the end, we disguise ourselves from ourselves."[13] We may find that ignoring or denying our goals helps us to achieve them—maybe because it makes us feel better about ourselves. People started to see that hypocritical deception may be happening within individuals rather than just between them.[14] In this view, hypocrisy came to look more like our best attempts to grapple with the relationships between our impulses, self-image, and the demands of society.

Despite these changes, the model of a deceptive, scheming, immoral hypocrite still shapes much thinking today.[15] Indeed, one study that analyzed forty dictionary definitions of hypocrisy found that deceit and pretense were the most common themes, with immorality and inconsistency following behind.[16]

So you will find commentators saying things such as, "Hypocrisy, by definition, refers to virtue or goodness," or that hypocrisy "fundamentally involves deception of some kind that is in the immediate interest of the hypocrite alone." If that's not enough, "a hypocrite *must* be self-conscious at least to a certain degree."[17]

But are they right?

MAYBE WE SHOULD ASK SOME PEOPLE WHAT THEY THINK?

Despite its long history, a common complaint until very recently was how little research had been done on hypocrisy.[18] This concept is so familiar to our everyday lives, yet it has remained "puzzling" and "deceivingly complex" even to experts.[19] And when researchers started to take a closer look in the 2010s, they realized that thinkers had been getting a lot wrong.

Here's the thing. How ordinary people think about hypocrisy is fundamental to understanding what it is. Hypocrisy is not like the outer realms of physics, where nonexpert opinion may be interesting but irrelevant. Hypocrisy is bound up with the act of judging that it exists. Therefore, our attitudes and judgments are the crucial things to understand.[20]

So it seems strange that it was 2013 before researchers asked people what they actually think about hypocrisy. And it turned out to be quite different from what philosophers had been saying.[21]

You'll remember that deceit was a big factor in hypocrisy for dictionaries and philosophers. Yet when the researchers Sean Laurent and Brian Clark asked 913 students to define hypocrisy, only 5 percent mentioned lying or deceit. Violations of virtue also loom large in the traditional view, but just 20 percent of respondents cited them.

What instead emerges from these definitions as a key feature of hypocrisy? Inconsistency. More than 90 percent of definitions referred to someone contradicting a statement with their behavior—even though this only cropped up in about half of the dictionary entries. Imposing standards on others. This idea was present in half of people's definitions, although fewer than 10 percent of dictionaries picked it up. Giving a public signal of your beliefs. This came up in 88 percent of definitions, although a quarter of them also thought hypocrisy could be about acting contrary to a *private* belief that you hold.[22] I get similar results when I repeat this exercise with my own students.

Asking people for their definitions of hypocrisy is only a starting point, however. The next few chapters show what we can learn from scientific experiments on hypocrisy. This new wave of research gives us the base on which to build a definition that cuts through the puzzles and muddles. It clears away the tangled strands of morality and deception that have grown up to conceal the concept. A clearer picture emerges—one that can help you to understand what hypocrisy makes you feel and do.

4 NEW INSIGHTS INTO HYPOCRISY

The first insight from the new science of hypocrisy is that the concept has three parts.[1] One is *inconsistency*: when our thoughts, statements, or actions are misaligned in some way. For example, there could be a gap between our statements and actions (saying one thing and doing another), one statement and another (flip-flopping), or even actions in one place and actions in another (different faces for different places).

The second part concerns *benefits*: when the person's inconsistency brings them benefits. The two main kinds of benefits are a boost to someone's social status (how they look to others) or to their self-image (how they look to themselves).

The final part is *injustice*: when these benefits appear unjust or unfair in some way.[2] For example, if someone gains social status through sending false signals or feels better about themselves than they deserve to. We often see the root of this injustice as a rejection of the idea that people are fundamentally equal and should be judged on the same terms.

Inconsistency is the core part. You can have situations where there are few benefits or little injustice, and we still think that inconsistency makes someone hypocritical—we just don't judge them so harshly. But I'm not sure you can have hypocrisy without inconsistency.

Yet it's injustice that is most integral to how we *judge* hypocrites. People are strongly motivated to believe in a just world, where people get what they deserve—and they hate people free riding on the trust of others.[3] If inconsistency is at the heart of how we define hypocrisy, injustice is at the heart of how we judge it.

Then we move onto the second big insight: Hypocrisy is a *process*—of perceiving and judging. As I explained earlier, seeing hypocrisy as a process is also what allows us to spot and avoid the hypocrisy trap.

When going through that process, we first notice inconsistency. Then we decide whether we think it's hypocritical and how strongly we feel about it.[4] That judgment is based on the three core parts—inconsistency, benefits, and injustice—as in: How glaring does the inconsistency seem? How much did someone's status or self-image get a boost? How justified was that boost, anyway?

The final insight is that when we say "hypocrisy," we can mean two different things. That's why the concept is so confusing.

The first thing we mean is a process I call *common-standards hypocrisy*. This is where we perceive the core elements of hypocrisy I just outlined: we identify that someone has been inconsistent, which has produced unjust benefits at varying levels. We then may call the person out on it.

What's the link to common standards? Well, when someone is being inconsistent in order to benefit themselves, that often violates the principle that everyone should be treated fairly, according to common standards.[5] Often it's making the exception that *creates* the benefit for you. Repeatedly violating this principle can bring all the bad effects listed earlier: trust and stability in society are undermined; abuses of power are enabled.

Of course, calling out hypocrisy too much can bring the other bad effects listed earlier: purges, cruel inflexibility. But the process here tries to support the common standards that many people value. Therefore, it can strengthen and underpin liberal democracies through the principle that people should be judged equally.

Let's go further and provide a definition of *common-standards hypocrisy*:

> When we judge that someone has got unjust gains by being inconsistent.

As I mentioned, we use the term *hypocrisy* broadly and frequently. The traditional view can miss this range of uses—it focuses too narrowly on deception and morality. But the framework here is flexible enough to do the job. Let's see how it can handle both a classic case of hypocrisy and something less obvious.

In George Eliot's novel *Middlemarch* (1871–1872), Mr. Bulstrode is a banker who presents himself as a pious pillar of the community. He is always critical of how others fall short of his high standards. Because of his superior ways, seeming like "the Ten Commandments are not enough for him," he's widely disliked.[6] But he also has secrets. Long ago, he made his fortune through handling stolen goods; he cheated the rightful heir out of this fortune so he could keep it; and he is involved in the death of the person who blackmailed him about these facts.

Bulstrode's hypocrisy is created by an *inconsistency* between his public claims to be a decent businessman and the behaviors of handling stolen goods, robbing an inheritance, and being complicit in someone's death. This inconsistency brought him the *benefits* of high social status in his community and material comfort. He also deceives himself into thinking he is a good person. Yet these benefits are *unjustified* because he claims to obey a Christian moral code and criticizes others for not doing so, but he has not made the sacrifices that were needed to live up to this code.

Now let's take a different example, one with much of the morality stripped out. Imagine you are on a first date. You weren't sure what to put in your profile, so you included music as one of your interests. During the date, you realize that the other person is *really* into obscure, challenging, and critically lauded bands. They show original taste, discernment, and commitment. Panicked, not wanting to look bad, you play along. You nod and join in when they criticize the unthinking generic tastes of others.

In reality, your tastes in music are incredibly derivative—you just listen to "Today's Top Hits" on Spotify and take whatever is there. There is *inconsistency* between the views you express (or condone) on the date and your actual listening behaviors. You get the *benefits* of social status as a music aficionado and maybe get a second date. But these benefits are *unjustified* because you have not actually invested the effort required to possess these skills and knowledge. Conscious of your hypocrisy, you frantically start researching once you get home.

Finally, let's imagine that you didn't go on a date at all. You just have an unspoken view of yourself as someone who has sophisticated musical tastes. You go around looking down on people whose tastes you think are more basic. But you also know you have a secret pull to trashy pop and, sometimes, when you need a break, you indulge in exactly the kind of music you scorn.

The *inconsistency* here is between your self-image as a connoisseur and your behavior of listening to critically derided music. The *benefit* is that you get a warm glow of satisfaction from thinking your music tastes are superior to others. That benefit is *unjustified* because you do not act in line with your rewarding self-image: you indulge in exactly the behaviors you condemn in others.

The last example seems very far away from the traditional view of a scheming and deceptive hypocrite. The only person being fooled is you. But as I'll show, there's evidence that people *do* think this case represents hypocrisy—and this framework can capture that reality.

These illustrations are simple ones. Later I will show you how various factors can be dialed up and down and how that makes us seem more or less bad and hypocritical.

The other thing we mean by "hypocrisy" is *double-standards hypocrisy*. Here, the inconsistency, injustice, and benefits to self are baked into our judgments. We judge ourselves, or members of groups we are in, differently from the way we judge others—while still paying lip service to the idea that everyone should be treated the same.

Here, the *inconsistency* comes from the way you treat an act based on who is doing it.[7] The *injustice* comes from rejecting the idea that, at some basic level, people or groups should be judged on equal terms. Instead, you're applying different rules for yourself or your "side" than for the opposition. And the *benefits* are that you can deny that's what you're doing.

Here's an example. Imagine that your favorite sports team loses a series of marginal refereeing decisions after they were overturned on video review. You go on social media and argue passionately that the on-field calls need to be sacrosanct, that video reviews are deeply flawed, and that victories based on overturning calls are illegitimate. You stress that your comments are about the health of the game, not about who benefits.

Your team ends up having a great season and is fighting to win the league title. The final game is level in added time, when your star player seems to score the winner. Devastatingly, the referee rules it out for a foul in the build-up play but, after a lengthy video review, lets the score stand—and your team wins the league. You go on social media and celebrate the victory, praising the players and officials.

There was *inconsistency* between how you perceived the first video review, which benefited the opposition, and how you viewed the second one, which benefited your team. You got *benefits* by appearing to be principled in your original posting and because later you did not admit that your team's victory might be tarnished in any way. These benefits were *unjustified* because you did not act in line with your stated principles when it was your team that benefited. By failing to admit or even see the inconsistency, you were not respecting the idea of fair play and a level playing field.

There's a complication here, though. As I have implied, the person may actually *see* things differently according to who benefits. A classic study found that supporters of Dartmouth and Princeton's football teams saw the same game completely differently based on their affiliations.[8] What looked like a foul to Princeton supporters was rarely seen the same way by Dartmouth fans, and vice versa. They did not even realize they were applying double standards.

But sometimes a person may use double standards deliberately, even strategically, to benefit their side.

"Let's let the people decide."

These words from Senator Mitch McConnell sparked a firestorm.[9] It was 2016, and President Obama had just nominated Merrick Garland to replace the late Justice Antonin Scalia on the Supreme Court. But McConnell, the Republican Senate leader, refused to hold a hearing for the nominee.

His justification was that the vacancy had come up nine months before a presidential election—and so Obama's successor should handle it instead. That successor turned out to be Donald Trump, who put forward someone else, someone to McConnell's liking.

Fast-forward to 2020. The death of Ruth Bader Ginsburg triggers another Supreme Court vacancy. This was just *six weeks* before the next election, so surely McConnell would have to wait, based on his previous argument.

Wrong. McConnell immediately said that Trump's nominee would have a hearing and a vote. There was no mention of the people having a voice this time. The position was filled a little more than a week before the election.

McConnell gave some reasons why the situation was different this time, but none of them explained why the principle of letting the people have a say should no longer apply. It's hard not to agree with the Republican senator Lisa Murkowski that the decision was "a double standard" deliberately used to gain an advantage.[10]

It's tough to find a single word that covers both the knowing and unknowing use of double standards, but *judgment* is the closest I can get. So the definition for *double-standards hypocrisy* reads:

> When someone gets unjust gains by being inconsistent in their judgments.

You or your group get a boost from these double standards. Perhaps they are real benefits, such as preferential treatment. Perhaps the benefit is just feeling good about your team, despite the fact they did something you would normally consider bad. You can see how things get flipped around, and the unjust benefits become bound up in your views and actions—rather than being the thing you perceive.

Here's a way to contrast the two kinds of hypocrisy in your mind:

The first one is about judging inconsisten*cy*.
The second one is about judging inconsisten*tly*.

You can see the contrast between the two in the table.

Type of hypocrisy		Definition	Example
Common-standards hypocrisy	"Judging inconsistency"	When we perceive that someone has won unjust gains by being inconsistent.	When a politician gets benefits from appearing to support "family values" actively, while at the same time having an extramarital affair.
Double-standards hypocrisy	"Judging inconsistently"	When someone gets unjust gains by being inconsistent in their judgments.	When I excuse that politician because I support his party but condemn his opponent for doing the same thing.

The two kinds differ in important ways. You can act in ways that make you look better than you deserve (common standards), while thinking everyone else is entitled to do the same (lack of double standards). Making this distinction allows us to target double-standards hypocrisy. Here's why we should do that.

The fact that double-standards hypocrisy pays lip service to the idea of equality is important. Rip away that idea, and double-standards hypocrisy becomes straightforward egoism or chauvinism: you openly think that you, or your group, are simply better than others. The lip service allows you to deny that you think this way—even to yourself. You can try to hide behind principles that people support, even as you violate them.

Imagine you are a partisan judge who amends their views based on whether they sympathize with the plaintiff or the defendant. But if anyone accuses you of that, you can act offended and say you are just applying the high-minded principle of "all are equal before the law."

That capacity for denial can make it harder to see how fragile the idea of equality is getting and how close society has come to a breakdown. Nevertheless, the very fact that people are still making these denials shows that we are not yet in the world of brazen power plays.

Right now, these dangers are obscured because we don't understand how hypocrisy works and what we need to do differently. So let's look at how hypocrisy functions—and, in the process, a clearer picture of human nature will come into view. We start with the base on which hypocrisy rests: inconsistency.

5 INCONSISTENCY

> The only completely consistent people are the dead.
> —Aldous Huxley, *Do What You Will*

Inconsistency is "the heart of hypocrisy." It's the core feature of the concept; take away inconsistency, and you lose hypocrisy. But inconsistency is not a simple light switch that is either on or off; it's a dimmer that gets dialed up or down to varying levels.[1] This chapter shows just how sensitive we are to changes in those levels.

The two main factors that move the dial are the type of inconsistency and the extent of the gap.

The first is about *what* is consistent: Is it our words and our deeds, our deeds and our thoughts, or our words here and our words there?

The second is about *how* inconsistent those things are: Have you done the exact thing you criticized others for or just violated a general principle you support? Is it a wrenching U-turn from something you just said, or have you plausibly changed your mind over time?

Explaining these factors can answer many questions about how we see other people in our everyday lives. I'll draw on the latest data about our perceptions of others, including new findings that haven't been seen before.

WHAT TYPE OF INCONSISTENCY IS IT?

Imagine this situation:

> A friend of yours says to you one evening that everyone should give money to homeless people in the street.
>
> Later that evening, they walk past a homeless person in the street—and do not give them money.

Hold that in mind and consider this situation:

> A friend of yours says to you one evening that everyone should give money to homeless people in the street.
>
> Later that evening, they are talking to someone else and they say the opposite: that no one should ever give money to homeless people in the street.

And finally:

> A friend of yours gives money to a homeless person in the street one evening.
>
> Later that evening, they walk past a homeless person and do not give them money, even though they had some left.

These three examples show three basic kinds of inconsistencies. The first one is between statements and behavior. Your friend said that everyone should give money to homeless people (statement), but they did not do so when they had the chance (behavior). The common idea of "not practicing what you preach" fits in here.

The second type of inconsistency is between one statement and another. Your friend said at one point that everyone should give money to homeless people (statement), before directly contradicting themselves later in the evening (statement). Cases where you switch your opinion according to whether it benefits you or your group would fit in here.

The final type may seem like a stretch. It's inconsistency between one behavior and another. Your friend gave money in one instance (behavior) but not in another (behavior), even though they had the opportunity to do the same thing again.

This last type can be harder to see as hypocrisy, mainly because it's tougher to attribute clear meaning to behaviors alone. But imagine a celebrity who is charming and polite to people in public (behavior), giving the impression that they are a kind person, yet is cruel and rude to employees out of sight (behavior). Or a person who contributes to a charity for animals yet kicks their cat at home.

Do you react to these kinds of inconsistency differently? One study asked people to rate scenarios of statement-behavior (S-B), statement-statement (S-S), and behavior-behavior (B-B) contradictions, a bit like the three scenarios I gave earlier. The researchers found a clear pattern. S-B examples were seen as highly hypocritical, S-S examples as moderately hypocritical, and then B-B ones as not very hypocritical at all. This matched what happened when people were asked to define hypocrisy: 91 percent of people referenced S-B clashes, 20 percent mentioned S-S conflict, and just 5 percent cited B-B contradictions.[2]

The takeaway may seem clear, but let's pause a second. When it comes to hypocrisy, there's an obvious difference between saying something out loud (or writing it down) versus just thinking it. In the latter, you're not making a claim to anyone—your opinion remains inside your head. So we also need to bring in thoughts as well as statements. And *what* you say obviously matters. You could claim that you always do the thing in question, or you could say that other people should do it. The first one could seem closer to a basic lie about your behavior rather than hypocrisy.

To find out if we care about these differences, I ran an experiment that tested different versions of the scenarios involving giving money to homeless people. I'm going to explain the experiment, but the main findings are also given in the box on page 92.

I added three more scenarios to the three given earlier. One captured the "private hypocrisy" of thinking something but not doing it. That's where your friend just thinks to themselves that everyone should give money, but they don't tell anyone. In another, rather than saying that everyone should give money, your friend simply says that *they* always give money. And the final scenario shows complete consistency: the friend says that everyone should give money and then gives money themselves. This last scenario allowed me to test how people react to the opposite of hypocrisy.

The table shows how all the scenarios compare.

Category	Type of inconsistency	Scenario
Consistency	Statement (Others)–Behavior	Friend says everyone should give money. Friend gives money.
Inconsistency	Statement (Others)–Behavior	Friend says everyone should give money. Friend does not give money.
	Statement (Self)–Behavior	Friend says they always give money. Friend does not give money.
	Thought–Behavior	Friend thinks to themselves that everyone should give money. Friend does not give money.
	Statement–Statement	Friend says everyone should give money. Friend says no one should ever give money.
	Behavior–Behavior	Friend gives money. Friend does not give money.

In November 2023, 6,158 people from the United Kingdom saw one of these scenarios as part of a longer online survey.[3] They were then asked to answer two questions:

- How hypocritical do you think your friend is, on a scale of 1 to 7?
  1 = not at all hypocritical, 7 = extremely hypocritical
- How do you feel about what your friend did, on a scale of 1 to 7?
  1 = I think it's totally fine, 7 = I think it's totally wrong

How did people react? Figure 5.1 shows the scores they gave.[4]

Inconsistency Between a Statement and Behavior Is Seen as Very Hypocritical

For both of the first two pairs of bars in figure 5.1, your friend said that everyone should give money to homeless people. But only in the second pair does the friend not live up to their statement. The figure shows that simply switching the friend's behavior like this raises hypocrisy ratings from 2.70 to 5.51. That's a big gap for a seven-point scale, particularly when you remember that everything else in the scenarios was kept the same. This gap shows the central role that inconsistency plays in hypocrisy.

Of course, the claims that we make vary. In the third group, labeled "statement (self)–behavior," the friend instead says that *they* always give money, without commenting on what others should do. People see behaving

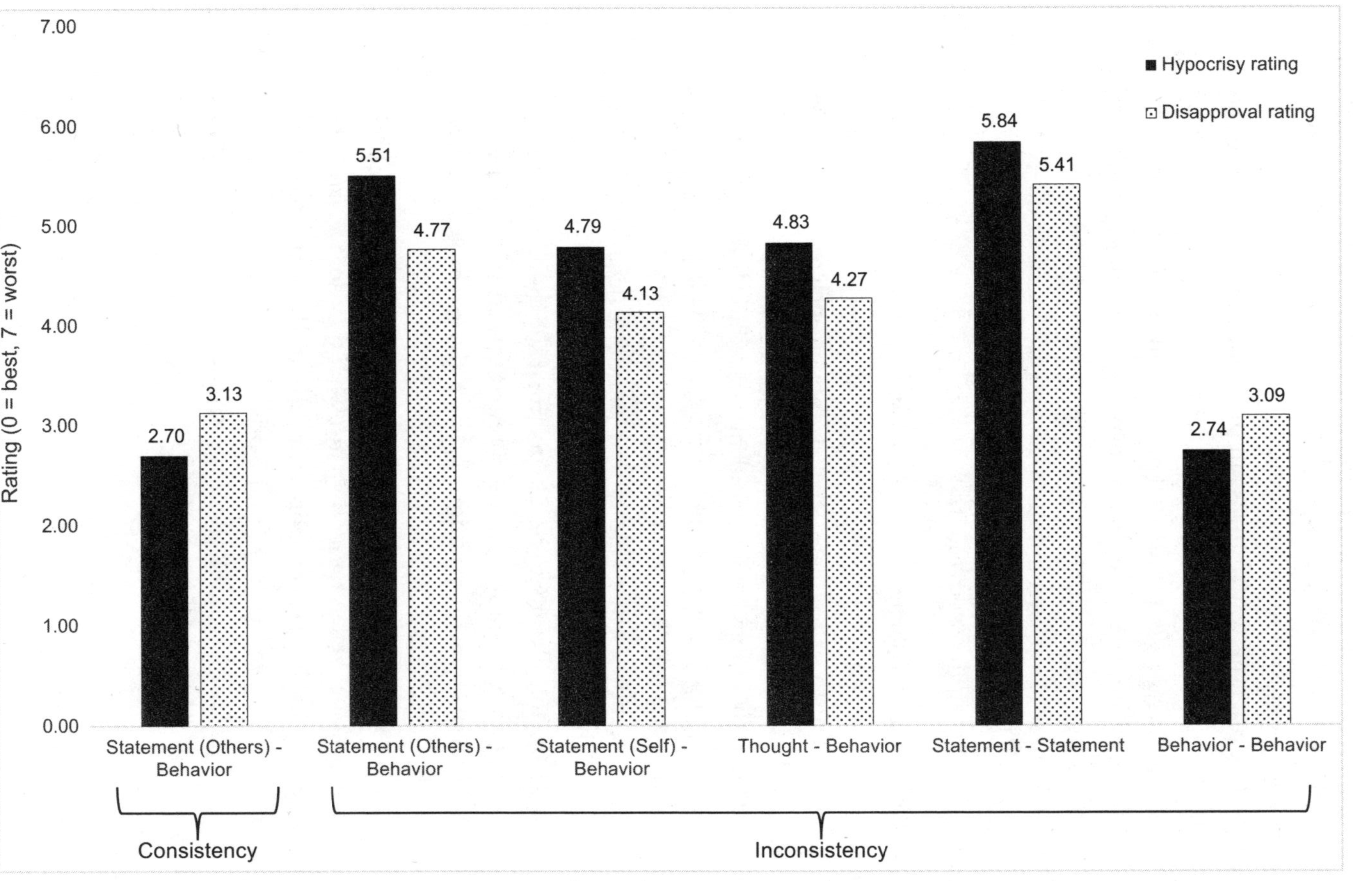

Figure 5.1

Overview of hypocrisy and disapproval ratings.

inconsistently with this statement as less hypocritical and wrong. The third pair of bars are lower than the second pair.

Why do we react this way? It turns out that condemning others for not doing something is a more convincing signal that you do that thing than directly stating that you do it. Put another way: you come across more like you give money to homeless people when you say "everyone should do it" than when you say "I do it."[5] That claim brings you greater benefits upfront, but can mean more blame later if it turns out you don't *actually* do it. That's why the group who talked just about themselves had lower hypocrisy and disapproval ratings in the experiment.

You Can Be a Hypocrite Inside Your Own Head

What about people who act out of line with thoughts that are never expressed to anyone? The fourth pair of bars, labeled "thought-behavior," show that respondents placed them squarely in the realm of hypocrisy. At 4.83 out of 7, their hypocrisy ratings are almost identical to those for the statement (self)–behavior group.[6] "Private hypocrisy" registers with people; you can be a hypocrite inside your own head.

This result confirms other studies that you don't need to be making public claims to be considered a hypocrite.[7] Most people judged someone who smoked cannabis illegally to be a hypocrite if she thought illegal drug use was wrong, even though she hadn't expressed this view to anyone else.[8] Around a quarter of hypocrisy definitions people give refer to contradicting privately held beliefs.[9]

We *choose* to see things this way. We choose to care about people's "real" motivations and "true" beliefs rather than just what they do. You could have a world where we just judge people on their actions. Remember the lawyer who volunteered to give legal aid despite privately blaming those she was helping. We could say that she did all the right things, and that's all that matters. But that's not the world we've created. We care about the gap between thoughts and actions.[10]

Private hypocrisy does seem to be judged less harshly than public hypocrisy.[11] In my study and elsewhere, it gets "moderately high" ratings for hypocrisy and wrongness.[12] People seem to judge those who look good unjustly worse than those who feel good unjustly.

Being Inconsistent in What You Say Is Judged Harshly

Perhaps the most surprising result is how harshly people judged inconsistent statements. This is where the friend said that people should always give money to homeless people but then said the reverse later in the evening. Inconsistency between statements was rated worse than the other kinds of hypocrisy—even worse than not practicing what you preach to others.[13]

In a way, this judgment seems odd. Unlike the other forms of hypocrisy, there's no evidence that these people didn't do the action in question. All they did was say something in support of it one time and something against it another time. They may have given money to homeless people, and in one sense that's the issue at stake.

But we may think that the person is simply weak, unable to maintain consistent beliefs, vulnerable to whatever new challenge comes along. Or we may think that the person has changed their statement to get an unfair advantage. Suppose you are at a work party, and as you talk in a corner with your colleague, you berate vegetarians as smug attention seekers. However, when you end up talking to your vegetarian boss, who's reviewing your promotion next week, you praise vegetarians as enlightened altruists. This kind of hypocrisy edges into flattery and snobbery, two vices that we also despise.

I tried to test whether making a self-serving motive explicit would influence people's views. To do this, I created a second round of questions in the experiment. After seeing the first scenario, people then saw a modified version that gave more detail. It clarified that your friend was "talking to someone important who was against giving money to homeless people," and your friend agreed "in order to please them."

This change tried to make it seem as if the friend were speaking against what they believe just to get an advantage. They said one thing to you, as a friend, and another thing to an important person to please them. What's interesting is that people's views hardly changed after seeing this updated scenario, as you can see in figure 5.2.

I'll be honest: I was surprised when I saw this result. I thought learning this motive would lead to even harsher judgments. My guess is that people

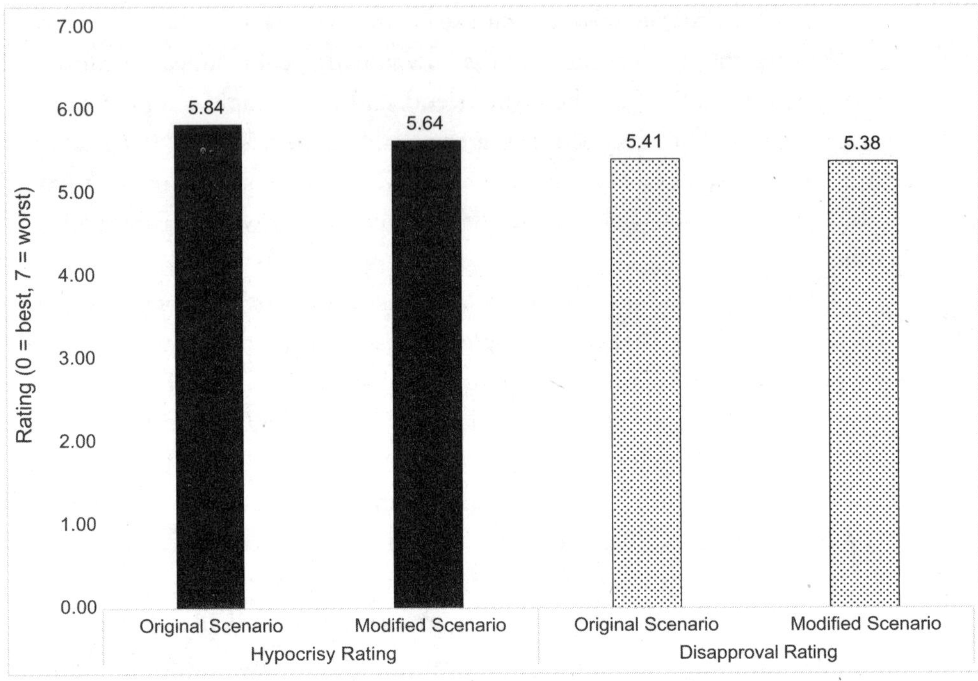

Figure 5.2
Statement-statement inconsistency, with and without clear self-serving motives.

still needed more context. It could have been that the important person had some power over your friend, and so your friend felt that they couldn't disagree. Or maybe there was some other goal at stake: remember how Diana nodded along to Jeff Hatch so she could help her nonprofit. In other words, the outcome may justify the hypocrisy.

We Don't See Inconsistency in Behaviors as Very Hypocritical–Unless We Think That It Brings an Unjustified Benefit

Let's end by talking about when behaviors conflict. Check back to the results in figure 5.1. The first pair of bars, labeled "statement (others)–behavior," shows that when the friend is completely consistent, the hypocrisy and wrongness ratings are relatively low (2.70 and 3.13 out of 7).[14] What's interesting is that the ratings for inconsistent behaviors, shown in the last pair of bars (2.74 and 3.09), are almost identical. This comparison seems to confirm that people do not rate inconsistency of behaviors as very hypocritical.

One possible reason is that people find it hard to decide *why* people have changed their behaviors and whether that change is justified.[15] First we perceive inconsistency, then we decide how we feel about it. Without much to go on, we can't move to the second stage.

I modified the scenarios to test this idea. The people who had seen the consistent scenario, where the friend did give money, were given an additional statement. It clarified that "your friend is just acting in line with their principles, rather than trying to feel good about themselves." In other words, the friend is not gaining any benefits from their action, in terms of either social status or self-image. Clarifying these good intentions should make the friend seem less hypocritical.

The people who had seen the scenario with inconsistent behaviors were told the opposite: the friend felt good about themselves after giving money the first time. They thought that "they are the kind of person who always gives money to homeless people." But, of course, that's not true: they failed to give money the second time. They are feeling better about themselves than they deserve.

Putting unjust benefits into the mix changes things. In the second round, shown in figure 5.3, hypocrisy ratings for the consistent group drop to 2.48, whereas those for the inconsistent-behaviors group rise to 3.67, creating a significant gap.[16] Inconsistent behaviors can rise to the level of hypocrisy, even if other kinds seem worse to us overall.

I think this finding lines up with our experiences. You can imagine cases where people signal principles with one set of actions and then violate them with another. Consider Rio Ferdinand, a footballer who sued a newspaper for invasion of privacy after it accused him of having an affair. He lost the case, and a major reason was that he'd accepted the position of England captain, who the authorities had insisted must be a role model both on and off the field. The judge decided that the act of taking the job meant "he was making a strong, if implicit, assertion that his private conduct by that time met the prescribed norms."[17]

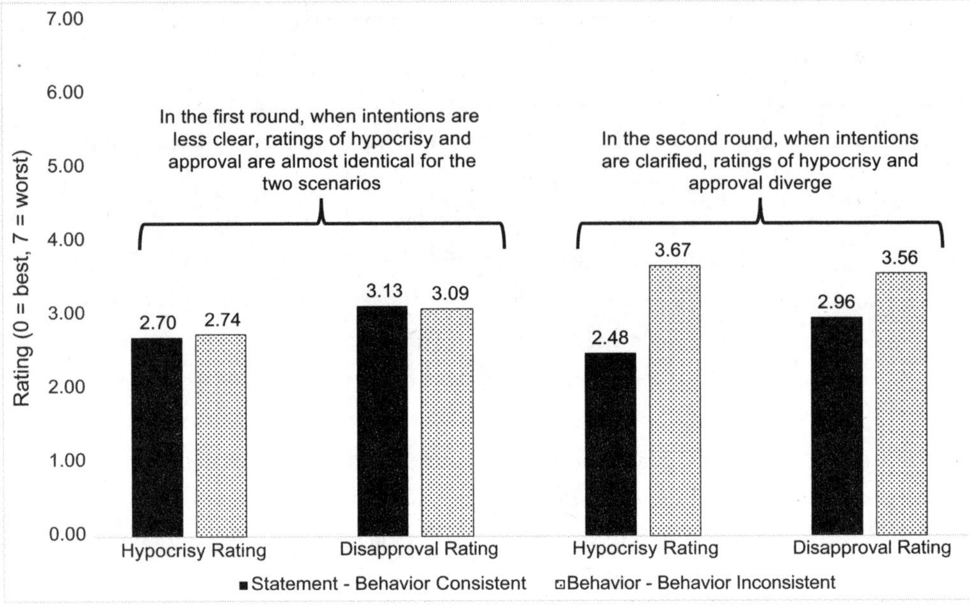

Figure 5.3

The effect of clarifying motives on perceptions of consistency and hypocrisy.

> **How Do We Judge Different Types of Inconsistency?**
>
> Inconsistency between a person's words and their behavior is seen as very hypocritical.
>
> Not living up to the standards you propose for others is seen as worse than contradicting a claim you've made about your own behavior.
>
> We see inconsistency in statements as hypocritical even without details about why it has happened.
>
> We don't see inconsistency in behaviors as very hypocritical—unless we think that it is bringing an unjustified benefit.
>
> You can be a hypocrite inside your own head.

WHAT'S THE EXTENT OF THE INCONSISTENCY?

We care about the kind of inconsistency we see—but we also care about the size of the gaps between words, thoughts, and actions. It turns out that three main things make that gap seem bigger. Does the person do the complete opposite of what they said, or is the contradiction more debatable? What order does the practicing and the preaching come in? Is the contradiction instant, or does it play out over a longer period? Let's find out why those things matter to us.

How Misaligned Are the Inconsistent Parts?

In a classic episode of *The Simpsons*, Marge gets worried by the level of violence in the children's cartoon *Itchy and Scratchy*.[18] (If you've never seen this show-within-a-show, she's got a point: the mouse Itchy often ends up decapitating the cat Scratchy.) She forms a protest group that pickets the studio and forces the producers to cut the violence from the show.

Then an exhibition of Michaelangelo's *David* comes to Springfield. Members of Marge's protest group want her to call for the show to be banned because they find its male nudity offensive. She thinks the statue is a masterpiece and refuses. Going on local television, she admits that her position is hypocritical: she wanted to ban one form of creative expression but celebrate another.

The obvious point, though, is that Marge is not against *violence* in one creative setting but for it in another. She is not supporting an exhibition of Hieronymus Bosch's medieval painting *The Last Judgment*, which depicts people getting skewered and shoved into ovens, neither of which would be out of place in *Itchy and Scratchy*. She condemns depictions of violence but condones ones of nudity.

In the show, it's implied that "creative expression" is the common factor that makes the inconsistency exact. Marge was for it one time and against it another. But that only works by going up a level of abstraction; you could argue that she consistently supported different *kinds* of creative expression: pro-nudity but antiviolence. Of course, Marge would tolerate nudity only if it's "high art," but let's park that point for now. The main takeaway is that, in my view, Marge seems less hypocritical because the mismatch is antiviolence/pro-nudity, not antiviolence/pro-violence, which would be really hard to explain away.

In my experiment, the scenarios always had an exact mismatch between two parts. People said everyone should give money to homeless people in the street and then either did not do that precise thing or said the exact opposite later. The statement was not "give money to homeless people when it's convenient" or "give something to homeless people." It was about money, given in the street, and it was not done.

In real life, things are rarely this simple. Usually the contrast is not so glaring. Maybe you included some caveats to your statement about giving money, such as you don't need to do it always. Or say you supported a related principle that has similar features. Perhaps you said that people should help abandoned cats in the street, and maybe you do that often.

Making the mismatch less exact will not stop accusations of hypocrisy. "You think it's worth spending your money on helping animals, but you have nothing for humans in need. What a hypocrite." But the fuzziness can blunt their force.[19]

Evidence from the psychologist Mark Alicke and his colleagues supports this idea. They showed people a scenario where a student ate three cheeseburgers for lunch. Then the participants were told that the student did one of three things afterward: walked in a relay to support the fight against heart disease; aided a community program raising awareness about exercise; or helped an antipornography drive.

When people were told that the student had acted against heart disease, 62.5 percent of them thought he was hypocritical. When he was volunteering to promote exercise, the figure was 35.1 percent, whereas just 4 percent said so for the pornography version.[20] Eating three cheeseburgers directly encourages the heart disease that the student campaigned against later. When it comes to exercise, the mismatch could be in terms of promoting healthy living—in general—while not eating healthily, but it's less strong. And possibly the cheeseburger–pornography link is something to do with self-control, but it seems tenuous.

We expect and experience greater blame when the mismatch is exact.[21] Companies who claim to have good governance get penalized more harshly when they have a governance scandal compared with those who have a governance scandal after emphasizing a different strength instead.[22] I think we know this and use strategies to lessen or disguise the inconsistency. For example, my mother once pointed out to me that she has an unfavorable view of the way Amazon treats employees. But sometimes she needs the speed and range of products it offers, so she gets my sister to order things for her. Routing the purchase through my sister made her feel less hypocritical.

How do we make these judgments about the level of mismatch? In a way, this is like asking how we connect one idea to another. I think there are three ways people form these connections when building an accusation of hypocrisy.[23]

Logic. Sometimes we reason out an inconsistency. If you support *x*, and *x* supports *y*, then you must support *y*. But you don't . . . so you are a hypocrite. Since any action has many aspects, people can apply this reasoning widely. Take someone who campaigns against illegal drugs. If you take the elements of campaigning, drugs, and illegality, you can use reason to identify many potential mismatches. Maybe the person gets drunk and assaults a police officer (mismatch covering drugs—defined broadly—and illegality). Or maybe they don't also campaign against illegal firearms (mismatch covering campaigning and law-breaking stance).

You often see this approach in attacks on political opponents. The attackers can usually make a logic-based case that someone will buy. If you search online for any well-known politician and the word *hypocritical*, you will find dozens of examples. Try it.

Instantly I found a national leader being attacked for arguing against fossil fuels on the international stage, while approving oil and gas exploration at home.[24] The usual setup is that the critic identifies a governing idea (here, tackling climate change) and then identifies an inconsistency within it (here, an action promoting fossil fuels and a statement restricting them). The success of the attack is how convinced we are by the match between governing idea and inconsistency.

These attacks are often useful, as in the trust machine. But the logical approach can seem inhuman and remorseless. It can strip away context and complexity, the nuances of real life, in pursuit of the abstract connection between ideas. Remember the purity regime's capacity for cruelty.

Doctrine. Often, we don't have to make the connections ourselves. We can point to clusters of attitudes that society has already established. The obvious examples come from religion and politics. If you become a Muslim or identify as a libertarian, that involves adopting or supporting a set of beliefs and practices. If you then do or say things that contradict the doctrine you've adopted, that can trigger an accusation of hypocrisy.

If you embrace a doctrine, you can get the benefits of seeming pious or enlightened or committed, and so on. You may even get these benefits by invoking just *part* of a doctrine, as in saying that you will buy only electric cars in the future. Yet if you don't adopt the rest of the doctrine in line with the signals you are giving, those benefits will seem like unfair gains. This is the root of the common criticism of "limousine liberals" and "champagne socialists," who want to look as if they care about the environment or inequality—without giving up their cars or paying more taxes.

The success of these accusations depends on a few things, though. The first is: How reasonable is it to expect that you've signed up for the whole package? Maybe the package is simple and you explicitly committed to it all. Medical colleges make their students take a modernized version of the Hippocratic Oath, which is short and consistent.[25] But the Old Testament and New Testament are quite different from each other: Are Christians expected to be consistent with both? In politics, enforcing absolute fidelity to a governing philosophy can seem impossible, given the everyday compromises politicians must make.

The second factor is how far the doctrine is set and defined. Some religions have a clear statement of belief and a single leader who maintains the doctrine. Catholicism has the pope and the Nicene Creed. Political parties often have leaders and platforms. But other cases may rely on our personal perceptions and intuitions. If you fly 5,000 miles to make a decisive intervention at a climate summit, does that action support or contradict your environmental principles?

Affiliations. Sometimes the mismatch comes from a relationship, not an idea. We often think that having a personal connection is a sign that you approve of an individual or organization. Then we extend our search for inconsistency through these networks. It's no longer just "Are you inconsistent?" but "Are your connections consistent with you?"

Family members can be one source of accusations. In 2023, a car with an expired temporary license plate was photographed in the driveway of a local lawmaker who had proposed greater enforcement against fake or expired license plates.[26] The car belonged to her son, but the inconsistency was enough to attract a news article, presumably because such a close connection implies some shared responsibility. My strong assumption is that the impact of this kind of accusation drops off quickly for connections outside the immediate family. They are the ones whom you are expected to know better and influence more.

Being an employee or club member may also seem to signal that you implicitly endorse the organization's values. In one experiment, people were told about one of two firms that consulted for law enforcement agencies.[27] Half the people learned about a firm that tried to reduce drug trafficking, half about a firm that focused on sex trafficking. Then they learned about a male employee of each firm who had been arrested for either drug possession or soliciting a prostitute. So for half the people the employee's crime was exactly mismatched to the organization's mission.

When this exact mismatch was present, the employee was seen as much more hypocritical and worthy of blame. The effect was even stronger if the employee was an executive at the firm, as opposed to an accountant. Again, this points to the principle that the strength of connection is driving the result, and it runs on a sliding scale.

Our judgments are informed by logic, doctrines, and affiliations, but we apply these criteria flexibly to serve our motivations. Remember the example of Marge Simpson. If you interpret her campaign against *Itchy and Scratchy* as being about freedom of expression, then she looks like a hypocrite. If you interpret it as being about violence, then not so much. We can frame it either way according to our preferences.[28]

And this is what people do all the time. They zoom out and say that a politician's argument against gambling was really one about the need for self-control and personal responsibility, so his abuse of prescription drugs makes him a hypocrite. Or they zoom in and say that the case they made for greater funding applied specifically to schools, not to fire brigades. I'm more sympathetic to the second approach: details and context matter; hypocrisy is in danger of being devalued; and, as I explain in the book's third part, our expectations of consistency may be unrealistic.

Which Came First: The Practicing or the Preaching?

Suppose you turn on the radio and hear someone called Pat talk about how he's started volunteering to promote healthier lifestyles in your local area. Pat says we need to be proactive about improving our diet and exercise. Two weeks later, you find out that Pat has been glued to his couch since the announcement, guzzling pizzas and watching TV. How hypocritical would you think he is?

Let's try it the other way around. First you learn about Pat's two dissolute weeks spent on the couch. Then you hear him on the radio, saying that he is taking up a volunteer role promoting healthy living. The statement and behavior are the same, but the order in which they occur is reversed. Do you judge him differently?

When a team of researchers showed people either one of these scenarios, the participants thought Pat was more hypocritical and wrong if the preaching came first.[29] That made it seem like his appearance had been insincere and that he actively does not live up to the standards he set for others. But when he went on the radio *after* the couch, people were more likely to think he had changed and "turned over a new leaf."

When judging hypocrisy, the distance between someone's statements and their behavior matters. But so does the order in which the statement and behavior happen.

If you ask people, the most common definition of hypocrisy they give is "saying one thing and doing another." This wording implies the statement comes first, followed by the inconsistent behavior.[30] This is the sequence that we judge most harshly.

We see companies the same way. Brands manage their image carefully; perceptions of corporate hypocrisy can be poisonous. At the same time, 77 percent of consumers want to buy from companies committed to making the world a better place.[31] So a lot is riding on how companies can come across as responsible rather than inauthentic.

One big strategic choice is whether you promote your positive image proactively or reactively. Some companies go out making claims to get good headlines in the absence of any bad news. The car company Volkswagen heavily promoted its environmental record in the early 2010s. For example, in 2014 it touted its "achievements in sustainable development and environmentally-conscious business practices." The same year, the company ran ads showing its engineers sprouting angel wings each time a car hit 100,000 miles.[32]

These efforts paid off: by 2015, the Dow Jones Sustainability Index had named Volkswagen the leading company for sustainability in the automobile sector.[33] A massive scandal erupted just a few months later. It turned out that Volkswagen had been fitting its diesel cars with devices that tricked official testing. The cars were actually much more polluting than they were allowed to be. The company suffered massive damage to its reputation and faced criminal prosecutions: by 2020, the scandal had cost the company €33 billion in fines and settlements.[34] Maybe devil tails would have been more appropriate than angel wings.

Other companies launch campaigns to respond to a problem that has already hit the news. For example, in 2008 the telecom company Ericsson was hit by revelations of dangerous working conditions and child labor in a supplier's factory in Bangladesh. The company then put out a report saying that the scandal meant it had adopted a new Supplier Code of Conduct sooner than planned, and the issue was now on the "top management agenda."[35]

Do people apply the same principles for companies as they do for Pat? It seems so. To test this, another research study invented a fictional store called Power-Mart, which sells electronic goods such as TVs and computers.[36] People saw the same two pieces of information. One was a company email newsletter about Power-Mart's sustainability, announcing that it gets all excess packaging professionally recycled. The other was a report in the local paper saying that Power-Mart had been caught dumping excess packaging in an overfilled landfill, causing water pollution.

The only difference was which came first: participants were told either that the newsletter came two weeks earlier or that the news report had. In line with what we've seen already, the people who saw the email *then* the article saw Power-Mart as much more hypocritical.

What's going on here? I think we are making two assumptions. The first is that Pat or Power-Mart felt bad for their past behavior. If there has been remorse, guilt, and suffering, then we feel that the person has earned the right to make their statement. Any status benefits they get as a result seem more justified.[37] The second is that they are sincere, they will live up to their statement, and there will be consistency in the future. The statement coming second makes us think about the future.

The ordering trick doesn't sort everything, though. Even if your statement comes after your behavior, you can still take a hit and be seen as a hypocrite. Just less of one. And several other things can influence how ordering affects our judgments. An explicit admission of your past failings will likely boost the impact; directly criticizing others may mean people give you less of a break. These factors are interrelated, and there's a strong connection to the final one I will discuss: how much time has passed.

Over What Period Did the Inconsistency Occur?

In 2017, a right-wing Irish politician was defending himself against accusations of hypocrisy. His argument was all about the passage of time. He said: "Some people on Twitter raised the issue recently suggesting I was a hypocrite because my own relationship broke up and I campaigned against divorce [in 1995]. . . . I don't think it's hypocritical to have changed one's mind between 1995 and now on the issue of divorce." This change of mind, he said, was "partly due to my own experience."[38]

I recently went to Iceland for my mother's seventieth birthday.[39] She wanted to go somewhere new, and Reykjavik is both beautiful and between the United Kingdom, where she lives, and the United States, where I live. For complicated reasons, my mother ended up holding a scone in the street. When she took a bite, I recalled how much she had disapproved of people eating in public when I was a child, thirty-plus years ago. When I pointed this out to her, she just said, "Times have changed, Michael."

The common factor here is adaptation over time. The politician says he gained experience that changed his mind. My mother adjusted her behavior to society's changing norms. And in both cases, the inconsistency was spread over more than twenty years.

People can defend themselves against hypocrisy by saying they've changed over time. And the more time involved, the more effective this excuse should be.[40] Imagine if your friend walks past a homeless person a decade after giving their opinion, rather than after just a few hours. Although I did not test this alternative scenario, my strong suspicion is that it would get much lower hypocrisy ratings. Maybe you think this, too. If so, what explains our intuition?

For a start, we often accept that people should change as they learn from experience.[41] We have evolved to be good at adjusting to our environment. You may think that all red berries are benign, but it's best not to keep thinking that if one nearly kills you. More time means more potential prompts for change and learning.

To make this clearer, imagine that there's no time gap. Someone thinks one thing at the exact same time as they say the opposite. We would think this is a clear case of deception. Saying you disapprove of people buying fur as you head to the checkout with a mink stole looks craven or bizarre, absent any other explanation.

But as the amount of time increases, we find it easier to imagine that the person is consistent *now*, at the second point in time. And that doesn't seem so hypocritical. After all, it's possible that you were completely consistent at point A *and* at point B. Suppose your inconsistency about buying fur happened between 2008 and 2010. We can mentally chop up your life into Person A, who was against fur and didn't buy it, and Person B, who was pro-fur and did buy it. But we'll struggle to do that if the reversal is between 4.18 p.m. and 4.20 p.m. in the afternoon.

People think like this about their own lives. If you ask people to reflect on how they have fundamentally changed over time, they become more likely to confess to past misdeeds and less likely to try to justify them. Mentally carving off our past selves helps the admission ("I did it"), while protecting our current selves ("But that's not who I am anymore").[42] And a bigger time gap makes the carving process easier.

I am not saying that we regularly think people flip from one consistent person to another. It's more a question of *deniability*—the possibility that a significant change has occurred. The more time that elapses, the more convincing the deniability becomes.

This chapter has shown how inconsistency is core to hypocrisy. But "we don't go around perceiving everyone as a hypocrite just because they don't always act consistently," as Daniel Effron, a professor at London Business School, told me.[43] Remember that there are two other factors that shape our judgments: injustice and benefits to the self. Of the two, the one that annoys us the most is *injustice*. The next chapter digs out the roots of our fury at hypocrisy—and it turns out that they go very deep indeed.

6 INJUSTICE

Injustice powers our hatred of hypocrisy. But it's injustice made to a particular recipe, heavy on ingredients such as perceived unfairness and inequality. This dish started simmering during our evolutionary past; the era of democracies brought it to a boil. If you dive beneath the surface of this seething resentment, the world looks something like this:

The benefits that people get should reflect their actions and efforts. When we think someone has gained social status or self-satisfaction without paying the right price, that feels like an unfair exchange. It violates our sense that people should play by the same rules on equal terms.

Democracies made this idea of equality explicit in the rule of law, but the concept has an older origin. In our hunter-gatherer pasts, collective punishment emerged to stop individuals cheating or becoming abusive. Over time, we internalized the lessons from this punishment and made it a moral code.

So the hatred we show for hypocrisy was born from our original desire to punish cheaters and free riders, who got benefits without paying the costs. We may talk about hypocrisy in moral terms, but these terms rest on an older dislike of someone getting gains through an unfair exchange.

When we judge hypocrisy, we apply this worldview in two main ways. We look at someone's motivation: What do we know about their intentions? Were there any extenuating circumstances? And we also look at the nature of the outcome: Did the hypocrisy cause any harm? Were there competing values at play?

Our perceptions of injustice therefore vary depending on how we answer a set of questions. That's similar to how we grade inconsistency. The difference is that inconsistency is the base on which hypocrisy rests—you can't get rid of it completely. In contrast, you can feel little sense of injustice at someone's action and *yet still think it is hypocrisy*.

Remember the "victim hypocrites" I mentioned earlier. Persecuted groups may be forced to conform to societal standards they find abhorrent just to survive. There is inconsistency between their thoughts and their actions, and they do get benefits as a result. They are hypocrites, but few people would see the benefits they get as unjustified.

WHY WE HATE FREE RIDERS

People are strongly motivated to believe in a just world where people get what they deserve.[1] But what does it mean to "deserve" something? One answer is that our gains should relate to our actions and the effort we make to perform them. In this view, justice is about getting a fair exchange.[2]

Imagine a singer who rose to fame through her vocal talent. Hundreds of thousands of people pay to see her. Her fame means she gets special treatment such as skipping lines and enjoying private openings of shops or museums. These are inconsistencies—it's one rule for her and another for someone else—and she definitely benefits from them. So that's two of the elements of hypocrisy.

But we are likely to think she has earned this treatment, so it's not *unjustified*. It would be weird to call it hypocrisy. In contrast, if she went around saying how fame hadn't changed her and how she worked hard to keep an ordinary life, we would judge her very differently. She would be getting the social benefits of seeming authentic and grounded without paying the costs (having to get in line like everyone else). Our sense of injustice would trigger the accusation of hypocrisy.

If someone has acquired benefits without paying the costs that we think are due, we feel they have exploited us and others.[3] As I explain later, we see this as *free riding*: the person reaps the benefits created by everyone else's sacrifices without making any themselves.[4] It's like criticizing people who don't give blood, while secretly not doing so yourself, and then expecting a transfusion when you're hit by a bus. We want to punish free riding to correct the imbalance and warn others for the future.[5]

The idea behind punishing free riding is that we all must contribute. You shouldn't be able to get rewards without effort unless that's been collectively agreed. We see free riders as rejecting the underlying principle that people should be held to the same rules and standards. They want different rules for themselves, ones where they get benefits on the cheap.

You can see why we hate this idea. We accept rules and constraints, even though we don't like them, as long as they apply to everyone. Why would we let others get an advantage while holding ourselves back?[6] We fear that if the rules apply to some people only, then soon they will become a tool for exploitation—before collapsing entirely.

The desire to stop people making exceptions for themselves is reflected in moral laws that explicitly apply to everyone. This impulse is found in many religions, but a clear example is what Jesus says in the Sermon on the Mount: "Do not judge, or you too will be judged. For in the same way you judge others, you will be judged, and with the measure you use, it will be measured to you. . . . How can you say to your brother, 'Let me take the speck out of your eye,' when all the time there is a plank in your own eye? You hypocrite, first take the plank out of your own eye, and then you will see clearly to remove the speck from your brother's eye."[7] Here, Jesus makes it explicit that hypocrites "violate principles of human equality."[8] That is, they want to be judged differently and escape the costs they would impose on others.

WHY DEMOCRACY PUTS US ON ALERT FOR HYPOCRISY

This idea of moral equality—that our abilities make us equal players in understanding what we should and should not do—raises questions about how the world should work.[9] If we are equal moral persons, then we deserve equal consideration when setting up and enforcing the basic rules of society.[10] In response, modern secular societies embraced (but did not create) the idea that everyone is treated equally under the "rule of law," without exceptions.

But what should those laws cover? How do we give people an equal chance to decide that? One answer makes us fixate on hypocrisy more than any other: democracy.

In May 1831, a young French nobleman set sail for the United States with a commission to study its prison system. In truth, his goals were bigger. Democracy had appeared as the alternative to the monarchies of Europe, but it wasn't clear how it worked in practice. Alexis de Tocqueville wanted to understand how democracy had shaped America, and vice versa.[11]

And here's the very first thing he writes in his book on the topic: "Among the new things that attracted my attention during my stay in the United States, none struck me more forcefully than the equality of conditions. . . . It creates opinions, engenders feelings, suggests customs, and modifies everything that it does not produce."[12]

Tocqueville recognized that the equality of conditions did not extend to everyone. The existence of slavery, the treatment of Native Americans, and the lack of votes for women made that plain. But he saw a widespread belief among the people he met that, fundamentally, they were their neighbors' equals.[13] Of course, even those who had this "equality of conditions" didn't all have the same wealth and standing; people felt that keenly every day. Instead, people saw themselves more as equal in theory or potential.

So what happens when people believe that they are fundamentally equal to others, yet all the time they see others getting things instead of them?

On the positive side, Tocqueville thought that this setup can create drive, exploration, and striving to make things better. He wrote of the "restless ambition to which equality gives rise."[14] But something else emerges, which is more relevant to hypocrisy accusations: people get envious.

The key thing is that the envy we feel comes from a sense of equality. If we don't think the person is in the same league as us, the sting is lessened. Five hundred years ago Francis Bacon noted that "where there is no comparison, no envy; and therefore kings are not envied but by kings."[15] Modern psychology backs him up. The more that someone thinks "it could have been me," the more envy they feel.[16] When your old neighborhood friend succeeds, it hurts because there are fewer excuses for why you haven't done the same.

Tocqueville saw that this tug between equality and envy could shape whole populations. In his view, democracies "develop the sentiment of envy in the human heart to a very high degree[;] . . . [they] awaken and flatter the passion for equality without ever being able to satisfy it to the full."[17]

When you see these envious pressures, things that seemed puzzling in earlier chapters make more sense. Why are we always checking for the slightest changes in the social pecking order? Because the idea of basic equality makes people more sensitive to even tiny status distinctions. Equality means that "every citizen will be aware of certain dominating presences around him and will focus his attention stubbornly on these. . . . When everything is more or less on a par, the slightest inequality becomes an eyesore."[18]

Now we can return to the question of why democracies fuel the search for hypocrisy. As the political thinker Baron de Montesquieu wrote a few decades before Tocqueville, "Though real equality be the very soul of a democracy, it is so difficult to establish."[19] Democracies create a starting base of equality that makes us sensitive to the gains of others, along with the sense that there are standard rules that should apply to everyone.[20] So we really hate people breaking those rules for their own benefit. What's worse, we realize with regret and fury that we could have easily cheated to get these gains, but we didn't.

Hypocrisy is not unique to democracies, of course. They just strengthen a link between equality and injustice that was forged much earlier, back in our evolutionary past. That's where the final part of the story is told.

HUNTER-GATHERERS ON THE LOOKOUT FOR HYPOCRISY

Since long before modern democracies, humans have existed in another type of society that is strongly egalitarian: hunter-gatherer groups. These are relatively mobile groups that go out to forage food or hunt wild animals. They stand in contrast to agricultural societies that focus on growing crops and raising domesticated animals, mostly staying in one place.

Although agricultural societies dominate the world nowadays, hunting-gathering has had an enduring influence on humans. That's not surprising when you realize it was dominant for more than 90 percent of human history. If agriculture has been around for 500 generations, we have been in hunter-gatherer bands for around 100,000 generations.[21] That's enough time for natural selection to have shaped our instincts into ones that fit with hunter-gatherer practices.

Those practices would have encouraged the sense of justice as a fair exchange and the hatred of free riding. The term *hunter-gatherer* is quite broad, so there is some variety, but it's clear that most of these groups were strongly egalitarian. Resources were shared out among the group, and individuals were rarely allowed to dominate.[22] As a member of the Ju/'hoansi people put it, "Each one of us is headman over himself."[23]

In a way, that's surprising: after all, any one person has a strong incentive to compete and get on top through force. Then they can make others give them benefits without doing any work themselves. Or they can get to the same place through skilled free riding: getting a share of the meat after only pretending they did their part on the hunt.[24] The explanation for why this didn't happen shows how fairness, morality, and hypocrisy became woven together.

Hunter-gatherer groups, which shaped our instincts over millennia, *required* cooperation to function. Foraging and hunting needed many adults to collaborate, which meant they had to be nourished, and so food had to be shared.[25] If one person tried to dominate and hoard food, that would threaten the functioning of the whole group. The same goes if someone tried to free ride in a hunt, which could threaten the success of the kill.

All this meant that those who seemed like they were trying to free ride or get an unfair allocation were punished. Members of the group gossiped about them and denigrated their reputation. They could be shunned and ridiculed. We know this happened because it still happens today in existing hunter-gatherer groups. For the !Kung people in Africa, the worst accusations you can make are those of hoarding or arrogance. For the first, you force the hoarder to give "till it hurts," while for the second you burst their bubble of conceit through put-downs and back-handed compliments.[26]

If the free riders or exploiters did not take the hint, then the group could gang up to exile or even kill them. That's why this process of group control has been called "moralistic aggression." It served the evolutionary purpose of warning those who try to exploit and free ride and even offered a mechanism to remove them.[27]

What's interesting about this anger is that it often seems "out of all proportion to the offenses committed," just like our reactions to hypocrisy seem surprisingly harsh.[28] Things make more sense when you realize that we are drawing on an evolved instinct that has served us well.

Over time, this control mechanism became something more—it became the foundation of whole moral systems. Prosocial behavior got you status in the group and a store of goodwill that you could use if you fell ill. The people who couldn't do this were punished and were less likely to reproduce. Over generations, these rules and incentives became internalized as a sense of right and wrong; our consciences were born.[29]

Charles Darwin made this connection, writing in *The Descent of Man* (1871) that "the social instincts . . . naturally lead to the golden rule, 'As ye would that men should do to you, do ye to them likewise;' and this lies at the foundation of morality."[30] We therefore loop back to Jesus's Sermon on the Mount via evolutionary history and cross-cultural evidence.[31] Similarly, others have suggested that Christian morality emerged from the realization that the weak could overcome the strong if they banded together, just like in moralistic aggression.[32]

So our sense of morality and justice was fashioned in a context where equality and fair exchange were dominant. It started with a system where the group came together against the individual to control violations such as free riding.

This origin explains the core sense of injustice that hypocrites trigger in us when they get undeserved benefits. We have a deep-rooted hatred of unfair exchanges.[33] Evolutionary psychologists have made the connection with hypocrisy explicit. In their words, "our hypocrisy circuit makes no sense logically, but makes evolutionary psychological sense . . . [because] it is as if a cheater proposes a social exchange."[34] This evidence backs up my point that hypocrisy is about more than morality: morality itself sits on an older concern about social exchange that hypocrisy sparks off.

With all this in mind, remember that hypocrisy is linked to one flavor of justice in particular—and other ones do exist. For example, you might think that someone's noble birth or religious office justifies their actions—they don't have to earn anything or make a fair exchange. This is a hierarchical concept of justice, and we can't ignore that recent human societies have been highly hierarchical—think of pharaohs and kings, feudalism and tyrannies. Hierarchy seems to be one of our mental models as well: we require less time and effort to understand hierarchies than other types of social structures.[35]

The desire for hierarchy seems to sit alongside the wish for equality. Human evolution has been seen as a U-curve in terms of inequality: in our earliest beginnings, there was hierarchy and violence, much like we see in chimps today; then came the long period of hunter-gatherer equality; that era was followed by renewed inequality in large agricultural societies. So we have a heritage of both hierarchy and egalitarianism.[36]

Which we choose may depend on how the trade-offs map against our immediate needs. Hierarchies can work well when we need to solve coordination problems, avoid costly conflicts over resources, and address external threats.[37] But if we make that trade, the ambivalence in our nature will always be there. As we watch those above us get the plaudits, there will always be the ancestral tug to pull them down, to punish and break them. Calling out hypocrisy is an easy way of doing that.

With that in mind, let's see how our sensitivity to injustice plays out in practice. As I mentioned earlier, there are two main things we consider: the hypocrite's motivations and what kind of outcome the motivations produced.

MOTIVATION

Intentions

When we are judging any action, we often consider whether someone meant to do it. Just think how many legal systems distinguish between murder and manslaughter. Even when the action is an admirable one, we care about whether someone is doing it for the right reasons or just to look good.[38] To show how hypocrisy is not an exception, let's go back to the experiment I ran.

In one of the scenarios, the friend says that *they* always give money to homeless people. You could say that the motivations here are ambiguous.

The person *could* be trying to deceive us, but maybe they just aren't very aware of their own behavior, or their memory is bad.

To see how motivations might affect our judgments, I tweaked the scenario and showed it to the same people again. I emphasized that the friend does not realize that they've ignored the second homeless person and that they continue to think they always give money. Now it's clear that the friend is unaware of their behavior—and therefore it's likely that their intention was not to deceive.

This change had a bigger impact on people's judgments than I expected. I thought people might see the friend as smug and deluded and judge them more harshly as a result. In fact, things moved in the other direction. You can see in figure 6.1 that people saw the friend as much *less* hypocritical and *less* worthy of disapproval.

Other studies support the basic idea that intentions matter. In one example, people were told about someone who had been active in antiracist

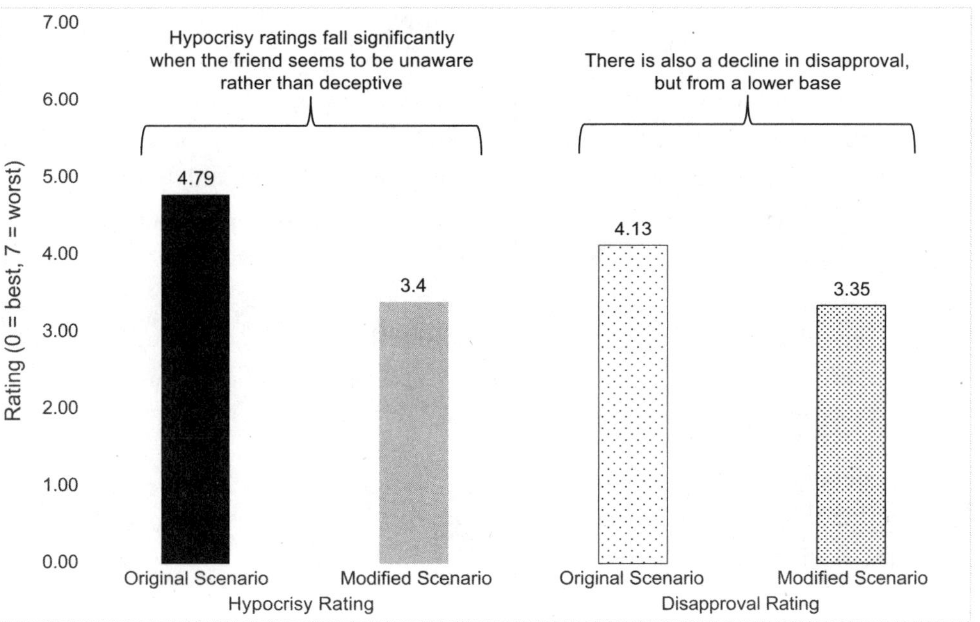

Figure 6.1
Effects of intention on hypocrisy judgments.

organizations but who had to interact with relatives with racist views. When she hid her disgust to avoid conflict, around a third of people thought she was being hypocritical; if her motivation was to gain their approval, that proportion rose to more than half.[39] Other examples related to smoking, drug use, and premarital sex showed similar patterns. Intention is linked to how intensely we judge people. But most results also showed fairly high rates of perceived hypocrisy even when there was no deliberate deception.

Of course, we can't always look inside people's heads. So what external evidence do we use in order to judge intentions? Sometimes we look at what a person has done or said in the past—their track record.

Consider an executive who has to promote five out of seven employees to management positions; two employees are Black, five are white, and the five white employees are the ones who get promoted. The researchers who created this scenario varied it in two ways. First, half the people who heard about it were told that the executive had a history of implementing reforms to increase the diversity of hiring at the organization; the other half heard that the reforms had been on a different topic. Second, some of them heard that the executive gave a blatantly racist rationale for the promotion decision; others were told that he said the decision was based purely on performance.

Unsurprisingly, when people heard about the past diversity initiatives followed by the blatant racism, they judged the executive harshly and thought him hypocritical. But when he claimed that the decision was not about race, then his past diversity activities worked in his favor. The researchers concluded that people thought the situation was more ambiguous and used the track record as a signal of his true intentions.[40] In this way, surrounding actions can build up our "moral credentials" that affect how others see us—if there's some leeway in the interpretation.[41]

Extenuating Circumstances

The other thing we look for are barriers or pressures that might have stopped people from fulfilling their intentions—or led them to be hypocritical against their will.

> Imagine the scene: Jennifer is riding on the subway one evening. The carriage is completely empty. Just as the doors are closing, a

man gets on. Although they don't know each other, he sits close to her and starts talking. He's talking about jury duty—how he did it recently, how it's an important civic duty. And what does she think about jury duty?

Jennifer finds all this unnerving—it's just them in the carriage, he seems odd, and she just wants to get off at the next stop. With all this in mind, she says what she thinks he wants to hear: that it's wrong to get out of jury duty.

It works; he's placated. By coincidence, Jennifer is called up for jury duty the next day. It's really inconvenient for her, so she tries to get out of doing it.[42]

Jennifer's words and deeds are inconsistent, but that's because she felt uneasy and even threatened by the stranger. When people see this scenario, created by the psychologists Jillian Jordan and Roseanna Sommers, they think that's a valid excuse. They rate Jennifer low on hypocrisy and disapproval. In fact, their ratings are no different from a scenario when the man simply tells her about jury duty, and she doesn't feel threatened or say *anything* in response.

Jennifer's situation was transitory, but obviously people may be locked into power structures that force them to pretend to protect themselves—or their loved ones. Religious persecution is an obvious example. In Spain during the fifteenth and sixteenth centuries, there were campaigns against the Jewish population that gave them the choice of exile or conversion to Christianity. Many chose the latter but continued to practice Judaism in private.[43]

You may also develop reservations about your native traditions and culture but feel unable to act on them until you are older and have an escape route. Suppose you were raised in a racist family environment that you are now questioning. Until you have the confidence or resources to act on your new principles, you will continue with the same words and actions, just without the belief—in other words, as a hypocrite. Falling short of principles can mean that you have adopted new principles, and so there's a new chance of progress.

But we might also identify other structures, such as poverty, that stop people from acting on their principles. That's the theme at the heart of the neorealist movie *Bicycle Thieves*, which came out in 1948.[44] Often considered one of the greatest films of all time, the narrative is depressingly simple. Times are tough in Italy, but Antonio has finally found the job that will save his family. He also has the bicycle that is essential for the position—until someone steals it from the street. He sees the thief and angrily accuses him in front of a crowd, but it's just one person's word against another, and the bike is nowhere to be found.

Eventually, desperate, Antonio sees an unattended bicycle and jumps on it, thereby becoming a thief himself. Circumstances have made him do the exact thing he furiously condemned.

He is caught instantly. Spared prosecution but with no job or prospects, he and his son are shown trudging into a dismal future at the end of the film. Although Antonio is a hypocrite, the injustice he's experienced makes it hard to judge him harshly.

There are many reasons why we might see inconsistency as more or less justified. The situation might have changed over time; you may be stuck in a role where you must advise against things that you do, as in doctors who smoke; you may be hampered by bureaucratic obstacles or feel powerless in the face of disapproval by others. But there is one reason that demands a closer look: weakness of will.

We all know about failings of willpower. We intend to do things, but we get tempted or distracted, or we fail to make the effort. Our fruit rots, and our bicycles rust. The key thing about weakness of will is that we had an intention that we failed to turn into action—and that inconsistency can be hypocritical.[45] Two things seem to affect how we judge weak-willed hypocrites: how often they miss their intentions, with hypocrisy increasing the more often people lapse; and how much they really care about their goal, with people who violate strong convictions being judged worse.[46]

For me, the key insight about weakness of will is that it doesn't excuse hypocrites from being judged—your good intention alone does not save you.[47] Instead, it's all about whether your weakness gets you benefits. Imagine a vegetarian who expresses their views ardently but also, occasionally, has a secret burger when drunk because they miss the taste of meat. If they continue to claim the social benefits of seeming strong and consistent, we are likely to condemn them. But consider if they get drunk with others who are pressuring them to cave, and they eat the burger while admitting how tempting it is and how conflicted they feel. That seems more like weakness and less like hypocrisy.

So motivation does matter. Your hypocrisy can have noble intent, like parents who try to present a good example. But that won't stop you being judged, especially if you are holding on to benefits from your hypocrisy. And I hope the ideas so far have complicated the notion of what an "intention" even is—perhaps it's a nonconscious impulse from our evolutionary past rather than a considered aim.

Perhaps because of these complexities, people also look at outcomes when judging the injustice of hypocrisy.

WHAT HAPPENED BECAUSE OF THE HYPOCRISY?

In the 2003 movie *School of Rock*, Dewey Finn is down on his luck after getting fired from his band just before the big Battle of the Bands contest. To make rent, he pretends to be his friend Ned and becomes a substitute teacher at a local preparatory school. He soon realizes that many of the kids in his class have musical talent. He hatches a plan to turn them into a rock band, with him as lead singer, and compete at the Battle of the Bands.

This is a comedy, so everything works out. The pupils put on a great performance, proving the doubters—especially their parents—wrong. Dewey's deception is rewarded rather than punished, and everyone seems to flourish. It's a happy ending for all.

Yet you could argue that Dewey is pretty hypocritical. He presents rock music to the pupils as a way to express themselves and break out of the classical music straitjacket. In his words, rock is about breaking the rules, freedom, and "sticking it to the man."[48] But he doesn't give much freedom to the children or offer them many options, at least at the start. He assigns them all roles in the band as part of a deceptive plan to achieve his own goals. *He* is "the man," using them for his ends.

Obviously, this take seems ridiculous. The framework for hypocrisy shows us why. It's true that Dewey's deeds are inconsistent with his words, and he benefits as a result. Yet there seems to be little injustice because everyone wins. Since there's no real harm, the hypocrisy seems unimportant. But suppose one of the students—say Lawrence, on keyboards—finds that he has now lost all enthusiasm for the classical piano he used to love. Maybe he would even have made a career as a concert pianist—but no more. In this world, Dewey's selfishness has caused harm, and maybe we're more likely to notice how badly his orders sit with his rock rhetoric.

There's some evidence to back up this intuition. In one study, people heard about a parent who dropped out of high school, regrets it now, and won't let his son do what he did. In fact, he pushes him hard, demanding lots of study and piano practice. When people were told that the son became a concert pianist, just 18 percent saw the father as hypocritical; when they heard that the son had developed emotional problems and dropped out of school because of his father's restrictions, the perception of hypocrisy shot up to 55 percent.[49]

In general, the more severe the harm, the more hypocritical people are seen to be.[50] Equally, the better the outcome, the more justifiable the hypocrisy seems. These findings match others that show that people think deception is ethical and desirable if it prevents unnecessary harm.[51] It seems that many people think as in the world of everyday compromises, where the end often justifies the means—like Diana's fundraising for her nonprofit. In contrast to the inhuman consistency of the purity regime, we think that hypocrisy where you do the right thing for the wrong reason might be OK.

The problem is that we disagree over what harms or benefits are and who deserves to get them. A cynical view might be that we approve of whatever benefits us. It's true that we judge people who cheat as more moral when we benefit from their cheating; we reproach liars less if they are lying to advance a cause we support.[52] But, notably, people also condemn leaders who backtrack on their moral commitments *even if they agree with the leader's new position*.[53] Agreement doesn't always wash away the taint of hypocrisy.

The underlying issue here is that people have competing values that are hard to prioritize—our views on them shift and conflict. Clashes cannot be avoided.[54] A police officer may have the principle of always putting family members first, but if one of them commits a crime, that code comes up against his duty to the law. We may owe loyalty to a company that's treated us well, while also feeling the need to blow the whistle on the bad things it's doing to others.[55]

At the same time, competing value systems are playing out at a massive scale in society. For example, in June 2020 US conservatives accused public-health officials of "social-distancing hypocrisy" because many of them were supporting people's right to gather and protest against systemic racism. The conservative argument was that many of these same officials had recently condemned people gathering to protest against COVID-19 lockdowns. The officials said the situations were different but also argued that the protests were justified, given the public-health impact of systemic racism.[56]

Here, as so often, hypocrisy looks like the battlefield for a clash of values and priorities. This comparison reinforces the idea that not only is hypocrisy grounded in people's perceptions, but it also helps to widen some of the critical fault lines in modern societies.

Yet many cases of hypocrisy are not about a clash of abstract values. They are about a person being inconsistent to get benefits that we think they don't deserve. So, having explored why we think that way, the final piece of the puzzle is to understand what hypocrisy can get you.

7 BENEFITS

English was Joseph Conrad's third language, and he didn't learn it until he was in his twenties. Despite this fact—or perhaps because of it—he became one of English literature's greatest stylists. Those gifts brought to life two characters who embody the twin ways we benefit from hypocrisy. The first one gets social status based on a reputation for integrity that he does not deserve. The second is filled with self-satisfied dreams about his heroic character that are brutally punctured by reality. Let's meet them.

NOSTROMO'S NEED FOR RENOWN

Nostromo, published in 1904, is a novel about the fictional South American republic of Costaguana. Nostromo is a charismatic sailor who has a reputation for being both brave and honorable.[1] Throughout the novel, everyone stresses how much people see him as "perfectly incorruptible" and how his integrity "seemed to be a part of the man, like his whiskers or his teeth." What's more, it's clear that Nostromo himself lives for his reputation. His great joy is to "ride through the streets, recognized by everyone, great and little."[2] As one character notes, "The only thing he seems to care for . . . is to be well spoken of."[3]

Nostromo's love for his reputation leads to hypocrisy and tragedy. At first, he lives up to his billing—he leads a daring mission to evacuate the silver from the local mine to stop it falling into the revolutionaries' hands. After his boat is struck in the dark, he and his confederate Martin Decoud have to hide the treasure on a small island just off the coast. Nostromo has to get back to shore but returns some days later to find Martin missing—along with four pieces of silver. What we discover, but he never does, is that Martin has killed himself, using the heavy silver pieces to weigh down his body in the sea.

Everyone on shore thinks that the treasure was lost overboard. Nostromo realizes that if he tries to return it, everyone will think that he stole the four pieces. He will be seen as a thief. His reputation will never recover, and that's the thing he prizes most. To keep people thinking he is incorruptible, he becomes corrupt: he cashes in the silver over years, getting rich slowly to avoid suspicion.

His secret actions are the exact reverse of his public image for bravery and integrity, and the hypocrisy tears him apart: "Nostromo had lost his peace; the genuineness of all his qualities was destroyed. He felt it himself, and often cursed the silver of San Tome. His courage, his magnificence, his leisure, his work, everything was as before, only everything was a sham."[4]

Nostromo gets the benefits of social status, which he craves, by falsely signaling that all his actions match his incorruptible image. His external adulation brings him internal torment. Interestingly, this is the opposite of what happens for Conrad's second hypocrite, Lord Jim.

LORD JIM'S IMAGINARY HEROISM

Lord Jim (1900) has been called the first modernist novel. The story is told out of order by multiple narrators and from weird angles.[5] But we get a pretty clear picture of the way Jim thinks about himself at the start. He thinks he's a hero.

At school, Jim sees himself as one who "quelled mutinies on the high seas, and in a small boat upon the ocean kept up the hearts of despairing men—always an example of devotion to duty, and as unflinching as a hero in a book." He will rise to meet the crises that come. When he becomes an officer on a ship for real, his confidence continues. Standing on the deck of the ship, he smiles and thinks of his imaginary achievements, sure that "there was nothing he could not face."[6]

We soon find out that Jim's "unbounded confidence" in himself is all false. Jim does not know what to do in a crisis; he does not act as a hero; his deeds do not match his thoughts. Just a few moments after he smiles in self-satisfaction, his ship hits something in the water. The bulkhead begins to bulge, the vessel starts to drop in the water—any second and it's going to sink completely. There are 800 people on the ship but only seven lifeboats, and that means, Jim thinks, there's no time to save anyone. Meanwhile, the dissolute captain and his craven officers have loosened a lifeboat for themselves and are shouting up at Jim to jump now, to save himself, and why not, Jim thinks, the ship is doomed already . . . In the darkness and confusion, with the ship going down under him, Jim finds himself in the lifeboat.

Cut to later. The twist: the ship didn't sink. It's eventually found by another vessel. The officers are picked up after a few days, publicly vilified, and put on trial. Jim is disgraced for abandoning ship—his actions have shown him to be the exact opposite of what he imagined.

The inconsistency is between his self-image and his actions. The benefit is feeling better about himself than he deserves. Conrad makes clear to us that Jim thinks he is above others and is the kind of person who would do the right thing. Just before the accident, he is "contemplating his own superiority" and literally feels good about it, "as though all the blood in his body had turned to warm milk."[7]

All these are *internal* benefits—he doesn't tell anyone about them before the accident; he's not boasting. In that sense, Jim's internal conceit is very different from Nostromo's need to fake his reputation. Maybe Jim's case is not our typical view of hypocrisy, but we do see it as such—and we do judge it.

In the end, Jim shows the power of the "induced hypocrisy" approach I discussed earlier. When confronted with the gap between his principles and his behavior, he uses that experience to change: the second half of the book is about how he becomes a hero for real and lives up to his self-image in the end.

The hypocrisy of these two characters takes different paths. Nostromo starts out as a self-satisfied person of integrity and becomes a guilt-wracked hypocrite. Jim starts out as a self-satisfied hypocrite and becomes a guilt-wracked person of integrity. What these examples also show is that the two types of benefits can be in tension: you can look good but feel bad or feel good while looking bad.

But when we think about hypocrisy, we generally imagine someone getting plaudits they don't deserve. In line with that intuition, it does seem like undeserved social status is the thing that annoys us most. Why is that?

SOCIAL STATUS

We do not like others to deceive us; we do not think it fair that they should be held in higher esteem by us than they deserve.
—Blaise Pascal, *Pensées*

Why Status Matters

Your status matters. People with higher social status get more resources, more attention, and more say in decisions. Status underpins your sense of well-being and esteem. Losing status can mean losing your health, since our nervous system worries about our rank. Feeling relatively low in status triggers systemic inflammation, which may increase chronic diseases related to aging.[8]

Status concerns may also harm you through violence. Contests over even small indicators of status can make you a threat or a target. Status disputes are the most common cause of murderous conflicts between men, and they often start with an argument over apparently trivial things—say, who has access to a pool table—that nonetheless signal who has the upper hand.[9] In a survey of college students, just less than half of college-age men and women said that "status/reputation concerns" had caused their most recent act of direct aggression (a face-to face fight or argument).[10]

The drive for status appears to be universal across cultures.[11] When you consider that status may also shape our values, conventions, and perceptions of beauty, there's a lot at stake.[12] It might be surprising to learn, therefore, that we don't talk about status—it's unpleasant, even taboo. Part of the reason for this silence is that direct attempts to achieve status reduce your status. People think less of you if you are blatantly trying to claim a higher rank; we are unimpressed by people who try to impress.[13] That means we have to give other reasons for our status-seeking behavior. You could even say that all status-seeking is hypocritical.

What is this thing, "status," that is so important but so elusive? A study tried to answer that question by asking 2,751 people from fourteen countries with widely differing cultures. The survey found a surprising amount of consistency: specific acts and traits had very similar impacts on status across cultures.[14] The most status-enhancing things included being a trusted group member, being intelligent, being an exceptional leader, and having a wide range of knowledge. The things that damaged status most included stealing, being unclean, and having a sexually transmitted disease or bad manners.

If you look at the things that bring status, they concern qualities that are generally useful to others—trust, knowledge, and willingness to share resources. Indeed, these results support the idea that status is based more on competence (the perceived benefits people can bring) than on dominance (the costs that people can inflict on others).[15]

This competence or "prestige" view of status is about respect and admiration. People give you deference without being forced to; they value what you can do for themselves and others.[16] Some obvious examples of people with this kind of status are doctors, singers, scientists, entrepreneurs, artists, and pilots. We also give it to people who we think are "good," such as charity workers and faith leaders, but morality is just one way to get status.[17] Not all hypocrites are trying to look morally good.

When it comes to hypocrisy, the point is that we *give* status—it can't just be taken. In fact, status is a social *exchange*: we give it to people on the basis that they can and will provide something in return.[18] But we make that award to people who appear to have value, not necessarily those who truly have it.[19] It takes effort to check this all the time, so we rely on signals instead—such as whether your financial adviser has a decent office, or any office at all.

And, finally, we give status at a cost to ourselves. As I mentioned earlier, status is a relative ranking: as someone else rises, your position seems to sink in turn. Status is a zero-sum game.[20]

If you put these factors together, you can see why status is linked to hypocrisy. We give status to people at a cost to ourselves, expecting a fair exchange. But people can simply appear to have these qualities and therefore get the status benefits at little cost. We call these people who free ride on our system of status "hypocrites."[21] And their main tool is called *false signaling.*

False Signaling

Signals are ways of sending information about yourself to others. The term *signal* is used to explain how people (or companies) show they have qualities that others are likely to value. Signals can be used to get status. Driving an expensive car may signal that you are wealthy. Students compete fiercely to get into famous universities. Companies put prestigious people on their board to try to increase the value of their initial public offering.[22]

Here's the important thing about signals and hypocrisy: you can signal that you have a quality that you don't actually have. You can walk around holding a renowned book in a foreign language that you can't read. Or you can refer to the charities you support even though you just spend money on yourself. These are false signals.

Hypocrites send false signals about their status, and this is a major reason we hate hypocrisy. Take the case of Becky, who is talking on the phone to her friend Amanda. They are discussing another friend, who Amanda mentions often downloads music illegally. Imagine this situation ends one of three ways:

1. "Shortly after their conversation, Becky goes online, and downloads music illegally."
2. "*Becky says that she thinks it is morally wrong to download music illegally from the Internet.* Shortly after their conversation, Becky goes online, and downloads music illegally."
3. "Becky says that she thinks it is morally wrong to download music illegally from the Internet, *but that she sometimes does it anyway.* Shortly after their conversation, Becky goes online, and downloads music illegally."[23]

In the first scenario, no one says anything about the behavior—there's no signal. The second is a clear case of a hypocrite sending a false signal. The third is exactly the same as the second one—there is still criticism—but no false signal is sent: Becky is an "honest hypocrite."

A team of researchers led by Jillian Jordan found that people who saw ending 2 judged Becky much worse than if she had said nothing (ending 1). That's unsurprising. What's interesting is that people who saw her honest hypocrisy (ending 3) judged her no worse than if she said nothing. Taking away the false signal also removed the penalty for hypocrisy. This result holds across several studies and seems to be real.

Yet this study just sees hypocrisy in terms of morality: it concludes that hypocrites falsely signal moral goodness only. Maybe your instincts lie this way as well. So let me argue that it's *status* that hypocrites get unfairly, and morality is just one part of that status.

Morality and status are related. Remember that many moral systems were founded on the principle that individuals should contribute to the group. Prosocial actions bring us status. People buy environmentally friendly products to look better in the eyes of others—and it works. Some communities have rituals of potlatching, where leaders compete to give away their stuff in order to win respect and status.[24] In other cultures, rich people visibly donate money to causes and institutions that try to do good.

But morality is just one kind of status; hypocrites can use false signaling to get other kinds as well. Sometimes looking like a rebel, a maverick, a cynic, or a dangerous freethinker can get you status. Take a teenager who tries to look cool, as if he doesn't respect authority or care about the future, but goes home and diligently does his homework.

In fact, you could argue that some parts of culture are all about creating new sources of status against traditional moral values.[25] Take art: it could be that the more transgressive and shocking a piece is, the more it's celebrated. Moreover, the people doing this celebrating are often established members of the society whose values are getting challenged. You can see a world where they hypocritically signal that they love images that in fact make them feel deeply uncomfortable.[26]

Hypocrisy comes from being inconsistent with the status claims you make, whatever they are.[27] But I think a false signal requires something else to make it hypocritical and take it beyond a simple lie. Hypocrites falsely signal that they would do, say, or think the same thing in other situations or for other people. Their claim goes beyond the immediate situation. They signal *consistency*.

Being consistent and trustworthy makes you valuable to others. We are always trying to work out what other people are *really* like. If we think someone holds to their stated principles in other situations as well—that a vegetarian isn't secretly scoffing burgers—we are more willing to give them credit. After all, that means they are paying the appropriate costs, and the status we give them is a fair exchange.

So if you claim more consistency, you also claim more status. Making a contrast with lying is helpful here. Some lies are just about the immediate situation: "Did you steal that newspaper?" "No." Those lies are not so hypocritical. The hypocrisy creeps in once you start sending signals that go wider—about the kind of person you are in general. Your character. "No. I would never steal anything. Stealing is wrong, and we should crack down on all kinds of theft."[28]

Remember the example of the person whose date knows more about music than he does. Saying that you've heard of the specific band she's mentioning? Simple lie. Following this up by saying that you diligently follow the latest releases from independent record labels? More hypocritical. Criticizing people who just listen to chart hits? Even more hypocritical.[29]

The stronger the signal, the more likely it is to become false—that is, a gap will emerge between your presentation and your reality. A bigger gap means more blame when the hypocrisy is exposed.[30] Moral claims often come into play here—not because hypocrisy is always about right and wrong but because moral claims are an easy and popular way of signaling consistency. They are literally rules about the world that are meant to hold true in all situations.[31]

For example, think how leaders can justify their decisions on either moral grounds or pragmatic grounds—say, a politician opposed gay marriage on the basis of tradition versus the cost to change government systems. Studies show that if you reverse your decision after making a pragmatic decision, you are seen as much less hypocritical. False signaling explains why: you are just responding to the situation in front of you rather than making a claim about what you would do elsewhere.[32]

In contrast, moral statements are seen as signals about *what you would do in the future*. As I mentioned earlier, if a politician takes a strong moral stance against lying, people take that as a signal that the politician won't lie in the future—even after they've been caught lying![33] But there's a way of strengthening the moral signal even further, which some people think is the height of hypocrisy: condemning others.

Strengthening the Signal by Condemning Others

There's plenty of evidence that we see hypocrites who criticize others as the "worst" kind.[34] For example, a recent study analyzed 370,000 posts and 11 million comments from Reddit's "Am I the Asshole?" forum—a unique place to see what people really dislike in others.[35] It found that scenarios where the author disparaged or judged someone else triggered especially negative reactions. Simply being an imperfect person who criticizes others was enough for commenters to label someone "the asshole."

When people were asked to define hypocrisy, around half of study participants mentioned the condemnation of others. Telling others what not to do (37 percent) was cited much more often than telling them what to do (10 percent).[36] The evidence from my earlier experiment backs this up. Some people saw a modified scenario where their friend actively criticizes anyone who doesn't give money to homeless people, calling them selfish and uncaring. People reacted to this change by seeing the friend as more hypocritical and less admirable (see figure 7.1). They gave the highest hypocrisy rating of the whole experiment to this scenario.

Condemning others fits into the story of signaling status and consistency. The reason? It sends a stronger signal that you wouldn't do that thing.[37] Imagine there are two athletes, Jessica and Nicole. If Nicole speaks out against performance-enhancing drugs, while Jessica remains silent, people will view Nicole as more likable and trustworthy. More importantly, they'll assume Nicole is less likely to use drugs in the future. Hypocrites can use the power of this consistency signal to get unearned status benefits.[38]

In fact, condemning others sends an even stronger signal than making claims about yourself. Even if Jessica explicitly states that she never uses drugs, people still prefer Nicole's approach of condemning others. This

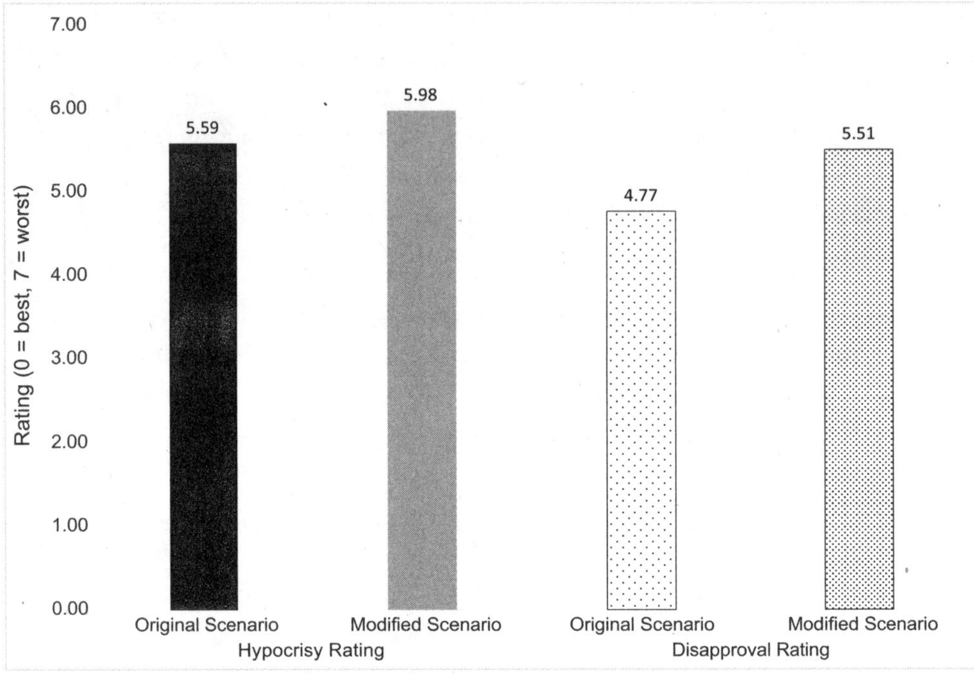

Figure 7.1
How people react when hypocrites criticize others.

might be because we don't like people who directly claim status—talking about yourself can seem like bragging, while criticism of others makes the same point more subtly.[39] Regardless of the reason, condemnation is a more persuasive signal of consistency and status.

There's an ironic twist: the people piling on to criticize false-signaling hypocrites may be falsely signaling, too. They may be giving the impression that they are better than they are. Again, there's an evolutionary explanation here. Remember that moralistic aggression emerged to take care of cheaters and free riders. Well, once that happens, "sham moralistic aggression" emerges as a new form of cheating.[40] In other words, you can free ride by condemning hypocrites—looking good while paying few to no costs.

In fact, you may be joining in to assuage your own guilt. Maybe you've done the same thing as the hypocrite at some point. In one study, people who felt guilty about using sweatshop-made products were more outraged and more eager to punish offending companies than those who didn't use the products.[41] Expressing outrage helped restore their positive self-image, effectively transforming their guilt into righteous anger.

The process can also work in reverse. Sending false signals can make you feel guilty inside.[42] Imagine you are offered the chance to make some money by giving a stranger a nonfatal electric shock. Whatever you choose, you are then asked to judge someone else who did take the money. People who decided to blame this other person *after doing the very same thing* reported more moral conflict and showed greater guilt-related brain activity.[43] Or, as Joseph Conrad put it, "Nostromo had lost his peace."

These two examples show how concerns for social status and self-image interact with each other. Which means it's time to explain how self-image concerns drive hypocrisy.

SELF-IMAGE

You can be a hypocrite without sending false signals. You might secretly disapprove of something you do often or never do something that you secretly support. So what benefits do "private hypocrites" get?

Well, just as we want to look good to others, we also want to look good to ourselves. Having a positive self-image feels pleasant and helps us function; it's one of the main drivers of our behavior.[44] But what does a "good" self-image look like in most Western societies?

It's often related to the same things that bring us social status and prestige: feeling competent, moral, authentic, and consistent.[45] We are motivated to think of how we are better than others in terms of these qualities. The issue is that we tend to inflate our abilities in our minds, leading to an inconsistency that other people view with scorn.[46] For example, imagine that John thinks it is wrong to cheat at exams, even though he does it often. He never tells anyone about his beliefs, though. In this world, around 50 percent of people think John is being hypocritical. But if you add in the idea that he secretly looks down on others who cheat, this figure jumps to 91 percent.[47]

We think private hypocrites feel better about themselves than they deserve to.[48] That's the undeserved benefit they get, and it comes about in two main ways. One is through self-deception, which leaves them secure and complacent in their self-image. The other is through "licensing." That's where they see they aren't perfect, but they do or think something that allows them to feel good about themselves anyway. Let's take licensing first.[49]

Cleansing and Licensing Yourself to Feel Good

Meet Celeste, who lives in New Jersey. She's forty and works for a consultancy that finds new ways to get people to spend more on sports gambling apps. Celeste's business is doing very well. It has found a clutch of prompts that get people to spend longer in play and bet more each time. But Celeste starts looking at the data and sees how big and frequent some people's bets are—and what time of night they are coming in. It is not hard to see that some players are in trouble.

Celeste starts working ten hours a week at a nonprofit that helps people dealing with gambling addiction and warns of the risks. She volunteers anonymously from her personal computer. She also starts giving $150 a month to addiction support services—again, without letting anyone else know. She can afford this because she got promoted, and her employer is paying out bigger bonuses.

When people find out Celeste is doing this, they think it's hypocritical. They think she's trying to "purchase a clean conscience on the cheap."[50] Since there's a direct connection between Celeste's public behavior, which may be causing harm, and her private attempts to be altruistic, people think that she's trying to feel better about herself than she deserves.

We know this because a team of researchers, led by Kieran O'Connor, tested what happens if public and private actions are *not* linked. Imagine if Celeste's consultancy focuses on boosting tobacco sales rather than on gambling—but she's still volunteering to support gambling addiction. In this case, it seems less likely that she's just volunteering to feel better about her job.

That's what people thought. If the "bad" public behavior and the "good" private behavior are about the same thing, people see Celeste as more hypocritical. They think that she's trying to alleviate her guilt without sacrificing enough.

In fact, we can say more: it's not the *attempt* to reduce her guilt that people don't like; it's if she *succeeds* in clearing her conscience. Imagine if after her volunteering, Celeste feels just as bad—maybe worse—than before. The guilt stops her sleeping at night. Compare that to a situation where she straightaway starts feeling better about herself. She doesn't feel guilty about her role in promoting gambling anymore. She sees herself as a better person and starts sleeping more soundly at night. In both cases, Celeste is driven by guilt. But people rate her as much more hypocritical when she succeeds in clearing her conscience. They also think she feels much better than she deserves and praise her less.[51] Why?

We think that if you feel guilty, you are paying a mental price—and the exchange seems fair. Otherwise, it feels unjust that Celeste is still getting the bonus and benefits from her job without paying the price of feeling guilty, even though she's aware of the harm she may be doing. The balance is off. Maybe if she did enough good stuff privately, the balance would swing back, and a clear conscience would seem deserved.

Oscar Wilde's novel *The Picture of Dorian Gray* (1890) has a nice—but weird—example of how this internal bargaining drives hypocrisy. Dorian Gray owns a portrait of himself as a young man, locked away in an upstairs room. For the past eighteen years, Dorian has not aged—but the portrait has. Every sin that Dorian commits mutates the portrait, making it look crueler and more hideous every time. And Dorian's been committing a lot of sins: murdering the artist who painted the portrait, driving his lover to suicide, blackmailing a friend, and generally indulging in every vice he can find.

But now, having seemingly evaded all retribution, Dorian has a change of heart. He decides he wants "a new life." He thinks that because he has done one good thing—not breaking the heart of his current lover—he might have changed already. He thinks of the portrait in the room: it would no longer torture him. In fact, "he felt as if the load had been lifted from him already," so he goes to check it, feeling that it must be looking better: "A cry of pain and indignation broke from him. He could see no change, unless that in the eyes there was a look of cunning and in the mouth the curved wrinkle of the hypocrite."[52]

If anything, the painting is worse than before, with a new flourish of hypocrisy. The reason for this, Dorian reflects, is that he was driven only by the wish to escape his guilt and feel better, not by genuine remorse. And he still has all the benefits from his crimes: he looks great, and he's gotten away with murder. In that situation, feeling that "the load had been lifted" looks like hypocrisy.

Deceiving Yourself

We've all seen them. The teacher who criticizes pupils for the exact same thing he does—without even realizing it. The self-satisfied businessperson who is oblivious to how far she falls short of the principles she claims to hold. The preacher who is secure in the knowledge that anything they might have done is justified and forgiven.

Self-deceived hypocrites who don't even face up to their inconsistencies. People who are so sure they are good that they are unaware of their flaws—or so unaware of their flaws that they are sure they are good.

This kind of hypocrisy can pop up anywhere, even for fleeting moments. In the film *Oliver!* (1968), the title character has the nerve to ask for "more" food than the measly rations given to children doing forced labor. When he is taken to the authorities they are appalled at his greed, even though we can see they are large men sat at a table groaning with half-eaten pies, wine, and meat. The scene lasts a second but says a lot.[53]

In James Baldwin's novel *Go Tell It on the Mountain* (1953), the preacher Gabriel Grimes urges others to avoid the pleasures of the world, repent, and be saved. He spares no one. But earlier in his life he had had an affair while married, resulting in a son whom he never acknowledged or supported and who died in a fight at age seventeen. Gabriel never confesses or even repents, either, because he thinks he has been chosen by God as one of his elect.

When his sister confronts him with the truth, Gabriel gives no ground. He claims, "I been doing the will of the Lord, and can't nobody sit in judgment of me but the Lord." But he has no answer when his sister asks him if God has ever said anything that Gabriel *didn't* want to hear. And when he argues that the Lord "sees the heart"—his true self, his true intentions—she agrees but says that Gabriel himself cannot see.[54] He has deceived himself about himself.

We've already seen that hypocrisy can emerge even without deliberate intent. We know this from our everyday lives. If a friend said to you, "I've just realized what a hypocrite I've been," you wouldn't find their epiphany odd—we are not always aware of our inconsistencies.[55]

Recent research supports the idea that many people see hypocrisy whether someone is deluded or not. Take a student who criticizes his classmates' commitment to their education, not realizing that his partying makes him a bad student as well. Three-quarters of people see him as a hypocrite regardless of his lack of self-awareness.[56]

The way we judge self-deception is both straightforward and subtle. On the obvious side: we don't like how self-deception helps people feel better about themselves than they deserve. Self-deception comes from a desire to see the self and the world in ways that favor you; it prevents or removes reasons to feel bad.[57]

We dislike this unfair deception, even though people are doing it to themselves. Part of the reason for this is that we only grudgingly allow people to feel good. We are less likely to think that the behavior of others earns them the right to feel virtuous, compared to our own.[58]

At the same time, the presence of self-deception does seem to make us judge hypocrisy less harshly. Intention makes a difference. Remember the experiment I ran: if your friend was not aware that they had ignored the homeless person, this greatly reduced judgments of their hypocrisy. In general, we think that propping up your self-image through self-deception is less bad than deliberately sending out false signals.[59]

Here's the subtle part. Yes, self-deception may take the edge off our anger at hypocrisy, but the trade-off may be that we lose respect for the person as well. Even though self-deception happens in various ways, the common factor is that we see it as a failure of the self.

Say that the cause is a lack of awareness: you simply don't realize that you just walked past a homeless person in the street. Much of our behavior happens without our knowing. Habits are a good example: you can commute from the office almost on autopilot and only realize when you are back home that you meant to stop at the shop.

One view is that this kind of thing happens all the time, so it shouldn't be judged harshly. But that view cuts against the idea of the consistent, coherent self that we prize. If someone asks you why you forgot the shopping, and your best answer is, "I was on autopilot," they aren't going to think more of you.

Or maybe self-deception comes from the need to reduce pain. As we've seen, being aware of hypocrisy is painful, and you can make some mental maneuvers to lessen the hurt.[60] Maybe that's just part of being human. But when others do this, we may be tempted to see it as weakness, a pitiful coping mechanism that helps them to evade their responsibilities.[61] If people cope by projecting their defects onto others instead, we may even see this way of coping as a psychological flaw.[62]

Comedy provides clues that the erosion of respect is real. Any writer can get an easy laugh by making a character miss the contradiction right in front of their face. It can be the basis for a one-liner or for a whole character. In one episode of the 1980s sitcom *Cheers*, the barfly Norm is imploring Woody to tell his girlfriend Kelly about the play he's acting in. Norm says, "You can't go sneaking out nights on somebody you love. Woody, you have to believe that truth and—" (the phone rings at the bar—when Norm is told it's his wife, Vera, without missing a beat he says, "I'm not here") "—honesty are the cornerstones of any relationship."[63]

When someone's status takes a hit because of their self-deceptions, they become a candidate for our contempt. Contempt is when we dislike something that we see as weak, laughable, or unworthy of respect. You can contrast contempt with hate, where there is also dislike, but it's directed at something that we think is powerful or threatening.[64] So while we may judge a self-deceived hypocrite less harshly, that's because their failings make us see them with derision, pity, or contempt.[65] They've been downgraded in our eyes.

Self-deception does not always backfire, though. If the gap between your self-image and reality is not obvious to others, then deceiving yourself can work out well. If you deceive yourself that your abilities are better than they are, it can make you perform *better* in practice. Being overconfident can make you more persuasive and increase your social status. The self-deception can be so convincing that it convinces others as well![66] Faking it until you make it can work.

In a way, there's an obvious path from deception to self-deception. Constantly deceiving others by sending false signals is exhausting work. So why not start believing in them, thereby freeing up your mind for other things?[67]

You may think that this self-deception can lead you into trouble and danger—in terms of survival, it's not helpful to believe that you are a faster runner or better swimmer than you truly are. But if that's true, then it seems odd that evolution did not get rid of self-deception by making people learn about its pitfalls the hard way. The evolutionary biologist Robert Trivers gives a startling explanation why: self-deception evolved as a better way of deceiving others and getting ahead of the pack.[68]

Suppose you're at a big job interview. You're trying to become the manager of a team of engineers in a rival company. You know that this business has a reputation for keeping things tight and running projects to budget. So you make a big play in your presentation about the importance of keeping control of costs and timescales. You're going to crack down on project managers who are wasteful and inefficient!

If, while you are saying all this, you are also aware that you have never been great as a project manager, that's going to hurt your pitch. The knowledge of your deception will make you nervous. Your heart will start going; your throat may get tight. Your ability to think in the moment will be harmed by the mental effort of dealing with memories of you busting through budgets.[69] You're less likely to get the job.

Self-deception makes all this go away and frees you to function better. That's why it can be used tactically to get gains. There's some evidence that people even distort their own memory when they're asked to deceive high-status people—but not low-status people.[70]

Again, this example shows how the two kinds of benefit—status and self-image—are connected in complex and unexpected ways. Sending false signals can boost your self-image, or it can make you feel guilty. Feeling better about yourself can harm your social status if glaring gaps make you a figure of contempt, or it can enhance your standing by removing internal conflict. But, in the simplest terms, sending *false signals for social status* seems to be the benefit that enrages us most about hypocrisy.

* * *

Inconsistency, injustice, and benefits to the self: we've broken down those building blocks of hypocrisy and seen how they work in detail. But there's one final aspect of hypocrisy that demands a closer look. Double-standards hypocrisy is full of inconsistency and injustice, but it puts them together in a particularly dangerous way. We need to understand how that happens and what we must avoid.

8 DOUBLE-STANDARDS HYPOCRISY

In New York City, as in many large cities, there is a bike-hire system: you take a bicycle from one dock, ride along, and return it to another dock. But you can choose between two kinds of bikes: a standard one or an e-bike, which is more expensive. When getting around, I'd take one or the other, depending on what was available, the weather, how I was feeling, and so on.

Here's the thing: when I took the standard bike, I would often see people zooming past me on the e-bikes and silently judge them as lazy and weak-willed. Why couldn't they just take a normal bike? Isn't exercise part of the point? Aren't these e-bikes sort of heavy and dangerous?

But when *I* took the e-bike, I would be thinking that it was a good decision: I need to get around faster this time; this journey is actually quite far; it's really humid, and there are some hills; I've been getting a lot of exercise recently. Why wouldn't you pay a small fee to go so much faster?

I judged the e-bike as a justified and smart decision *when I was riding it*; I judged it as a pathetic and maybe harmful indulgence *when I wasn't*—perhaps especially when I hadn't been able to find one available.[1]

This is just a small example of double-standards hypocrisy, which is when someone gets unjust gains by being inconsistent in their judgments. They criticize another individual (or group) for something that they excuse in themselves or their team—without admitting that's what they're doing.

In my case, my judgment of e-bikes varied according to whether I was riding one at that moment. In both cases, I felt like my choice was good and justified. In fact, I found it easy to switch between these opposing views with no sense of conflict or concern.[2]

This ease reflects the unjust gains we get from double standards: we feel that our exceptions are justified somehow, that we've maintained our principles overall—and we get to keep claiming this publicly to others as well. We want to tell ourselves and others that we aren't driven purely by self-interest; we aren't being cruel or bigoted; we have principles! Any exception we make is for a good reason or isn't really an exception at all—because we're actually sticking to some other, deeper principle. This tendency of ours was captured by Adam Smith, the founder of economics: "Though it may be true, therefore, that every individual, in his own breast, naturally prefers himself to all mankind, yet he dares not look mankind in the face, and avow that he acts according to this principle."[3]

It's easy to criticize the way we try to make sense of the world. When anyone tries to justify treating themselves or their group differently, they may be able to come up with some good reasons. Context matters; many things affect our judgment. And justification may come down to values: one person's justified resistance is another person's violent law breaking. We may not even know at the time which side of history we are on. This reinforces the idea that it's our perceptions that create hypocrisy.

But one thing remains clear: it's only hypocrisy if we disguise the factors that are driving our judgments. If we don't hide them, it's open prejudice or selfishness—but that often doesn't pay off for us. So we need to come up with other, acceptable reasons for our inconsistent judgments, although we may not even be aware of the truth.[4] The rest of this chapter explains how we come up with those reasons. First, I show how double standards emerge between yourself and others, and then I show how they emerge between your group and your opponents.

"RULES FOR THEE BUT NOT FOR ME"

Many people cheat: around one in five people say they have been unfaithful to their current sexual partner.[5] But this figure counts only the people who said they had "sexual interactions" with someone else. Not only is that term vague, but people have varying ideas of what counts as infidelity in general.

Does texting count? Going for dinner in secret? Looking at dating apps? People will make different judgments about where to draw the line.[6]

They will also draw the line in a different place for their partner than for themselves. In psychology, making more lenient judgments on yourself than on others is called the "actor-observer bias." Infidelity is a good place to look for this bias because most people don't want to think of themselves as unfaithful.[7]

In one study, people were asked to rate potentially unfaithful actions on a scale from 1 (not at all unfaithful) to 7 (very unfaithful). These actions were in four buckets:

- **Sexual or explicit behaviors.** This category included the clearest examples, such as having sex with someone, touching them, or having a shower with them.
- **Online behaviors.** For example, sending and receiving explicit messages, signing up for a dating app, looking at it alone.
- **Emotional or affectionate behaviors.** Receiving close emotional support, watching movies in a dark living room, sharing secrets, sharing a casual dinner.
- **Solitary behaviors.** Watching pornography alone, masturbating, admiring the looks of others.[8]

As you may have guessed, people were asked to imagine either that *they* were doing the behavior or that *their partner* was. Overall, participants did show double standards: they rated a behavior as less unfaithful when they were doing it, as opposed to their partner.

You can tease out self-other double standards in less direct ways as well. For example, imagine you are asked to give an instance of when you've been hypocritical. Would you answer in a different way if you had been asked about someone *else* instead?

The evidence says yes. People use far fewer words when describing their own hypocrisy, often leaving the answer blank. They are stricter about what counts. They include more excuses and justifications. Or they tell self-affirming stories that don't show much, if any, hypocrisy (*"I served my country in the military but voted for a Democrat because I felt he had the best plan"*).[9]

But we can dig deeper; there's something else going on here. Let's go back to the infidelity study. It turns out that the gap between self and others shows up for only two of the four categories I mentioned earlier: online behaviors and affectionate behaviors. These are the ones rated firmly in the middle in terms of severity, which indicates that they are ambiguous. They could fall either side of the line. In contrast, explicit sexual behaviors clearly cross the line—whereas solitary ones generally don't.

Ambiguity opens room for judgment, and that's how double standards creep in. The same behaviors may seem like infidelity in some contexts but not in others.[10] For example, here are some of the behaviors that show the biggest gaps between self and others. Let's see how details can make them seem quite different.

Watching movies in a dark living room with someone. How close are you sitting? What movie are you watching? Is there anyone else there?

Sharing secrets with someone. What kind of secrets, in what context? Are we talking about work gossip in a public place or your heart's true feelings? Are you betraying the confidence of your main partner?

Creating a profile on a dating website. Was it done as a joke or a dare, at a party, surrounded by your friends, who also did something similar?

It's possible to think of reasons why ambiguous actions (but not explicit ones) might fall on the right side of the line. And we find these reasons easier to imagine for ourselves, in part because we think we are more complex and multifaceted than other people.[11] Excuses come to mind more readily when it's our own behavior in question. The actor-observer bias explains this tendency as follows: we often blame our failings on the situation or context but the failings of others on their qualities or intentions.[12] For us: *I failed the driving test because I had a bad driving instructor and the weather on the day of the test was lousy*. For them: *He failed the driving test because he's a bad driver who didn't even try hard to learn.*

We find it easier to bring reasons to mind for ourselves because, well, it's our mind. Memory gives us access to our reasons and how the situation affected our decisions.[13] We can easily imagine similar situations for ourselves. But this is much harder when it comes to other people, thanks to our lack of access. So, instead, it's easier to see their failings as the product of their personality or character. Since we don't know what we don't know, we may not even realize that we are adopting these double standards.[14]

Take the example of "phubbing": looking at your phone in social situations ("phone" + "snubbing"). I'm sure this has happened to you; I'm sure you've done it. One study from 2018 found that phubbing happened in 62 percent of conversations observed in a restaurant, an average of three times a conversation.[15] When the other person used their phone, people thought the conversation was less intimate, but not when they used it. In fact, phubbing is annoying to the person being phubbed, and it damages relationships by creating exclusion and resentment.[16]

Much as we resent others looking at their phones, we love doing it ourselves. Phubbing is therefore one of those actions that looks different depending on your perspective. If your partner is looking at their phone while you're watching a TV program together, you may see them as being rude or disengaged. But if it's *you*, you're likely to think about your phone use in terms of good intentions and positive contributions. You're just looking up something about one of the actors, and you'll probably share it after the episode ends.[17]

A recent study confirmed that this is how we justify our phubbing double standards. People thought their phone use, compared to that of others, was more related to positive social reasons (contributing to a conversation) and positive personal reasons (individual enjoyment). They also thought that they were better at multitasking while using their phones than other people. Given that phone use made things worse for others, these assumptions are bad.[18]

We seem to see more good intentions for ourselves than for others and give ourselves more credit for them as well.[19] We look a bit like James Baldwin's preacher Gabriel Grimes, justifying himself through his true intentions. Or we come up with reasons why things that benefit us are good. If a lie advances the causes we care about, we're more likely to excuse it than if the liars were on the other side.[20]

As these examples suggest, double standards often arise from bias in our judgment. That means we may not even be aware of double standards because we generally have a "bias blind spot": we think that other people may be biased, but we are not.[21] For example, various biases can affect who is recruited for a job. One is called the "halo effect," where recruiters latch onto a single positive aspect of a good candidate (such as a good first impression) and use it to create a "halo" that outshines any defects. When experienced Swiss recruiters were told about these kinds of biases, they thought their colleagues might be susceptible. Themselves? Not so much. (But they were.)[22]

The bias blind spot emerges for the same reasons that we apply double standards to others. We spend too much time thinking about our good intentions and feelings and not enough about what we actually did.[23] So, ironically, not only do we have double standards when it comes to judging behavior, we also have double standards for perceiving double standards!

"BLOOD IS THICKER THAN WATER"

We form groups naturally. You can confirm this claim just by walking around a city with your eyes open. A church is emptying; a football stadium is filling; the bars are busy at night. Bonds tighten through singing, shouting, and talking.

Decades of social psychology research have shown that the results can be profound: we react emotionally as if "the group becomes a part of the self, and the self becomes a part of the group."[24] Moreover, these bonds don't need to be forged by personal history, a common origin, or a shared set of values. They can form quickly (even when the group has only just been created) and arbitrarily (even when the group is simply formed by chance).[25]

A key part of any group's identity is that it is not another group. You define yourself against something else, at least in part. Strangers in the street align into allies and enemies. As you can guess, one thing these group members do is excuse the actions of their teammates and blame their opponents. In fact, people think the sins of their fellow members are about as acceptable as their own—even if the club has only just been established.[26]

These contrasts help explain the balm we spread within our groups and the venom we throw outside of them. Humans are much more cooperative and agreeable than our primate ancestors, yet we are capable of extreme and horrific cruelty toward outsider groups. The anthropologist Richard Wrangham has called this the "goodness paradox," and it comes from our hunter-gatherer past, where we were in relatively small bands that competed with other bands for the same resources.[27] Evolution has driven us to adopt different rules for our group members.

But it's not just a case of "my group good, other groups bad." We may apply double standards regardless of our own allegiances. Just think of the many examples of discrimination by race, gender, and age embedded in societies. We often give less credit for the same behavior when someone from a lower-status group does it. Tax officials treat filing errors by entrepreneurs differently based on their social group. Men are expected to be more sexually active than women and get judged less harshly when they are. Even when a potential employee has the exact same qualifications and experience, employers are less likely to contact them if they are from a racial or ethnic minority.[28]

In modern democracies, we shy away from being open about these double standards. We have these intense group-based loyalties and dislikes, but we hypocritically pretend that we still treat everyone basically the same. Again, this shows how the drive against one kind of hypocrisy (double standards) may bend back around into a different kind of hypocrisy (common standards). We may try to treat people equally, but we end up sending false signals.

Yet this kind of hypocrisy can take us to a better place overall. Judith Shklar concludes that such a pretense may be essential if we are to accept the diversity of humans.[29] If we abandon it entirely, we enter the world of brazen power plays, where groups reject common rules and embrace discrimination, bigotry, and a simple struggle for dominance.

I will soon show a way out of this maze, but first I need to give one final insight: how this struggle for dominance reveals just what is so dangerous about double standards.

DOMINANCE AND PRESTIGE

When someone adopts double standards, they are effectively claiming that a rule applies differently to them—or not at all. That's a claim to superior status. They are placing themselves or their group at a higher rank. When someone openly flouts the rules that they want for others, what annoys us is the "air of superiority" that the flouting implies.[30]

Of course, we *do* accept that some people should be judged by different standards. If we tried to drive like a stunt driver, we would be seen as reckless, maybe suicidal. We accept that their superior skills make what they're doing acceptable. Adults are usually seen to have the ability to make reasoned decisions, but children are not—so we have different rules for them. We tend to listen more closely to people who have achieved excellence in their fields than to those who are less experienced or distinguished.

As I explained earlier, these skills, abilities, or achievements form a kind of status called "prestige" status. This is where people respect and value you for what you know and do; they find you persuasive, want to learn from you, and admire what you contribute to the group.[31] You may remember that hypocrites often try to get status by falsely signaling that they have these qualities when they do not.

But prestige is not the only way that humans achieve status. There is an older, darker, and crueler path available; it's called dominance. Dominance is about intimidating and coercing others to give you what you want. You operate through fear and force. You punch down on others, maybe literally.[32]

You will recognize the signs of someone trying a dominance strategy. They are the ones in a group who are trying to speak more loudly, more deeply, and more often; they stand or sit expansively rather than being hunched; they are aggressive or dismissive toward others and say their way is the best way.[33]

The character Jack from the book *Lord of the Flies* (1954) embodies this approach. When a group of boys are stranded on a desert island, Jack tries to seize control with fear, ridicule, and violence. When the characters Piggy and Ralph, symbols of prestige status, create a system that allows everyone to have a say, Jack smashes it. He thinks, "We know who ought to say things. . . . It's time some people knew they've got to keep quiet and leave deciding things to the rest of us."[34]

Prestige: I give you status because of what you can do *for* me. Dominance: I give you status because of what you can do *to* me.

Let's put these two things together. If you make a claim to be treated differently that people see as justified because of your prestige status, it's not seen as hypocritical. You are like the stunt driver. If you make a claim to be treated differently that is just a play for dominance and control, it's not seen as hypocritical either. You are like a chimp making a brazen power play. So what *does* make us perceive double-standards hypocrisy?

When you or your group make a dominance play that looks like a prestige claim. You claim that you *deserve* an exception from the rules based on merit or prestige—but we think that claim is not justified. Instead, we think you are just trying to get an advantage (whether you realize it or not). You want the power to do what you want, to be treated differently, while saying that your qualities make that OK. We see the shadow of self-interest within the shiny claim of justified superiority.

To see the danger here, imagine a religious group whose members think that they are intrinsically so good that the rules for how to live a moral life simply don't apply to them. Those rules are checks for other people. No matter what they do, regardless of its wickedness, they are in a superior, protected club.

This idea is called *antinomianism*—literally, the word means "against law."[35] Here's how the idea emerged, in very basic terms. If you think that salvation comes from your faith alone, then what you do on earth—your deeds—does not matter so much. You don't always need to do good works.[36] In fact, your faith means you can commit sins that will be excused and your slate wiped clean.

Some Christian thinkers took this idea even further. They said that before the world began, God had "unconditionally elected" one set of people to be saved and another to be damned.[37] The decision was already made, fixed forever, and separate from people's qualities or actions.

You can see the extreme conclusion hovering in the background. If you are one of the elect, you can do *anything*, and it will not affect your fate. Critics were aware of the dangers of these double standards. In his *Dictionary of All Religions* (1704), Daniel Defoe claimed that antinomians believe that "the child of God cannot sin . . . that murder, adultery, drunkenness, etc., are sins in the wicked but not in him . . . that a hypocrite may have all the graces that were in Adam before his fall."[38]

You can see how prestige and dominance are playing out here. Such a person wants the right to do whatever they want (dominance)—but also to claim that it's justified because of their superior status as one of God's elect (prestige).[39]

These double standards can have horrifying results. *The Private Memoirs and Confessions of a Justified Sinner* (1824) by James Hogg is a haunting novel that claims to be based on a manuscript found in a remote grave in the Scottish borders. The main character, Robert, is told by his father that he is one of God's chosen elect. Prompted by his shadowy friend Gil-Martin—who may just be part of Robert's mind—Robert gradually falls under the idea that legal and moral rules don't apply to him. His "justified and infallible state" means that he is allowed to use "that liberty by which the chosen and elected ones are made free."

The results are delusions and violence. Robert starts showing some extreme group double standards. As he says to his jailer, "If you are one of my brethren, I will take you into sweet communion and fellowship. . . . But, if you belong to the unregenerate, I have a commission to slay you." Prompted by Gil-Martin, he starts thinking about "the pleasure the Lord took in executing his vengeance on the wicked," until, he says, "at length I began to have a longing desire to kill my brother." We are never sure exactly what is real or not, but it seems that Robert acts on this desire, among others.

He ends up on the run, hiding as a shepherd, trying to cling to his faith in redemptive double standards but wracked with guilt about "whether or not I really had been commissioned of God to perpetrate these crimes in His behalf, for, in the eyes and by the laws of men, they were great and crying transgressions." He eventually hangs himself from a tree.[40]

THE DANGERS OF DOUBLE STANDARDS

Maybe singling out double standards isn't justified. After all, some double standards create hypocrisy that seems trivial. So what if I silently judge people on e-bikes? Is phubbing really a big deal? Can we really be expected to love our neighbors all the time as we love ourselves?

You could go further and say that a world without double standards, where everyone treats everyone else the same, would be an inhuman nightmare. We have bonds that we treasure; we have people we've vowed to protect ahead of others. A rootless, bloodless existence is not necessarily a better one. We have an innate desire to exert some control or power over others.[41] Why else is competition in games and sports so universal?

Fair enough; let me clarify. Double standards are dangerous because they always undermine the basic equality of people, which we often see as a central pillar of justice. In any single case, that may not be so bad, depending on how the other aspects of injustice stack up. One aspect is your intent: you can phub without meaning to, or you can do it deliberately to avoid helping someone in need. Another is the degree of harm: you can silently fume at people on e-bikes, or you can start playing games of chicken with them. We should target our criticisms on the most unjust double standards.

However, the risk is that even trivial instances are steps on a road to somewhere worse. Excusing your phubbing or your flirting may open cracks that lead to your relationship falling apart. Robert's faith that he is one of the elect gradually leads him to murder his brother. Doing what you want feels good, and our hypocrisy allows us to think it's justified, which maintains our positive self-image. The attempt at dominance starts to creep in ("the rules don't apply to me/us"), but under the cover of prestige ("and it's justified because . . .").

Double standards can therefore become self-reinforcing, escalating patterns of thought. As they spread throughout society, they start to shut off the paths for tolerance and reconciliation.[42] In their place come the unrestrained individualism and tribalism of brazen power plays. They are dead ends. If we want to broker compromises and deal decisively with emerging threats, we need to reach beyond our selves and our groups. We need to treat those with different convictions on similar terms—as hard as that can be.

Now we've fitted the final piece of the puzzle into place. We've revealed all the rules that govern how we react to hypocrisy. We've covered a lot, so let me bring it all together for you and show how you can apply these insights in practice.

9 THE MAP OF HYPOCRISY

People use the term *hypocrisy* as a loose and fuzzy condemnation.[1] That's not surprising. The idea is both pervasive and fluid. It can feel more like a shadow that creeps into situations, without a clear entrance or exit. Or like a noise in the background, surging and ebbing, never completely fading. Yet even slight changes to the details of a situation—or a shift in our focus—can wrench the dial so that the noise becomes deafening.[2]

But we are no longer helpless. The new findings I've set out can bring us more clarity and control. They provide a "map" that breaks down these judgments into parts, which come together to produce an overall level of hypocrisy.[3]

The Map of Hypocrisy

Inconsistency	Type	*Thoughts* *Statements* *Actions*
	Extent	*Degree of misalignment* *Order* *Time period*
Injustice	Motivation	*Intentions* *Extenuating circumstances*
	Nature of the outcome	*Extent of harm* *Competing values*
Benefits	Social status	*Strength of false signal* *Condemnation of others*
	Self-image	*Licensing* *Self-deception*
Actor	You or another	*Degree of ambiguity*
	Your group or another	*Strength of association*

Let's show how we can use this map to build a towering case of hypocrisy from a benign base. I'll start with an example that is really unhypocritical and then ramp up each category in turn.

> Sarah rescues and fosters animals in need in her spare time. She fundraises and advocates for people to treat animals with kindness and respect.

There's no inconsistency here. So let's start by introducing some.

> But she's a committed meat eater and often she goes online to post anonymous spiteful comments that denigrate vegans as naive extremists.

This change introduces a *statement-statement* inconsistency. You could argue: Why doesn't Sarah care as much about the animals on farms as the ones in cities?

Or we could create a *statement-action* inconsistency, which is perhaps the most powerful one.

> The truth is, Sarah doesn't always treat animals well—sometimes she keeps them in overcrowded conditions.

To make this change more powerful, we could make the *misalignment* even more exact. Rather than just saying that people should treat animals with kindness, we can make Sarah specifically condemn the exact behavior she is doing:

> This is despite Sarah saying that the worst thing you can do to animals is become an owner when you don't have the space or resources for them.

Then we can look at the *order* of things. Let's make Sarah preach something before practicing the opposite:

> Last month, Sarah used her guest slot on a podcast to make this message forcefully. She said that too many people were now keeping animals in small apartments. Two weeks later, she took in three more cats to her crowded apartment.

Two weeks? That seems to leave some wiggle room. Let's collapse the *time period.*

> That same afternoon, she took in three more cats to her crowded apartment.

Did Sarah mean to do this? Let's make her *intentions* clearer.

> That same afternoon, she took in three more cats to her crowded apartment. She knew that she didn't have the room. She knew that this was exactly what she had just told others not to do. But she did it anyway.

But maybe Sarah thinks there is no choice and that the animals are better off inside her apartment than outside. So let's try to rule out *extenuating circumstances.*

> She knew that she didn't have the room. She knew that this was exactly what she had just told others not to do. And she knew there was a shelter a mile away that could take the cats. But she hated the person who ran that shelter, so she took the cats in anyway.

We can also increase the *extent of harm* created by Sarah's hypocrisy.

> The cats that Sarah took in didn't behave well. Sarah ended up smacking them a few times when they tried to steal food from the other ones. Once she hit one maybe a bit too hard.

At this point, you could lessen the hypocrisy if you introduced some *competing values.* You could say that Sarah truly believed that physical discipline is a legitimate behavior-management approach, which would help cats be happier in the long run. But let's not do that and instead make things even worse.

Although Sarah has already sent a false signal with her podcast appearance, we can *strengthen the signal* further and have her *condemn others* at the same time.

> Sarah got a friend to nominate her for the award of Animal Welfare Champion in her local city. During her acceptance speech, she

	Sarah rescues and fosters animals in need in her spare time. She fundraises and advocates for people to treat animals with kindness and respect.
Word-word inconsistency	*But she's a committed meat eater and often she goes online to post anonymous spiteful comments that denigrate vegans as naive extremists.*
Word-action inconsistency	*The truth is, Sarah doesn't always treat animals well—sometimes she keeps them in overcrowded conditions.*
Degree of misalignment	*This is despite Sarah saying that the worst thing you can do to animals is become an owner when you don't have the space or resources for them.*
Order Time period	*Last month, Sarah used her guest slot on a podcast to make this message forcefully. She said that too many people were now keeping animals in small apartments.* *That same afternoon, she took in three more cats to her crowded apartment.*
Intentions Extenuating circumstances	*She knew that she didn't have the room. She knew that this was exactly what she had just told others not to do. And she knew there was a shelter a mile away that could take the cats. But she hated the person who ran that shelter, so she took the cats in anyway.*
Extent of harm (Competing values)	*The cats that Sarah took in didn't behave well. Sarah ended up smacking them a few times when they tried to steal food from the other ones. Once she hit one maybe a bit too hard.*
Strength of false signal Condemning others	*Sarah got a friend to nominate her for the award of Animal Welfare Champion in her local city. During her acceptance speech, she talked about how volunteers like her can make a difference and condemned anyone who shows cruelty to animals.*
Licensing Self-deception	*As she sat down and people applauded, Sarah thought about the times that she hadn't lived up to the ideals she preached. But then she thought about how much the animals owed her. Any slips she made were surely justified by her work overall. She relaxed, felt good, and drank in the acclaim.*
Self-other double standards	*After all, you couldn't judge her like most people with pets. This was her mission.*

Figure 9.1

How using the hypocrisy map can create a damning picture of hypocrisy.

> talked about how volunteers like her can make a difference and condemned anyone who shows cruelty to animals.

Let's add in some *licensing* of her own behavior that makes her feel better, even though it does not amount to full *self-deception* (which might make people more understanding):

> As she sat down and people applauded, Sarah thought about the times that she hadn't lived up to the ideals she preached. But then she thought about how much the animals owed her. Any slips she made were surely justified by her work overall. She relaxed, felt good, and drank in the acclaim.

Finally, we can add in an element of double standards between *self and others*:

> After all, you couldn't judge her like most people with pets. This was her mission.

By ramping up each of the factors, we've turned an admirable person into a monster of hypocrisy (figure 9.1). In this example, Sarah ends up as a cruel and deceptive person—but that's because I deliberately go to extremes. Hypocrisy does not require objectively bad things such as hurting animals. It's a wide-ranging idea.

Of course, this is a simplified example. Views on how the parts stack up will vary from person to person; some of these parts may counteract each other. Remember "victim hypocrites." They are getting one kind of benefit—social status—through conforming. But usually this is at the expense of another kind—their internal peace and self-image. The false signaling may tear them apart internally.

Moreover, the map only presents how we judge hypocrisy. It doesn't show what we need to do to escape the hypocrisy trap. We need a guide to which aspects of hypocrisy—which parts of the map—we should target and which we should tolerate. Part 3 of the book offers that guide.

III ESCAPING THE TRAP: WHAT WE CAN DO

10 TAKING A DIFFERENT VIEW OF HYPOCRISY

In Greek mythology, the Hydra was a giant, vicious water serpent with many heads. Born in the swamps of Lerna, it would slither onto land and "ravage both the cattle and the country."[1] But its true strength was hidden. If people tried to kill the Hydra—as they often did—they got a nasty surprise. When they cut off one head, *two* would grow back in its place. The harder they fought, the stronger the enemy became.

The hypocrisy trap works in a similar way. Attempts to kill hypocrisy only end up breeding more hypocrisy. Or they can lead to a collapse that replaces hypocrisy with worse outcomes: despair, deep cynicism, a struggle for power without rules.

Some people have reacted to these challenges by saying that hypocrisy has "maze-like inescapability."[2] No matter what you try, there's no way out.

I don't think that's true. There are three main things we can do: the first two are simpler; the last one is much trickier. All of them involve the idea that we can never kill hypocrisy completely. The real question is what kinds of hypocrisy we can and should live with.

The first path is to use new ways of increasing our own consistency. Behavioral scientists have started to show that this can be done by redesigning our environments and thought patterns. We make ourselves more likely to stick to our claims and principles; we reduce our hypocrisy.[3]

The second path is to reduce the risk of *accusations*. Maybe the first route fails, and we can't find a way to be more consistent. In that case, we can still use the hypocrisy map to anticipate and avoid the things that will make others angry. We can downplay how good we're feeling, weaken the signals we're sending, or show how we're balancing competing values.[4] We can reverse all the things we did with Sarah's cat-rescue scenario.

This option is about reputation management, but it's not purely cynical. It's also about managing anxiety. Sometimes you're forced into being inconsistent. In those cases, this option can reduce the sick, cold fear that someone will call you out, that any status you have gained—even if it's modest or temporary—could collapse into the humiliations of hypocrisy.

Yet these two options deal only with your personal position. They lessen the effects of hypocrisy, while keeping its core dynamic the same.

We need to disrupt that dynamic by shifting when and why accusations do or do not occur. In other words, rather than just trying to change hypocrites, we also need to change how people see hypocrisy. The goal here is to find ways of keeping us in the worlds of the trust machine and everyday compromises, while avoiding the extremes of the purity regime and brazen power plays. This is the third path.

And this is where we hit the tricky part. The hypocrisy trap means that there's no simple way of unlocking a good outcome. Taking any one solution too far just makes the jaws of the trap close tighter.

Making accusations can benefit us by ensuring the trust machine works. But carrying the same tactic too far locks us into the rigid inhumanity of the purity regime. Over time, unrestrained accusations exhaust the concept altogether, and we enter the dark world of brazen power plays.

Holding off on accusations can keep us in the humane world of everyday compromises. Yet, taken too far, this restraint creates a complacent, self-satisfied state where hypocrisy loses its bite—and we end up with brazen power plays by a different route.

We don't get out of this trap by just reversing what got us into it. We don't exit the maze by retracing our steps. Instead, we need a guide. We need help to see the most corrosive forms of hypocrisy and condemn them, while holding off on the ones that are irritating but less harmful—and that may even be beneficial. That way, we can preserve the power of accusations, so they have impact when they need to.

Our guide can be the hypocrisy map (chapter 9)—specifically, the injustice part. We should look for the kinds of hypocrisy that rank high in terms of injustice and sharpen our knives. For cases where injustice seems to be low, we should step back.

The map highlights four injustice factors: intentions, extenuating circumstances, the extent of harm, and competing values.

For intentions, we should ease off on accusations where a person or company is genuinely aiming for something better and failing to live up to their goals. Take a father who criticizes smoking in front of his children out of concern for their health, while secretly struggling with his own habit.[5] However, we also need to prevent people from distracting us with malign deceptions that end up destroying trust in society.

For extenuating circumstances, we should check the barriers that might have stopped people from being consistent. These barriers could be poverty, social pressure, or bureaucratic obstacles. The most extreme create "victim hypocrites" forced to act against their will—but in most cases we will have to judge how real we think the barriers are.

In terms of harm and competing values, we need to look past how annoying hypocrisy can be and consider its impact instead. How has the inconsistency hurt a living being, directly or indirectly? Some hypocrisy directly allows people to commit horrible abuse. Take the famous British publicist Max Clifford, who was well known for decades. He was also a campaigner against child sexual abuse and participated in the trials of at least two offenders, whom he called "manipulative and arrogant." He felt he had "a moral right to expose others who are duplicitous and hypocritical."[6] When a well-known TV presenter was exposed as a pedophile, Clifford gave interviews saying that many more names would come out.

His name was one of them. Two months later, he was arrested for a string of offenses and was sentenced to eight years in prison. Jurors at his trial were told that one victim had written him a letter years before his exposure, identifying his campaigning as a "double bluff" to distract attention from his own pedophilia.[7] His hypocrisy created a "smokescreen" defense until he finally pushed it too far.

In contrast, should we really care if someone does the right thing for the wrong reasons? Maybe in principle, but the bigger goal might be to retain the power of accusations for when they matter. And that means letting some relatively harmless hypocrisy go.

Finally, underpinning this idea of justice is the principle that people are fundamentally equal and should be treated as such. That puts double-standards hypocrisy in the firing line.

So, we can see three kinds of solutions: increase our consistency, reduce accusations against ourselves, and change views of hypocrisy. The following chapters show how these three play out in three domains that are essential to modern life: politics, business, and relationships.

By setting out these solutions, we will discover other things. For example, we might recognize that we make contradictory demands of politicians, companies, and other people—and therefore that some hypocrites are just doing what we ask. We may start to think that the way we talk about "hypocrites" is not so helpful because hypocrisy is not so much a fixed character trait as a judgment we make. (I recognize that I use the word *hypocrite* often in this book—I am one!)

We could even end up questioning whether our expectations of consistency are realistic. Non-Western cultures show a much greater acceptance of the need to vary one's views from social context to social context. Findings from behavioral science show that we are much more inconsistent than we like to think. If we get convincing explanations for why our thoughts, words, and deeds often diverge from each other—without our even knowing—we might begin to reassess our ideas of the self.

So, yes, we all are hypocrites—and that can sicken us. But it does not mean we can or should kill hypocrisy. Instead, we need to retain the benefits that it can bring, while being realistic about how behavior happens and fighting off the corrosive urges of double-standards hypocrisy.

The Hydra was not invincible. Defeating it was one of the labors of Hercules. It should be one of ours as well.

11 POLITICS

WHY DO WE SEE SO MUCH HYPOCRISY IN POLITICS?

Look away from the page, clear your head by thinking of a pear, and then try to come up with an example of hypocrisy.

Odds are that your example is related to politics. Unless there's some obvious pear-related hypocrisy I've missed.

Hypocrisy accusations are woven into the fabric of politics—they are probably the most common attacks that politicians make.[1] As the political thinker David Runciman notes, hypocrisy is what you reach for "if you wish to do the maximum possible damage to your political opponent in thirty seconds of airtime."[2]

One side will point at, say, right-wing bastions of law and order who want leniency and special favors when their rule breaking comes to light. The other side will mock wealthy left-wing advocates of equality, diversity, and social justice who maneuver furiously to ensure spots at elite universities go to their children, not to those whom they claim to care about.

These attacks are so common because they are so easy. You don't need to engage with or debate someone else's principles on their own terms—that's hard. All you have to do is say that they have not lived up to those principles, *whatever they are*.

Call it the "simple inconsistency" ploy. With it, you can avoid seeming to take a position. You're not trying to push your own position on taxes or abortion. But you can give the impression that you've understood your *opponent's* position because you've spotted an inconsistency that they apparently missed.[3] "So you're in favor of taxing *x* but not *y*!"

If we are making these kinds of attacks, we're already in trouble. There's no attempt to engage the other side on the issues and convince them they are wrong. A polarized era gives you few incentives to do that. But even if we can't agree on any shared values, we can still attack the other lot for not living up to *their* values. That still has some bite. As Judith Shklar put it, when you don't have a shared moral knowledge, "the contempt for hypocrisy is the only common ground that remains."[4]

So hypocrisy accusations may be a symptom of breakdown and dysfunction. In a polarized world, you want to fire up your side with fury. Hypocrisy is a reliable source of fuel for the flames. As the temperature rises, you look around for even more stuff to chuck into the fire, and so the cycle continues.

The problem is that, as we saw, polarization crushes trust. When you point out the gap between your opponent's words and deeds, on the slightest pretext, you aim to destroy trust in them. But they're trying to do the same to you. As more accusations pile up, the effect is to reduce trust in politics and people in general.[5] If everything and everyone seems fake, the public can end up casting around desperately for people who seem real, for escape routes to authenticity. Unfortunately, as I'll explain, those routes may lead to the purity regime or brazen power plays.

What's a better way forward? Well, let me say upfront what I'm *not* proposing. It would be quite simple to do a contrarian take that we all should just relax about political hypocrisy: "Let it go! We're all being too uptight!"

But there's too much at stake to slip into easy, empty cynicism. The hypocrisy of malign deception can break down society's vital systems until they fail completely.[6] You can see it in countries that have slipped into autocracy, such as Hungary and Venezuela, while all the time their leaders claim that people are making free democratic choices. For that reason, we can't just let the trust machine wind down.

Nor can we simply stamp out hypocrisy in politics. Instead, we need to keep bouncing between the politics of the trust machine—without letting them get out of hand—and the politics of everyday compromises—without letting them get cruel and complacent. Let's look at how we can work toward this goal through the three main types of solutions: increasing consistency, reducing the risk of accusations, and changing views of hypocrisy. Each one is promising.

DUMBFOUNDING YOUR OPPONENTS

First, we can try to make people's thoughts, words, or deeds more consistent. In fact, this goal often drives our criticism of political opponents, even if we don't realize it.

Let's say you are trying to call out left-wing hypocrisy about marriage and family. In the 2022 American Family Survey, only 30 percent of college-educated liberals ages eighteen to fifty-five agreed that children are "better off" with two married parents. This is the lowest share of any group. Yet if you look at this group's behavior, it's quite different—69 percent of parents in this group were married. When it comes to their *own* plans and the expectations of their peers, marriage seems very important to educated elites.[7]

What are you doing if you wave this contradiction in their faces? At least some of your desire is to *change views*. You want to convince people that their real stance is revealed in what they do, not say, because that's where the costs come in.[8] You want to shake your opponents out of their misguided opinions by showing them a raw inconsistency that they cannot deny. You want them to admit that they believe marriage is important for children.

Remember the idea of "induced hypocrisy"? It's a similar impulse: make people feel unpleasant cognitive dissonance, which they are driven to relieve. Except in this case they relieve it by changing their opinions to match their behavior—which brings them into line with you. You convert them. You win.

The bonus for you is that this may not be a nice process for your opponents. You want to destroy the status that comes from appearing to be consistent and coherent; you want to reduce your opponents to a state of confusion. You're aiming for a reaction similar to what the social psychologist Jonathan Haidt calls "moral dumbfounding."

Imagine you are told about the following situation: "A man goes to the supermarket once a week and buys a chicken. But before cooking the chicken, he has sexual intercourse with it. Then he cooks it and eats it." Most people who hear this feel a sense of disgust. They instinctively condemn the action as morally wrong. But, as Haidt points out, no one apart from the chicken buyer knows what's happened. You might think that the man is not harming anyone, so it's OK in principle. If you think that way, then you may be in a difficult position. The action feels wrong, but there's no clear reason why. You start "flailing around, throwing out reason after reason" to explain your feelings, but they keep getting knocked down. You start sputtering and become speechless.[9]

What's going on when we get dumbfounded like this? We are layering post hoc reasons on top of a rapid, intuitive, and emotion-based judgment. When these reasons don't seem to add up, our ability to explain our stance starts to grind to a halt. Our claim to be consistent, coherent agents seems to crumble. Even our cognitive ability to solve simple problems may stall—if the correct answers challenge our existing convictions.[10]

This is what we hope will happen when we confront people with their political hypocrisy. At this point in our dreams, our broken opponents realize the truth, raise their red-rimmed eyes to ours, and say, "You were right." We have exposed their inconsistencies, and we welcome them to our arms, cured.

But do such dreams ever come true?

We overestimate how likely people are to convert. We keep thinking that once we confront and break them down, they will see the light. This way of thinking is called "naive realism": the belief that we see the world objectively and without bias, the way things really are.[11] Other people are biased or misled, but we are not. We just need to convince them to come round to our viewpoint.

But, of course, it's not that simple. We don't really see things "as they are." Our own perceptions are shaped by our background, experiences, and culture, just as our opponents' are.

All this means that a hard attempt to shock people into consistency is more likely to trigger pushback and conflict than an epiphany.[12] Many studies have shown that giving information is a weak way of changing your adversaries' views.[13] As we've seen, people have many tactics for batting away inconsistencies when they're revealed. When an approach like induced hypocrisy works, it's often because a supportive environment helped people change without judgment. That's the exact opposite of politics.

SHARE LESS, TRUST MORE

Here are two things we can try instead. First, pausing before sharing. Compared to politicians, people in their everyday lives are under less pressure to take a stance on every issue. But social media have made stance taking extremely easy: a quick click can give you a rush of righteousness. If we can sign up to fewer opinions, we're more likely to be consistent with the ones we retain.

What I've got in mind is the easiest kind of opinion taking: where you simply reshare or like an opinion created by someone else. Not only is this low effort, but you may also be boosting something that you can't, on reflection, fully stand behind. After all, it's content from another person that flashed across your screen for a second. Maybe you haven't engaged with it too deeply. Indeed, studies show that people will still share information even if they don't really believe it, despite saying that they care about accuracy.[14]

Given this context, simply urging people to share less won't work. These resharing behaviors are usually rapid and prompted by triggers in the design of platforms.[15] Instead, we would need to build in prompts that increase the *friction* of sharing.

Social media companies have been taking tentative steps in this direction. In 2020, Twitter (now X) temporarily forced users to "quote tweet"—that is, add something—rather than just resharing a post instantly. WhatsApp now does not let you forward a message to more than five people at the same time. Instagram introduced a feature that asks users "Are you sure you want to post this?" when hurtful language was detected in a post.[16]

Measures like these can influence behavior. Experiments with thousands of Facebook and X users found that "misinformation" sharing fell by 3 percent to 6 percent when digital ads simply prompted them to think about accuracy in general.[17] People who were asked to pause and explain a headline said they were less likely to share false information as a result. Another study concluded that the quality of posts would increase if some users got a short multiple-choice quiz about a platform's community standards before resharing.[18]

The underlying idea here is to create a pause, even a small one, that prompts people to reflect on whether the opinion at hand accurately represents themselves—in other words, "Do I really agree with this?" Maybe that means we don't end up sharing an opinion that is actually misaligned with our wider words, deeds, and thoughts (in a way, we avoid spreading "fake news" about what we really think).

That idea faces obvious headwinds. It's not realistic to expect social media companies to curb behavior that makes a profit unless there is external pressure. People may not care about creating contradictory or false impressions of themselves—or may not be sure what they "really" think anyway. A promising alternative approach is to provide reassurance that *others* are being consistent. Remember the "democratic hypocrisy" I discussed earlier. People start grasping for antidemocratic measures because they fear that the opposition will get there first. Lack of trust means they think that the other side is just paying lip service to democratic values as a tactic before the coup.

These fears may not be accurate—groups often think they share fewer values than they actually do. If you point out that fact, it can make things better. One US study surveyed politician partisans about how much they valued democratic processes and how much they thought their enemies did. For example, Democrats might be asked if they supported reducing the number of voting stations in towns that vote Republican, followed by if they thought most Republicans would do so for Democratic-supporting towns.

The researchers then surveyed another group of people. Half of them were simply asked how far they supported antidemocratic actions. The other half were first asked to guess what their opponents would say and then learned the real levels of support from the first study. Finally, they were asked how much they supported antidemocratic actions.

The people who had heard the good news about their opponents were 29 percent less likely to support antidemocratic actions, compared to those who hadn't (24 to 17 on a 100-point scale). This result held for both sides. They were also 14 percent less likely to support an antidemocratic candidate in a hypothetical primary election.[19]

Correcting misperceptions like these has produced similar results across many different countries.[20] In another study, this approach proved most effective at reducing support for undemocratic practices among twenty-five options tested.[21] The tactic is not infallible: another study found smaller effects; corrections may get swamped by competing partisan messages in the real world.[22] But it definitely promises a toehold to prevent us sliding into a world of dark cynicism.

THE DANGERS OF POLITICAL CONSISTENCY

Politicians are pushed toward making big claims. They are forced into taking public stances on a bewildering range of issues and are rewarded for making those stances strong. Voters want clarity and confidence, not nuance and qualifications.[23] An opponent will be waiting to exploit any ambiguities or admissions.

The problem with taking a strong stance is that democracies are about power as well as principles, meaning that ambiguity and compromise are inevitable. Democracies allow a range of groups to exist, such as unions, religions, companies, and cities. Each wants to hold power and advance its interests. To get them onside, politicians need to persuade them—but the variety of interests means politicians need to present things a bit differently to each.[24] That means inconsistency and compromise slip in.[25]

If you end up getting power, things get even harder. You need to deliver for your group's interests, which means you must be flexible, focused, and tactical. But, while being partisan, you also have to keep promoting principles such as freedom and equal treatment for all—and stick to the persuasive things you said to different groups in the past. Power needs to exist alongside principles; you can't just ditch one or the other.

Unfortunately, that combination is not popular. The public hates it when politicians don't live up to their big, clear claims. As Judith Shklar puts it, "Democracy generates disappointment, and a sense of always being deceived."[26]

The result can be a thirst for a "real," sincere, authentic politician to step forward. This person will offer the promise of a politics free of hypocrisy.

You can see this urge in the explosive rise of leaders such as Tony Blair and Barack Obama. The risk is that the greater the promise, the greater the toxic disillusionment that inevitably comes.[27]

But Blair and Obama showed this risk only in a milder form. To see the real issue, we need to look at two of the most surprising Western leaders in recent times: Jeremy Corbyn and Donald Trump. Their unexpected rises to prominence can be explained by the public's disgust with hypocrisy and desire for true consistency. The fascinating thing is that the two politicians responded to this desire in completely different ways.

Jeremy Corbyn became leader of the UK Labour Party on September 12, 2015. He had spent thirty years as a relatively obscure member of Parliament, strongly to the left of his party. He was not expected to be competitive in the leadership election: at the start of the race in June, betting on his victory would have won you $100 for a $1 stake, despite there being only four candidates.[28]

Three months later, he had won the leadership in a landslide, sweeping to victory on a tide of "Corbynmania." At music festivals, thousands of people chanted his name over and over.[29] And all this happened thanks to his stubborn antihypocrisy, which made him seem appealingly *authentic*.

From the start, the media and Corbyn's own team emphasized "that magical ingredient of authenticity that he seems to exude." His "priceless untouchable" authenticity was seen as the bedrock of his appeal. In contrast to slick, weak, artificial politicians who switched their positions shamelessly, he was the scruffy, unvarnished real deal. He pitched the country "a new type of politics; bold, authentic and principled." He spoke below the slogan "STRAIGHT TALKING. HONEST POLITICS."[30]

Corbyn was seen as authentic because he was consistent. This quality came across in two main ways, both of which will be familiar from part II. There was consistency over time. Corbyn was described as someone "whose political views haven't altered since 1983"—he had always believed what he believed, even when it was unpopular.[31] You knew what he stood for.

Then there was consistency between what he said on the public stage and what he did in private. Stories circulated that seemed to confirm that he really did practice what he preached. Various politicians from his party had promoted publicly funded schools but ended up sending their own children to privately funded ones. Corbyn was different. His insistence that his son went to the local public school was so strong that it broke up his marriage. In the media telling, this was strong evidence that he would pay a heavy price to be consistent with his values, even in his private life.[32]

For a while, these qualities brought results—mainly because he was pitted against people who lacked them. In the 2017 general election, he was lucky to face Prime Minister Theresa May, who was widely criticized as stiff, robotic, and deeply uncomfortable when campaigning.[33] Her desperate attempts to simulate likability clashed badly with Corbyn's straightforward answers. Labour unexpectedly won 40 percent of the vote, just 2 percent behind May's Conservative Party, which lost its majority.

But here comes the downside. Here's why the push for greater consistency by politicians ends in the trap of the purity regime. First, it shuts down the flexibility and compromise that political leaders need. The fact that Corbyn didn't change his views also made it seem as if he "lack[ed] the ability or the originality to adapt to a changing world."[34] Rigidity is not the same as strength. Principles can harden into dogma. As one of Corbyn's former colleagues complained, "Politics is about compromise, and he never wanted to be put in a position where he was expected to compromise."[35]

But as the leader of his party, he *was* in that position. The risk with setting high standards for consistency is that any whiff of pivot or compromise gets pounced on. And so when Corbyn was forced to make some compromises, he made them badly and paid a price. He campaigned for the United Kingdom to stay in the European Union despite having been a Euroskeptic for all of his career, and was so tepid and unconvincing that few people were persuaded. He was caught in an "authenticity trap" of his own making.[36]

The authenticity trap is created if you draw support from being consistent with principles, but you end up in a position of power. Arguably, the public wants politicians both to be authentic and to tell them what they want to hear at any particular time.[37] But politicians can't do both. Flexibility disillusions your supporters. Sticking to principles, even if they are unpopular, may make you, well, unpopular.[38]

Corbyn eventually entered this dead end, perhaps helped by media that were biased against him.[39] In 2019, he faced a different kind of opponent:

Boris Johnson. Johnson neutralized Corbyn's authenticity advantage by "being himself." Was his bumbling yet swashbuckling persona real or not?[40] Either people believed it was, or they *didn't think it mattered*—Johnson was entertaining and offered enticingly simple answers at a time when everything seemed stuck.

Johnson went all-in on the "What do people want to hear?" side of things and blew Corbyn away. The 2019 election was the worst defeat for Labour since 1935. Johnson's tactics—seem "real" without committing to principles—point to the other place that a yearning for consistency can lead to. And the Western politician who dominates that space is Donald Trump.

Hypocrisy is the key to understanding Trump's rise to power. More specifically, the sense that his opponent in 2016, Hillary Clinton, was a hypocrite—but that he definitely was not. As an article four months before the election put it, "Clinton has been dogged for years by what pundits like to call her authenticity problem. . . . To listen to her critics, the real Clinton is a shape-shifter, with any avowals of authenticity dismissed as the expedient work of a conniving opportunist. Trump, on the other hand, has polled as one of the most authentic candidates in this election, despite statements and behavior that might also be called brazenly inconsistent."[41]

These claims about Clinton were common. A typical article in the *Washington Post* said that Clinton's campaign was "breaking the hypocrisy meter" and that "all this faking sincerity is cringe-inducing."[42] The media seized on leaked speeches showing Clinton saying one thing to the public and another in private to donors and interest groups.[43] In one, Clinton literally said "you need both a public and a private position."[44] This is the exact reverse of the consistency Corbyn was seen to have. I think Clinton's statement is right in many ways, as I explain later, but in a contest that several media outlets called the "authenticity election," where frustration with the establishment was intense, this line of attack may have been the deciding factor.[45]

If Corbyn's response was rigid consistency with principles, Trump's was to allow people to think that principles don't really matter so much. If he was consistent in private and public, it was because he didn't *try* to be any better in public. He fired out shocking things that preceding politicians thought you had to disguise.[46] The *Financial Times* argued, after four years of Trump as president, that "Donald Trump has been wildly inconsistent during his presidency, and is often called a liar, a cheat, a fraud. Accusations of hypocrisy, however, don't tend to stick. That's because Trump doesn't take the moral high ground. . . . That gives him a kind of protection against the charge."[47]

Let's look at the hypocrisy map to understand what's going on here. It's harder to call hypocrisy because Trump is not falsely signaling consistency to gain status. Instead, he is claiming status regardless—the message is that we don't *need* to care about consistency in politics. Politicians don't have to worry about constantly shifting positions. They just have to be consistent with their personality, their will, and make others go along with that. If they're strong enough, that approach will pay off.

You can see the logic of brazen power plays at work here. It may feel like an exhilarating breakout but, as we've seen, this way can lead to cynicism and even nihilism.[48] Saying that someone should be taken "seriously, not literally" makes it harder for them to be called a hypocrite, since it becomes unclear what any particular statement really means.[49] And maybe it doesn't matter anyway, if it's all just a power play.

I'm not saying that you can't make a case that Trump has shown hypocrisy. Instead, my point is that a drive for total consistency in politics is not a good solution. It can open the door for someone like Trump to abandon the whole game of consistency. Or it can elevate someone like Corbyn, who marches into the dead end of the purity regime.

REDUCING THE RISK OF ACCUSATIONS

In politics, maybe we shouldn't be so insistent that everyone is consistent. If hypocrisy is necessary—sometimes—then we may need ways to fend off accusations. I'm not arguing for a deceptive politics of spin. Instead, I'm spelling out the tools that we all use in political sparring, whether we realize it or not.

The first defense we can use is "framing." Remember Marge Simpson's protest against *Itchy and Scratchy*. Was it about the narrow issue of violence or the wider issue of freedom of expression? Is the politician who drives drunk a hypocrite because he also pushes abstinence over birth control? Maybe he's not practicing his preaching about self-control, or maybe drinking and sex are just different things.

You widen the lens when you want to see hypocrisy and narrow it when you don't. You control that lens through how you "frame" things. You can defend your stance by framing things narrowly, focusing on the specific issue and context rather than on the bigger principle in the background. "Yes, I don't think we should eat animals, but I'm not a vegan—because using animal products is a different issue." You're trying to carve out a separate space and defend it.

Suppose you want to raise fuel prices through taxation in order to reduce car use, but you also publicly campaign for the rich to pay more tax in order to reduce inequalities. If the framing is about *taxes*, someone could attack you as inconsistent—it's often thought that fuel taxes hit those on lower incomes harder.[50] But if the framing is about *climate change*, you can say that you are preventing harm for those with fewer resources, who are likely to be hit hardest by rising temperatures.[51] You look more consistent in the second frame.

There are reasons to think these tactics work. They use "construal-level theory," which explains how we are strongly influenced by whether we think about something abstractly or concretely.[52] Am I doing home improvement (general, abstract), or am I hammering this nail into this wall (specific, context)? Studies have shown that in politics, having people think in general terms makes them more committed to basic values such as "fairness" or "tradition," while specifics make them more pragmatic.[53]

You can use the hypocrisy map as a guide to how others will attack. You can check out your vulnerabilities in terms of

- **Logic**. How could someone reason out a clash between your positions? How much could that convince others?
- **Doctrine**. What wider causes have you adopted? Is it reasonable that you've signed up for the whole package they present? How clear and defined is the doctrine?
- **Affiliations**. Do your relations, employers, friends, or associates clearly do or say things that contradict what you're doing and saying? How close are you to them?

Then you can frame your actions or statements to sidestep the attacks in advance. Yet politics remains a tough challenge. It has a tension between power and principles right at its heart. In politics, you will never escape questions about how your core values match what you do and say. So let's look at the two main ways of denying that your actions betray your principles.

Let Me Explain How My Decisions Are Actually Consistent with My Values

In 1988, Brazil launched its new Constitution, marking the country's shift from military dictatorship to democracy. The Constitution clearly enshrined the principle of universal health care by saying that "health is a right to be enjoyed by all and a duty of the State; it shall be guaranteed by . . . universal and equal access to all activities and services for its promotion, protection, and recovery."[54]

But a principle needs to become a plan in order to get anything done. If you're looking to create that plan, you'll quickly see that countries have applied the idea of "universal health care" in very different ways. The United Kingdom funds the National Health Service through general taxation; Australia has a mix of public insurance and private providers; anyone living in Switzerland is required to buy health coverage from nonprofit providers.[55]

All these choices are open to debate among supporters of the idea. You can claim that you are using competition to deliver universal health care better. Someone else will say that you are a hypocrite who invokes the ideal of universal health care because it's popular—only to undermine and betray it with your choices.[56]

You can see this dynamic in Brazil's debates about what the Constitution's principles meant in practice.[57] Critics attacked the choices that ensuing governments made as "radically opposed to the founding principles upon which the system was conceived."[58] The role of the private sector was a flashpoint. The Constitution allowed private companies to be involved in the system, but only in restricted roles: foreign companies were barred from running hospitals, for example.[59] When the government ditched this rule in 2015, was it allowing much-needed investment or betraying the health system's core principles?[60]

Deliberate deception—claiming that you are supporting a principle while trying to kill it—is the kind of hypocrisy we should reject. That tactic endangers a bigger principle as well: trust. But if you are honestly trying to make the hard compromises needed to translate an ideal into reality, then here's what you should do.

Keep relating your specific choices back to the big general principles. That's always easier to defend because there are so many ways of achieving those principles. If you try to defend a more specific principle—no role for private health care at all—then you are more likely to get caught up in claims of hypocrisy.

Of course, there's no hard line between general and more specific principles. It's more like you are planting a flag somewhere along a scale. Your opponents will try to say you made a more specific claim and have hypocritically betrayed it; you will try to push back the other way. And sometimes you will be forced into a second option: to admit you had to compromise.

I Am Consistent with My Core Values–but We Need to Compromise This Time

On March 23, 2010, Barack Obama sat down at a desk surrounded by supporters, the world's media—and twenty-two different pens. Letter by letter, he used those pens to sign the Affordable Care Act (ACA) into law.[61] By 2023, the act had brought health-care coverage to 40 million people, protected 133 million with preexisting health conditions, and enjoyed a 62 percent approval rating.[62] Supporters and opponents agree that it was a "big deal," to paraphrase Joe Biden.

But the ACA was not a total fresh start, unlike Brazil's Constitution. It did not fulfill the big promise Obama had made just three years earlier: the United States would have universal health care by 2012.[63] Millions of Americans were still uncovered and had to rely on their state expanding coverage. The plan was nothing like the "single-payer" plan that Obama had praised in the past, which would have created a government plan for all.[64] It did not even offer a publicly funded option that could have lowered costs for all. Obama had advocated for this option as late as 2009, before denying that he had campaigned on the issue.[65]

Yet I think Obama avoids the charge that his actions hypocritically betrayed his values. For a start, he could have campaigned on the principle of universal health care and then abandoned it as just too hard. In other words, it would have been easy to gain status by sending false signals. There were lots of incentives to do this; scared and scarred by the failures of past reforms, his most senior advisers had urged him to relent straight after the election.[66] Instead, he spent his political capital trying to turn principles into reality.

Second, Obama put caveats into his ambitions from the start. He said a single-payer system might not be possible straightaway. It would have been his ideal option if he were building something "from scratch," but he wasn't.[67] Switching away from the current setup would have involved replacing the insurance of millions—political poison. Even his big promise was a clever mix of idealism and realism. Universal health care, he said, "must not be a question of whether, it must be a question of how."[68]

The "how" was a ton of compromises.[69] Obama needed to pass a law through Congress. Although his party controlled Congress, members wanted different things. Some ideals would be compromised or sacrificed in negotiations.

Obama made his pragmatism explicit rather than claiming he had achieved perfection. Six years after the law's passage, he presented it this way: "It's like building a starter home—or buying a starter home. It's a lot better than not having a home, but you hope that over time you make some improvements."[70]

A policy is not a temple of values, the perfect realization of a vision. It's a starter home, made from everyday compromises and extenuating circumstances. It's flexible, not fixed, and that means it can be fixed over time.

The skill here is to show that your core values guide your actions even if your results don't realize them perfectly. The aim is to be the kind of politician "whose compromises are therefore not hypocrisy but instead a form of principled pragmatism."[71] Can we stomach that stance? Or do we just prefer a fighter? I think we might be able to get on board.

Earlier I shared a study that showed how people were *more* forgiving of hypocritical politicians. The setup was that a politician who says that it's "never" OK to lie but then is shown to have lied was judged better than one who says it's "sometimes" OK to lie. The "never" politician was seen as more hypocritical because they were sending false signals, but they were also judged as more moral and admirable. Saying "never" seemed to act like a strong signal of future honesty—despite the lie—while saying "sometimes" gave the impression that they might deceive.[72]

That's not promising. The study also tested another option: the politician says that it's "rarely" OK to lie. That retains a principle, an ambition, but it's not absolute. As the researchers say, this stance "might reflect thoughtful exceptions."[73] It could signal that you have good intentions that you are trying to fulfill—and when you make an exception, it's *justified.*

In the experiment, the "rarely" option conveyed honesty and fostered trust better than "sometimes." Did it also come across as less hypocritical than "never"? The experiment didn't give clear evidence that it did, but the authors think that it might work in some contexts.[74] So the questions become: Which conditions or caveats can people tolerate, and which annoy them? How do things play out with real personalities and deep loyalties?

It seems that there's a path to tread, but it's a narrow one, and the risks we saw with everyday compromises loom large. You can seem smug and complacent, satisfied that you are the grown-up who gets the balance right. You see yourself as the person rising above partisan squabbling. Whatever compromises you make, even if they are truly timid, can be rewritten in your mind as justified moves that show you to be the bigger person. People also don't like this kind of thing.

But perhaps changing what people do and don't like is part of the solution to hypocrisy in politics.

CHANGING VIEWS OF POLITICAL HYPOCRISY

We've missed a crucial part of the solution so far: the accusers. Our political environment is being damaged by unrestrained accusations of hypocrisy. This thread has run throughout the book, so let's just pull out three strands of it again.

First, we're creating cynicism by exhausting the concept. In politics, accusations of hypocrisy are relentless but not costless. We empty hypocrisy of meaning when we overuse it as an accusation. We make it just another term of abuse in the game of politics. As Judith Shklar explains, "In the unending game of mutual unmasking, the general level of sham rises. As each side tries to destroy the credibility of its rivals, politics becomes a treadmill of dissimulation and unmasking."[75] We end up mired in cynicism and distrust.

Second, we're distracting ourselves from the bigger issues. Ironically, these attempts at unmasking may end up missing things instead. If people are too focused on personal inconsistencies, they may not see how groups or institutions are creating a system where they can *afford* to play by different rules, with no consequences.[76] Hypocrisy accusations may be distractions based on naive assumptions about how power can be curbed.

Third, we're pushing ourselves toward the bad "worlds" of hypocrisy. If we hound politicians for the slightest inconsistency, decent people who are aware of their flaws won't enter politics.[77] Instead, we will get people who aren't aware of their flaws or who don't care about them. If we get angry at politicians for falling short of an impossible standard, that anger will become a flood that carries us to the purity regime or brazen power plays.

If all this is true, then we need to think differently about hypocrisy in politics. We don't have to *like* hypocrisy—it's so dislikeable. Instead, we need to accept that tolerating a certain level of hypocrisy in politics is the least-bad option overall.

The first step is to realize that hypocrisy is unavoidable, at least in democracies.[78] Anyone promising otherwise is also a hypocrite—of the most dangerous kind. So we need a reckoning with all the reasons that hypocrisy is baked into democratic politics: the need to balance principles and power; the need to disguise our feelings in order to be polite and tolerate differences; the rewards for making absolute claims.

Then comes the harder part. We need to edge toward an understanding that trying to stamp out political hypocrisy completely is both futile and self-defeating.[79] Implacable, blanket accusations boomerang back into hypocrisy.

"Tyrants and terrorists can no longer hide. We will see them. We will hear them. We will see and hear everything. If it happens, we'll know. . . . We will see it all, because knowing is good. But knowing everything is better."[80]

So says Eamon Bailey, a tech CEO with megalomaniac qualities, in the movie *The Circle* (2017). He wants to use his company to achieve a vision of total political transparency. Politicians will wear the Circle's cameras constantly, while making all their calls and emails accessible to the public in real time. The idea gets a rapturous reception around the world.

The movie is a heavy-handed satire about the power of big tech—but it captures the naive drive to destroy hypocrisy in politics. We get rhetoric that's so glib it's hard to argue with: "We need to know what the people who represent us are doing with their time, on our dime. To serve us better." In the novel the film is based on, we see the crushing pressure of the purity regime as the drive for politicians to "go transparent" goes "from polite to oppressive," with refusers being "treated like pariahs" within weeks.[81]

And we also get glimpses of futility. "Goodbye backroom deals!" exclaims Bailey's chief of staff in the film when introducing the first politician to make the switch. But the deals just find a new backroom. The meetings with the ever-present cameras become fake and scripted, while staffers out of sight do the real negotiations. As the philosopher David Runciman explains, this kind of reaction is entirely predictable: "The demand for that level of openness, of honesty, of being who you seem all the way through, drives politicians into greater secrecy. Transparency as a crusade does not produce open politics. Transparency as a crusade forces politicians and others to find places even more secretive where they can hide."[82]

Then comes the hypocrisy. It may not surprise you to find out that the Circle itself isn't completely transparent. The push for sunlight has just been a cover for a hidden agenda of profit and control. In the climactic scene, the movie's heroine, Mae, stands onstage and says she wants to end "the usual hypocrisy of the digital world," where everyday people upload their secrets into the cloud, accessible to tech leaders who nevertheless retain control of their own data. What this means is she's hacked into Eamon Bailey's secret email accounts and is about to share all the bad stuff with the world. After all, "knowing everything is better," right?

Just like the Circle, we, the public, demand standards from politicians that we ourselves cannot maintain—and we know it. One study that measured reactions to politicians saying it's "never," "rarely," or "sometimes" OK to lie also asked people which one *they* supported. It turns out that most people do not agree with the stance that it's "never" OK to lie, even though they reward politicians who adopt that position.[83] (In general, people think that deception is ethical if it prevents unnecessary harm.)[84]

Maybe your instinctive response is: "Yeah, but we're not the ones out there making big claims for ourselves. Politicians are different."

I hope you can see now why that line doesn't hold up. We are the ones who shape politicians' behavior through our demands and expectations. And those demands are inconsistent. We want politicians to be better than us but also to be like us. We force them to inflate themselves, to fight our causes, but also to hide their virtues, so they don't seem too superior or unrelatable. We want them to use power effectively, to compromise and get results, but also to stick to the purity of their principles. They are the screens on which we see our own contradictory political opinions played out, and we don't like the show.[85]

The final step, after seeing that hypocrisy is inevitable and our accusations are self-defeating, is to change what we do. If we need to tolerate *some* kinds of hypocrisy, which ones?

There are three things we need to do, and all of them are hard.

Reject Politicians Who Preach Antihypocrisy

Politics makes antihypocrisy seductive. It feels so good when someone promises to rip away the suffocating lies and replace them with something real. It can also feel like the right thing to do. If a politician is promising to uphold ideals, supporting their stance seems like a blow against pervasive political cynicism. Maybe we can believe, just one more time, in something true?

Time to steel ourselves and accept that antihypocrisy is a false promise. In fact, we are just choosing between one kind of political hypocrite and another.[86]

There are the ones who engage in some pretense as part of the normal run of democratic politics. Those are the hypocrites we usually get angry about. Think Hillary Clinton.

The other kind are the ones who deny that they ever act like this, who present themselves as unsullied by the dirty compromises of politics. They look down on the other politicians wallowing in the muck. They make a big, explicit play about *not* being hypocrites. Think Corbyn or—in a slightly different way—Trump. But hypocrisy in politics is unavoidable, so they can never live up to these claims—especially if they want to get anything done. Their criticisms bend back around into hypocrisy again; they are boosting their social status and self-image unjustly.[87]

So we need to change our views and see that these politicians do not offer an escape from hypocrisy but just serve it up in a more insidious form. They prey on our tendency to see ourselves as consistent, truthful people, and they claim that they, too, are just like that ideal self-image. In contrast, other politicians are toxic liars.

All this kicks away at our support for compromises that make democracies work. Instead, it offers a vision of politics as a quest for purity and truth. That vision is like a sweet treat that tastes good but makes us sicker in the end. The politician can never sustain it—democracy always disappoints—and that means an even more toxic collapse of trust later on.

Get Realistic About the Inconsistency of Our Political Demands

We need to come to terms with our part in creating political hypocrisy. We are inconsistent in the demands we place on politicians. We pull them between the logic of power and the logic of principles, depending on how we feel. But we *don't admit this*. Instead, we embrace the fantasy of a simple war of principles or adopt a cynical view that everything's just corrupt.

So we need to edge closer to understanding that democratic politics has to do contradictory things, and we play our part in that dynamic.[88] That means not buying in completely to the idea that politics is about seeking truth and achieving purity but instead retaining the sense that it's also *an act of collective problem solving*.[89]

That double view of politics is hard to face directly because it triggers the unpleasant dissonance discussed earlier. It's easier to keep switching effortlessly between demands for complete sincerity and demands to *just get something done*. But forcing either extreme breaks democratic politics.[90] We need to recognize that in politics inconsistency is a feature, not a bug.

It means realizing that we may not be choosing between truth and lies but between "politicians who are sincere but untruthful and those who are honest but hypocritical."[91] It means recognizing the value in flawed striving for something better, rather than rejecting the attempt altogether. And it means tolerating the flexing of absolute rules when the context demands compromise.[92]

I'm not urging desiccated centrism, stunted ambitions, or lazy complacency. We shouldn't abandon political convictions but rather see them as the framework for navigating trade-offs. But the path is not easy. It requires tolerating compromise, incoherence, and maybe even disappointment. That goes against our political instincts and incentives. But maybe those incentives will change if we realize how our overuse of hypocrisy takes us to dark places when it goes unchecked.

So there are some kinds of hypocrisy we should tolerate because they come from our inconsistent demands. For example, I think we should be more relaxed about politicians saying different things in different ways from context to context. Maybe they vary their accent, delivery, and emphases to please the audience in front of them. This practice is "universally derided"—and went down very badly in the experiment I ran.[93] But it's also been seen as a necessary skill since the dawn of politics and can be seen as a sign of respect for your audience.

The flip side of this tolerance is that we need to crack down on other kinds of political hypocrisy. In my view, the main target is double-standards hypocrisy.

Target Hypocritical Double Standards

In general, the most destructive form of injustice in hypocrisy comes from double standards. Unfortunately, they are rife in politics because there's a clear clash between opposing sides. Say your party is in power. If the economy is booming, you will think they are more responsible for that situation than if it's tanking. But if the opposition is in office, you'll explain away the good times as just luck (or deny that the times are good at all).[94]

The task of undoing double standards may appear hopeless: polarization and distrust seem to be entrenching them more each day. But there may be just a chink of light. The key insight is to make an emotional appeal; reason is not the driving force here. Although we often try to explain why our double standards are OK, we're usually just layering justifications onto our gut feelings.[95]

Before the 2004 US election, a pioneering study showed inconsistent words and actions by either George Bush or John Kerry to partisan supporters of either side. Unsurprisingly, participants were much more likely to see hypocrisy in their opponent and turn a blind eye to their guy. But the study was also scanning their brains at the same time. When people were confronted with their candidate's failings, they did not reason coolly. The parts of their brains that were firing were the ones dealing with distress, negative emotions, and threats.[96]

There might just be a chance to redirect these emotions. As I discussed in part II, we feel the need for fairness as an intense, almost visceral drive. At the same time, in many countries there is wide support for democratic principles such as equal treatment under the rule of law.

So maybe it's possible to highlight the gap between people's double standards and their beliefs in a way that turns the powerful drive for fairness back on themselves. Much like induced hypocrisy, making an emotive appeal to fairness in the abstract may trigger unpleasant feelings of cognitive dissonance that people must resolve. They may feel guilt at violating their own sense of fairness. And maybe they resolve that tension by choosing principles over double standards, although it's easier not to.

Even a long shot is worth pursuing, given the damage double standards can do. If politics is like a game, then a lot of political hypocrisy is about getting tactical advantages. You spot an opportunity to get on the scoreboard even if you don't particularly deserve it. But double-standards hypocrisy is like violating the basic rules of the game. It's like your coach putting an extra player on the field, confident that the referees will turn a blind eye. Even if they don't, she will have an excuse about why it was justified for her team to do this—but not for the opposition.

You can see that, over time, these moves mean that no one wants to play. The game collapses. The political system we created for sorting through and managing differences crumbles. Institutions—the referees of the game—can no longer impose any control. The teams don't even see why they should play, since they can just claim victory and try to enforce their perceived supremacy however they can.

These things are already happening. All around the world, there are examples of "democratic erosion" leading to autocracy.[97] The number of liberal (free) democracies fell from forty-two to thirty-four between 2012 and 2021. In the latter year, thirty-three countries were moving toward autocracy; fifteen were moving the other way. The result is that the democratic advances since the Cold War have been eliminated.[98]

As we saw, double-standards hypocrisy is the key way people justify supporting democratic erosion. Every time we break the rules for our side, every time we deny the opposition a fair chance, we're planting seeds that can grow into weeds and choke the playing field faster than we realize. So, yes, that means calling out *your* coach for cheating as well, and that's one of the hardest things we can do. But otherwise there will be no game left to play—and you may find that your coach has stopped listening to her players anyway.

12 BUSINESS

COMPANIES CAUGHT IN A TRAP

We judge companies just like we judge people. And over the past couple of decades, we've built a trap for them.

A frail, elderly woman named Joan lies confined to her bed. She used to garden and still cherishes her lawn, so she's hired John, who lives nearby, to maintain it. He talks smoothly but never lifts a finger. He just pockets the cash, knowing that Joan can't check his work.

A shameful act. But would you feel differently if Joan had been deceived by a well-known lawn-care company instead? To answer this question, a study scanned the brains of people as they heard about three scenarios: about a person, about a company, and about the workings of a neutral object—such as a lawnmower. It turned out that their brains responded in a "strikingly similar" way to actions by people and actions by corporations. The area of the brain concerned with "seeing people" was active for people and corporations, but not for the description of objects (such as the lawnmower).[1]

That wasn't a foregone conclusion: other studies show that this area of the brain becomes less active when we see pictures of excluded and dehumanized people, such as drug addicts.[2] But this doesn't happen with companies.

Other studies agree: we judge the hypocrisy of companies along the same pathways as those we use for people.[3] In the words of Alison Taylor, a professor at New York University's Stern School of Business, "We personify companies. We talk about them as if they're people with brains. We talk about Apple versus Microsoft and Pepsi versus Coke and whether a company is a hypocrite."[4]

In fact, we get even *more* enraged by hypocrisy coming from corporations. We use the same pathway as for people, but we go further down it. The brain-scan study I just mentioned also asked participants to rate their emotional reactions to each story. Strikingly, people had more negative feelings about bad corporate actions than about bad personal actions. Even when the story featured a positive act, participants gave companies less credit than people.[5]

But our relationship with companies is complex—it's not just about hate. We can fall in love with brands. They can provide us with support, comfort, a way to get closer to the person we want to be. We see brands as having distinct personalities, just like humans; they can seem alive.[6] They can feel like our friends.

What's made these ties even more volatile is that we have started to demand more from the relationship. Recent years have seen growing pressure for businesses to push forward with social change without waiting for governments to act.[7] We have urged companies to claim that they can help with pressing issues facing society.

That push is most obvious when it comes to the environment. In a global survey from 2024, a fifth of employees born after 1995 said that they had changed jobs or industries because of environmental concerns. More than half said that they and their colleagues were pressuring their employers to take action on climate change.[8] Two-thirds of consumers say that they are highly concerned about sustainability, with the average person claiming they'd pay a 12 percent premium for eco-friendly products.[9]

Companies have responded to this pressure with zeal. The past few decades have seen a torrent of promises about cutting carbon, reducing inequality, or increasing diversity. For Nike, "Equality should have no boundaries." Coca-Cola doesn't just want to quench thirst but also to "refresh the communities we serve." "As an independent house of luxury," Chanel is "committed to play a role in restoring nature and climate."[10]

And these claims have kept getting inflated further, in part because companies have competed to see who can look the most responsible.[11] But the claims also breed ever higher expectations for your company to fulfill: they create pressure rather than relieving it.[12] As ambitions get bigger, they increasingly get out of line with a basic reality: businesses need to be financially sustainable. They need to make a profit. One reason the Tom's footwear brand (slogan: "Wear good") got into financial trouble was its flagship commitment to donate a pair of shoes for every pair sold: 95 million of them by 2019.[13]

Now the trap comes into view. As consumers, we push companies to make bigger and bigger prestige-status claims about societal issues. They respond eagerly, sometimes in slightly sickening ways, but these claims cut further against the unavoidable need to make a profit. As gaps between words and deeds open up, we see hypocrisy flood in.

We're right to be skeptical. When regulators in the United Kingdom and Netherlands reviewed the environmental claims made on 500 global websites, they found that roughly 40 percent of them were false or misleading "greenwash."[14] Another analysis looked at what US publicly traded firms say about diversity and who they actually employ. Nearly 40 percent were "diversity washers": they talked disproportionately about diversity compared to how diverse their own employees were.[15] Often the gap is real.

THE DIFFICULTY OF ESCAPE

These waters are hard to navigate, even for companies that make major efforts to do good. Take the example of Patagonia, the US outdoor-clothing brand. Patagonia makes a big claim: "We're in business to save our home planet."[16] It sets high standards for the sustainability of its own products and mostly lives up to them. Since 1985, it has given 1 percent of its profits to support the natural environment and formed a nonprofit to encourage others to do the same. In 2022, its billionaire owner put his money where his mouth was and transferred ownership to a trust and a nonprofit in order to ensure all company profits would go to combating climate change.[17]

And yet "Patagonia has been accused of hypocrisy—the harder the company fights against the consumer society, the bigger its business grows."[18] Its ideals have proved effective at selling products. In 2011, the company launched a famous ad featuring a picture of a Patagonia jacket beneath the headline "DON'T BUY THIS JACKET." Smaller text explained the need to reduce, repair, and recycle clothing. But consumers seemed to ignore these messages: nine months after the ad, the company's sales had jumped by more than 30 percent.[19]

There were claims at the time that the ad was just a marketing ploy.[20] Patagonia's response was telling. It said: "It would be hypocritical for us to work for environmental change without encouraging customers to think before they buy. . . . It's not hypocrisy for us to address the need to reduce consumption."[21]

I hope you can see how this unique ad creates *more* hypocrisy, not less. It's sending an implicit signal to consumers that it's good to buy the jacket, while explicitly using ideals to deny that that's what it's doing. Again, trying to escape hypocrisy can just re-create it in a new way. And remember that consumer responses drive a major part of this hypocrisy. In 2016, Patagonia pledged to donate all its profits from Black Friday to good causes. Consumers responded eagerly: "Sales on that day exceeded $10 million, but in the following days many consumers returned their products to the stores. Often slightly embarrassed, they told similar stories: in fact, they did not need their purchases, but had rushed out to buy Patagonia products because they wanted to signal support for the company's message. And they got their money back."[22]

Patagonia made sustained efforts to do things better, but it still couldn't escape accusations of hypocrisy. When you send strong signals of principle, and your customers respond to them, then the basics of business can be a trap. Indeed, research shows that the more a company tries to be responsible and transparent, the more it gets hit with criticism and scrutiny.[23]

Any business taking a stand will struggle to align all its actions with its claims. And if its stand gets grander, customers are more likely to see a gap and become skeptical.[24] In recent years, they've been helped by

- **Transparency.** Recent decades have seen the release of much more information about companies. There's greater scrutiny from the media and advocacy groups. And that scrutiny has uncovered some big inconsistencies.[25]
- **Social media.** Employees can now post unfiltered views about how a company's external rhetoric does not match its internal actions. Think

of all the leaks about explosive all-staff meetings. We rarely doubt these accounts.[26]

- **Global supply chains.** Companies are caught in widening webs of connections. Consumers now judge those companies to be responsible for the actions of their suppliers. There's a chain of blame: if one of your contractors is being hypocritical, *you* may get boycotted as a result.[27]

It's no coincidence that confidence in major companies halved between 2000 and 2023.[28] Businesses need to get serious about these growing risks: they can damage a company's reputation, finances, and culture. Since consumers see brands as people, they react just as viciously to corporate hypocrisy as to personal hypocrisy. Demand for the brand's products falls; people will pay less for what it offers. Authenticity that can take decades to build up can be destroyed instantly, tainting everything a company tries.[29]

And don't think that diehard customers will save a business. In fact, the people who identify the most with a company, the true fans, are the ones who respond most violently when revelations emerge.[30] For them, it's personal. They have the greatest need to disengage to preserve their self-esteem: they need to cut the bonds quickly to avoid being dragged down as well.[31]

It's hard to escape the hit to the bottom line that hypocrisy brings.[32] That's one of the reasons why, after years of raising expectations, companies started to look for off-ramps in the mid-2020s. In the fourth quarter of 2021, 155 companies in the S&P 500 mentioned "ESG" (environmental and social governance) in their earnings calls. Two years later, just 29 did.[33] 2025 saw an active backlash in the United States against companies taking up progressive causes. On the internal side of things, commentators conclude that "corporate America would very much like its employees to be quiet now. Executives have had enough of the bring-your-whole-self-to-work and speak-up-at-the-office grand experiment of the pandemic era."[34]

But they can't escape the trap so easily. If you suddenly reverse your stance, it looks like you were just paying lip service to causes in order to look good—in other words, you were sending hypocritical false signals. Or people may think that if you *did* believe in the causes, your flipping means you are pathetically weak. As I mentioned earlier, a cynical stance acts like insurance against hypocrisy.

Whipsawed between opposing consumer demands, companies must be tempted to duck the debate altogether and try to keep a low profile. But that's not a failsafe plan: doing and saying nothing still looks bad to many employees, customers, and investors.[35] We see through it as a strategy. Experiments show that a CEO who deliberately says nothing is rated as badly as a CEO who made a strong moral claim and was then found to violate it.[36] People still want the things they buy to be inexpensive, but they also want to feel good about buying them. And, of course, people vary wildly in terms of which ideals make them feel good!

I think there is a way forward. If we judge companies like we judge people, then the insights from the hypocrisy map hold true. Companies can increase consistency, reduce the risk of accusations, and change views of hypocrisy. Here's what that would look like.

COORDINATE FOR CONSISTENCY

Imagine you are the CEO of a company, juggling hundreds of priorities. Legal, human resources, marketing, and finance are all busily working on their pieces of the puzzle. But then things start to crumble. Your marketing team, with an eye on social media, launches a bold campaign for gender equality. The problem is that they haven't checked in with HR on how your own pay gap looks. Suddenly consumers are pointing fingers and crying, "Hypocrisy!" The error is not a lack of good intentions—it's a lack of coordination.

It's possible that something like this happened between different parts of the fashion company Coach. In late 2021, a video went viral on TikTok showing Coach products that seemed to have been slashed and dumped by staff. The video pointed out that Coach itself urged customers to repair items instead of chucking them out. The company's website promoted its repair-and-reuse program because "it's another small thing we can do to keep bags out of landfill."[37] It seemed that the company was not following its own advice—the sustainability people may have become disconnected from the store managers. In response to the video, Coach said it was now sending all such items to its circular-economy programs instead.[38]

Some companies must grapple with the fact that they do a lot of things. Take Unilever, a $150 billion behemoth with 400 brands, ranging from baby food to soap to ice cream. It owns Ben & Jerry's, Knorr, and Vaseline. That diversity brings both strength and risk: look at Dove soap and Axe deodorant, two Unilever brands operating in the same space. Dove's "Real Beauty" campaign was famous for celebrating women regardless of what they looked like. But Axe's marketing had women shouting, "Bom chika wah wah!," and throwing themselves at men in a way that critics said "blatantly objectifies and degrades."[39] Unsurprisingly, Unilever got labeled with hypocrisy.

Unilever responded with a new corporate strategy based around consistent purpose. In 2016, it vowed to banish gender stereotypes from all its brands' marketing.[40] It went even further in 2019: every Unilever brand needed to have a clear social or environmental purpose—or it would be cut. The approach was successful: shareholders got a 270 percent return between 2009 and 2019. By 2022, Unilever was seen as the most sustainable business on the planet.[41] Even the most sprawling companies can get more consistent and be rewarded for it, given good strategy and leadership.

Problem solved? No: the reality is more interesting. It turns out that Unilever's ambition of total consistency of purpose may have been a stretch. In 2024, its new chief executive admitted that it had been trying to knit too many things together. He announced a new approach that involved focusing harder on fewer, more realistic priorities. Gone was the drive to fit brands into a single purpose. The consistency now came from sticking with priority issues over time (which critics saw as an excuse to do less overall).[42]

The Unilever example reveals that coordination is costly; you can't fix everything, so you need to make choices. And, in terms of priorities, there's one risk that applies to all companies, regardless of their size and complexity. I'm thinking of the gap between how a business presents itself and how it treats its own employees.

Just ask Nike. Its bold statement that "equality should have no boundaries" was aimed at racial inequality in sports.[43] But critics pounced, accusing Nike of hypocrisy for the inequality faced by workers in its supply chain in low-income countries. It seemed like some boundaries to equality were in full force. Nike scrambled to review its internal practices, but it had already taken a reputation hit.[44]

Or take Walmart, which proudly gave more than $1 billion "to support organizations that impact local communities around the world" in 2013. But it didn't get too much praise. Instead, the company was accused of hypocrisy because of the controversy raging over the wages it was paying to US employees, many of whom had to rely on government help to make ends meet. The gap is likely to have inflamed the protests and boycotts that were plaguing the company.[45]

This internal-external gap can be truly toxic because how you treat employees always matters—it's a meaningful action that can be opposed to your fine words. It's a direct opportunity to practice what you preach. And in the age of social media, employees can expose hypocrisy to the world with just a few clicks.

Closing the gap is not a luxury but a necessity. Data show that when external efforts start to outpace internal ones, employees start to leave.[46] The lesson is clear: get your house in order before making a grand public announcement. HR and marketing need to be talking to each other.

DESIGN OUT HYPOCRISY

But *how* do you "get your house in order"? If companies are made up of people, how can you help those people act in line with desired goals and values?

Behavioral science shows that leadership, planning, and good intentions are not enough. To align words and deeds, you need to build incentives and prompts into the everyday way your organization works. You need processes that nudge employees toward consistency, even when they're feeling less than heroic. That's just being realistic about what shapes what we do at work.

Experiments with financial advisers have shown the impact that building in consistency can have. Most financial advisers will claim that they want the best deal for their clients. Yet they often come across products that are inferior for clients but which make *them* more money—whether it's in stocks, pensions, or insurance plans. There's a clear chance for hypocrisy here.

Let's break down what's going on. An adviser learns two different things: how good the product is for their client and how good it is for themselves. A clever experiment showed that the order in which you find out these things matters. If you discover what's best for your client first, you find it harder to choose the selfish option. But if you hear about the selfish one first, you start down that path and find reasons to keep going.

Here's the part that matters. The researchers gave real financial advisers the option to get either the selfish or the altruistic information first. They found that 30 percent of them were willing to pay to learn about *the client's* best option first.[47] So some people really want to put up barriers to help them stick to their principles—in other words, to be less hypocritical.

But what happened next is more interesting. Some of the advisers who had chosen to get the selfish information first were denied: they got the client information first instead. When that happened, those "selfish" advisers ended up recommending the client-friendly option *just as often* as the "altruistic" ones did.

In other words, a simple reordering of information was enough to shift even self-interested advisers toward doing the right thing. When real money was at stake.

There's a profound lesson for companies here. If you redesign the "choice architecture" that employees encounter—say, the order of information or the timing of a reminder—you can make it easier for them to live up to promised values. Want to make your supply chain more sustainable? Don't rely on your procurement people to search for the greenest option—flag it in the system as a default.[48] Design out as much hypocrisy as you can.

Yet, of course, you can never design it out completely. That means sometimes companies have to manage the accusations being made about them—and there are better ways of doing that as well.

WEAKEN THE SIGNAL

How do some businesses talk about social issues without driving us crazy? Why do certain campaigns feel authentic, not fake? What allows some companies to fall short and get away with it?

The cynical view is that it's all about getting good at deceiving and deflecting. We don't have to turn that way, though; there's another path.

You can see the path's outlines in how Starbucks developed and presented its work to reduce the plastic it uses. Rather than latching onto the latest issue, it chose one related to its core business: serving drinks. Rather than making overblown statements, there was a specific promise to stop its use of plastic straws by 2020. Rather than claiming pure motives, the press releases were clear that the business *also* benefited: using less plastic saved money and got drinks out faster. And instead of saying that these actions absolved Starbucks completely, they were framed as "another step" in an ongoing journey to sustainability.[49]

This approach—admitting mixed motives, choosing a relevant issue, setting concrete goals, and being honest about the bigger picture—is key to building trust and credibility with consumers. It involves companies "weakening the signal" that they are sending. As we saw, that move reduces the risk and impact of getting called out for hypocrisy. So how is it done?

The first step: admitting that your company also benefits. You might think that companies should try to show that their intentions are pure. But that's a risky choice unless your business is taking a big, undeniable hit from taking a stand. We always have a baseline level of cynicism about companies' motives. The need to make a profit means we see inconsistencies no matter how hard they try. When the accusation comes, claims of purity look deceptive—and that's what we really dislike.[50]

Instead, consumers often respond better when businesses don't pretend they are acting out of the goodness of their hearts.[51] Starbucks flagged up its cost and efficiency savings. It may seem like a paradox, but trust and credibility can come from admitting mixed motives.

It follows that you should choose an issue that plausibly relates to your company's skills, activities, or values. People are more likely to think you are serious about a relevant issue, regardless of your mixed motives.[52] Drinks packaging is the core business of Starbucks, and it could point to a credible track record of sustainability efforts.[53] The implication is that you should choose a few relevant priorities, not dozens.[54]

In contrast, choosing a tangential issue is more likely to invite skepticism.[55] In 2017, Pepsi put out an ad in which the supermodel Kendall Jenner hands a can to a police officer during a political protest, he drinks from it, and everyone is happy. The ad was instantly criticized for trying to co-opt the imagery from Black Lives Matter and trivializing social justice issues by implying a soda could solve them. It was pulled after a day. Pepsi's lack of connection or track record with issues of race was also seen as a major reason the ad came across as inauthentic.[56]

The next steps are crucial. If you just promote a good act that relates to your business, you're actually inviting an accusation of hypocrisy. It may seem that you're trying to disarm your critics, like a cement company planting a few trees or a tobacco company funding teen antismoking campaigns.[57]

Therefore, you also need to be realistic about the scope of what you're doing and admit it won't solve everything. Make your claims specific and limited rather than vague and inflated. A study showed that people were less skeptical about a hotel that gave concrete goals, such as reducing water use by 20 percent through efficient new showers, compared to one that made fuzzier claims about the environment.[58] Again, think of the specific Starbucks goal for plastic straws.

You might think that vaguer promises are safer because they're more forgiving. It's not so clear to the public if you've failed to fulfill them.[59] If you're just trying to "support the environment," you could point at many things to claim you met that goal. But, as in the Nike example, that ability cuts both ways: critics can use an equally wide range of things as evidence that you have fallen short. And you may find that regulators get annoyed: the Norwegian Consumer Authority argued that H&M's "Conscious Collection" label gave a misleading impression of sustainability.[60] The best option is to focus, go concrete, and follow through.

If you do follow through, don't brag about it. Taking a self-promotional tone increases skepticism, while a "subdued approach" feels more authentic and less annoying.[61] That kind of tone fits with the final step: don't pretend that your actions make your company perfect—admit the imperfections and the distance still to go. Reduce the false signal. Starbucks is not saying it's solved the plastic problem or denying its footprint; rather, it's putting its improvement in context. An overly rosy story will just lead people to roll their eyes, particularly for brands in more controversial sectors.[62] Giving an honest picture of the overall situation and the direction of travel can preempt future accusations of hypocrisy.[63]

Sadly, it's still rare for companies to take this step.[64] But perhaps that's because we, as consumers, can't let go of our unrealistic views about how much corporate consistency is even possible.

CHANGING VIEWS OF CORPORATE HYPOCRISY

Portentous music and dramatic lighting. A cause that people believe in; a stirring story about overcoming adversity; a bold promise for the future. Then the logo appears on-screen, and you know, just know, that it's all image management, debasing shared values for private profit. You feel sick.

We've all felt this wave of nausea at some point, which means the case I'm about to make is hard and maybe unpopular.

We need to adapt our views of corporate hypocrisy. Right now we give companies even less leeway than we do people. We expect them to be consistent entities who respond to our demands, or we will go elsewhere. Yet sometimes inconsistency is unavoidable. Companies need to navigate

- **Audiences**. Companies have to speak to many audiences and vary the messages they give to each—just like politicians do.[65] Boards, investors, clients, consumers, pressure groups, and employees all demand commitments that may conflict with each other. We've already seen the growing tension between consumers' desire for action on social issues and companies' need for profit.
- **Locations**. Companies may have to operate across a range of places that make it very hard to be consistent. Say your fast-food chain bans trans fats globally, only to find out it's almost impossible to replace them in some countries. Supporting political protests may enhance your reputation in one place but kill it in another.
- **Bureaucracy**. It can be hard for organizations to turn intentions into action. Leaders may think that a change has happened when in fact

the project has become trapped in an internal turf war or held up by complex contract negotiations.

Hypocrisy may be the only way of handling these conflicts. When the demands of your audience clash, the obvious choice is to send signals to each group that you are responding to their concerns—whether in terms of words or actions.[66] If you don't try to manage the conflict, you get tied up in endless strife and chaos. So some people see hypocrisy as an "organizational obligation" rather than a sin to be avoided at all costs.[67]

I'm not saying that bad-faith deception is fine; companies can and should work to make their claims and actions more consistent. But companies are responding to conflicting demands made by consumers, too. Those demands also need to change—here's how.

HELP COMPANIES FAKE IT UNTIL THEY MAKE IT

Our model for thinking about corporate hypocrisy is often basic: talk is cheap, and what you do is what counts. Companies try to fashion an external image that may clash with internal "reality." So to avoid hypocrisy, they first need to execute "real" actions and then talk about them. Or at least they need to announce ambitions with a specific, credible plan for achieving them.[68]

But remember that hypocrisy is not that simple. Making a statement can force your behavior to change so it falls into line; you start to become what was originally a performance. Your words don't just reflect reality—they can create that reality.

In the same way, perhaps we should realize that statements are also signals that companies send to themselves: they can be "hopes, dreams and visions through which corporate actors hope to seduce themselves and each other."[69] It's easy to see communication efforts as just empty spin, but they may be an attempt to bring a new phase into being. Companies may be trying to jolt themselves into consistency through talk.[70] As one corporate vice president put it, "If you are sufficiently brave or cheeky to communicate a few inches ahead of the actual state of affairs . . . you can help to assure that reality follows suit."[71] Perhaps we should see that words can be a way of doing the work rather than avoiding it?

You may be skeptical, but consider if the following story is plausible. In 2013, the home-improvement big box retailer Home Planet is failing. Having found initial success with low-cost products from overseas, its 150 stores now look tired and are getting squeezed by online retailers. A new direction is needed, and the CEO sees it in consumers' growing concern for the environment. She announces that Home Planet will become "the most sustainable choice for your home." The slogan becomes "It's Your Home Planet"; a marketing campaign encourages people to "Plan It for the Planet"; and all the tatty signature-yellow store exteriors are repainted green.

The changes are a bit surprising. Home Planet didn't have a great track record in this area; it was known as the cheap choice, not the sustainable one. And, the truth is, at the time of the pivot, little had really changed. But the newly hired chief operating officer begins to dig into what might be done. The logistics people talk about fuel efficiency. Store managers are sick of the waste they're piling up. The facilities team starts thinking about the plummeting cost of solar power.

Then the environmental groups come calling. They're skeptical but want to see if there's any opportunity here. They start with the company's use of illegally felled wood and use its own language as leverage: "Ban it for the planet!" It's an eye-opener for the managers at Home Planet, and they start to wonder what else they hadn't considered. Twitchy investors start asking about plans to avoid a hypocrisy backlash.

The slogans have started to reshape expectations, control discussions, and provoke demands, both internal and external. The CEO knows she needs to go further. The COO gets the license to shift the organization closer to its new image, working with activist employees who see how rhetoric can become reality. It's slow work, but each change reinvents and strengthens the original idea. Consumers are willing to pay higher prices if they get credible stories about where the money is going. By 2025, Home Planet is the first retailer with an all-electric delivery fleet.

Now imagine if the whole response to Home Planet's changes had been geared around slamming hypocrisy. If environmental groups had just gone for easy points based on Home Planet's past failings. If employees had responded with cynicism and offered nothing because things weren't fixed already. If customers had looked at all this with scorn, thought it was fake, and given up on their own green goals. Would things have been better if they had all used accusations of hypocrisy to shut down the space for change?

We need to leave *some* room for companies to make everyday compromises as well, rather than insisting that practice and action always exactly align. Perhaps we can withhold judgment until there are credible signs of convergence—or not. If nothing emerges, then it's deception not aspiration. But demanding that everything is fixed behind the scenes in advance can backfire.

DRAW THE LINE AT INTOLERABLE HYPOCRISY

What if hypocrisy is just what we demand of businesses because we require them to respond to our conflicting wishes? People who claim to want "ethical" products often don't buy them. Instead, they get angry at the companies who supply the "unethical" products they do buy.[72] We want good feels but also good deals. Our demand doesn't always reflect our demands. That fact just encourages companies to be more incoherent and deceptive.

The obvious solution is for us to bring our purchases more in line with our principles. The market will then offer more products that respond to that demand. But what if we don't have much ability to change what we buy? People may genuinely want to buy ethical products—they just can't find or afford them. Say I want to buy an electric vehicle, but I have no way of charging it. Do we have any other routes for change?

If both consumers and companies can't avoid hypocrisy, then the key is to focus on its worst abuses. That means going easier on companies that make credible efforts, even if they make a profit as well. It means recognizing when they are trying to coordinate for consistency or to design hypocrisy out of their organizations. We may even need to give companies time to catch up with their slogans if they are moving that way.

Taking this approach can also help us develop our thinking about the world. For example, as employees we may start off by saying that we want a leader who is completely honest and authentic. Many business books have pushed "authentic leadership," where managers gain trust and success by showing their "true self." This desire seems to make sense: leaders who are perceived as hypocritical undermine their employees' trust, motivation, and performance; increase turnover and absence rates; and may end up promoting antisocial and unethical behaviors in their firms.[73]

But, as we saw with Jeremy Corbyn, leaders often have to make pragmatic compromises that they don't fully reveal to employees. The author and leadership coach Caroline Webb pointed out to me that a major task for leaders is to navigate ambiguity for others.[74] If you share every emerging risk or concern with your employees, no one will work for you. Therefore, leaders may need to be "inauthentic" in a shallow sense (putting a face on) in order to remain true to deeper principles (care for employees). And, at some level, employees understand this.[75] If we benefit from the results, why not focus our energies elsewhere?

The hypocrisy map can be our guide. We should look where the injustice is greatest: where there is clear deception from a company causing tangible harm to get private benefit. Volkswagen's cover-up of its polluting "Clean Diesel" cars is a paradigm example. This was criminal fraud that caused widespread harm. The emissions led to 45,000 years of healthy life lost due to ill health, disability, or death. Each cheating car per 1,000 cars caused the infant mortality rate to increase by 1.7 percent.[76] This is the kind of case we should use as a trigger to push for wider changes that mean such hypocritical cheating can't happen again. After all, accepting some hypocrisy means we must be even clearer about what crosses the line.[77]

13 RELATIONSHIPS

It took some time, but Ben did it. The hours spent on Facebook groups, scrolling through the latest studies, texting other parents—they paid off. The campaign was successful. His daughter's school is now going to be smartphone free.

No more phones vibrating in pockets or hidden behind textbooks. Now they'll be stored in lockers at the start of the day, to be retrieved at the end. No more endless silent scrolling in corridors. People will notice each other again.

The evidence he's seen is clear: the constant distraction stops us listening, thinking, learning. Staring at a screen cuts us off from those around us.

He moves his thumb to post a triumphant message on social media. Just then a notification pops up: "You used your phone for an average of 4 hours 39 mins a day last week."

He clicks on Screen Time. It tells him that he picked up his phone ninety-seven times while his daughter was at school.

He looks up at his daughter, sitting at the kitchen table, watching him. And thinks: "Maybe there's a bigger lesson here."

Ben is confronted by the gap between his stance that smartphone use should be limited and his intense use of his own smartphone. What's the best way of closing that gap?

Maybe he should just decide to cut down on his phone use and then try to resist the temptation. Use willpower, fueled by the fear that someone will call him out or by the belief that he's trying to do the right thing. That's the default way that people think about self-control.[1]

The problem is that "willpower is overrated."[2] In fact, faith in willpower alone might be the reason we see so much hypocrisy, such large gaps between principles and action.

The startling truth is that the people who are best at self-control don't rely on willpower so much.[3] They find ways of structuring their lives so they don't have to. They build desired behaviors into routines and make them habits; they anticipate temptation and plan around it; they remove choices or attach big penalties to them.[4]

Whether consciously or not, they are using the latest insights from behavioral science. Let's see how those lessons can help you practice what you preach.

MAKE A COMMITMENT AND PLAN AHEAD

The first insight is to fix a commitment in advance that makes it harder to deviate from your principles later. You increase the cost of being inconsistent further down the road. Katy Milkman, a professor at the Wharton School, suggests that these costs can come in four different kinds:

- **Soft penalties.** When you suffer a psychological cost (such as shame or guilt) if you fall short. Ben might make a public promise that he's not going to use his smartphone at all during the day. His status takes a hit if people find out that he did.
- **Hard penalties.** When you pay a material cost if you don't meet the goal. Ben might use an automated app service to ensure that $15 leaves his bank automatically every time he opens an app during the day. For added power, the money could go to a charity he dislikes, or the fines could increase each time he slips.
- **Soft restrictions.** When you put up barriers that make it harder to be inconsistent but that can be pulled down without too much effort. Ben might use a feature that blocks the use of apps during the day yet can be turned off with a passcode.

- **Hard restrictions**. When you do something that makes it impossible or very difficult to deviate later. Ben might delete Facebook or get rid of his smartphone.[5]

These tactics effectively build a trust machine for the principle at stake. But there's a problem. Maybe you're not surprised to learn that we choose the softer alternatives more often. After all, we like to keep our options open! The snag is that those alternatives are also *the least effective ones.*

The issue is obvious when you look at soft penalties. They can be surprisingly effective—mainly because we want to seem consistent to others. In one experiment, people who made a pledge to save more money did have higher savings six months later than those who just retained a savings account.[6]

But if soft penalties always worked, hypocrisy wouldn't exist.[7] People wouldn't gain status by making claims that are contradicted by their behavior later. No couples would break their wedding vows, and no vegetarians would ever eat meat.

We need to build bridges that help our statements become behaviors. The good news is that behavioral science has some blueprints ready.

The first one focuses on reducing wiggle room. The more specific the pledge is, the harder it is for us to fudge whether we broke it or not. Link the pledge to a clear outcome: you will not use your phone between 9:00 a.m. and 5:00 p.m. on weekdays except to make and receive calls.

Then you choose a way of proving you kept the pledge that is hard to fake, even if you are tempted. You might make a commitment to upload your daily or weekly Screen Time reports, which show what apps were used and when. You may even want to enlist an "accountability partner" who checks the reports occasionally.

The second tactic is to use "cue-based planning."[8] When we make pledges, we tend to focus on *what* we're going to do: "I won't use my phone during the day." We think less about the *how*. We don't consider all the things that prompt us to pick up our phones: notifications, moments of boredom, momentary panic on waking up.

That's a mistake. Much of our behavior is triggered by cues in our environment in ways we may not even realize. For many smokers, finishing a meal acts as a cue to have a cigarette. If the cue–behavior link is repeated often, we call it a habit. Ignoring these cues or underestimating their power means our pledges are likely to go astray—because we haven't come up with a plan that reflects how we actually behave.

Cue-based planning forces us to work through the cues that trigger our behavior—either to change them or to come up with new ones. As hundreds of studies have shown, that makes it more effective than the usual way we plan and pledge.[9] So how does it work in practice?

It's pretty simple. You take a basic goal, such as "exercise more," and make it specific, as I just mentioned. So maybe it will be "I will go to the gym every Thursday after work." Then you think about what happens around the time you want to perform the behavior. You're looking for a clear cue that you can attach the new behavior to. To make it easy, you can just complete the phrase: "When *x* happens, I'll do *y*." Maybe you have a finance meeting every Thursday that finishes at 5:00 p.m.: "When the finance meeting ends, I'll go to the gym."

The ideal is that this action becomes habitual over time. You don't even need to remember the pledge you've made or try to motivate yourself. You just respond to the cue without effort. That's how habits work, and therefore plans can be most effective if you attach the new action to an existing habit. If you have a habit of packing your work bag the night before, then you can say, "When I pack my bag on a Wednesday, I will include my gym clothes." You "stack" the desired habit on top of an existing one.[10]

If your pledge is to *stop* doing something—such as using your phone during the day—you should take a couple more steps. You need to work out the cues that prompt you to pick up the phone and then plan around them. Suppose you work from a desk at your home during the day. Having your phone in sight on the desk might be a cue to pick it up. So the plan might be, "When I sit down at my desk, I will put my phone in the desk drawer." You disrupt the existing cue and replace it with another one, which gets you nearer to your goal.

Putting your phone in a drawer is a type of "soft restriction," the second of the four kinds of commitment devices. For phones, a mini-industry of app blockers now sells inconvenience as a benefit. Users are receptive:

product-feedback scores show that people seem to *like* restricting their future selves.[11] Soft restrictions also seem to work. One study found that people who set Screen Time limits reduced their time spent on Facebook daily by more than a third over six weeks.[12] Even small increases in the effort needed to do something can have a surprisingly large impact.

But soft restrictions are always vulnerable to what I call the "Toad Problem." In Arnold Lobel's *Frog and Toad* books for children, the title characters are looking at a plate of delicious cookies.

"We must stop eating! We need will power," says Frog. To solve the problem, he puts the cookies in a box.

"Now we will not eat any more cookies."

"But we can open the box," says Toad.

So Frog ties some string around the box.

Toad points out that they can cut the string and open the box to eat the cookies.

Frog gets a ladder and puts the box up on a high shelf.

"But we can climb the ladder and take the box down from the shelf and cut the string and open the box."[13]

Every step does make it less likely that Frog and Toad will eat the cookies. But each one can be overcome. So Frog ends up taking the cookies outside and feeding them to the birds. Toad stomps home to bake a cake.

Frog has stumbled on a "hard restriction": he has stopped future cookie eating by destroying the cookies. He's forced consistency onto himself. For phone use, you can put your phone into a box called a kSafe.[14] You set the inbuilt timer and until it goes off, there's no way of overriding the lock and getting at your phone. In theory, you could find a hammer and destroy the box, but that risks destroying your phone—which, of course, would be the ultimate hard restriction.

Although these commitment devices may be effective, you may not want to boast about using them if you can avoid it. People may trust you less as a result.[15]

Imagine you hear about two workers completing online tasks: Rory and Sam. Rory uses willpower to stay focused, while Sam uses an app to block distracting websites. When people hear this setup from researchers Ariella

Kristal and Julian Zlatev, they think Sam has less integrity, and they are less likely to trust him. It's the *choice* that matters: the same results hold if Sam chooses the app, but it breaks, and he's forced to use willpower anyway.[16]

Why? It seems that when a person chooses a commitment device rather than relying solely on willpower, we think that they know their willpower has failed in the past. If they don't trust themselves, maybe we shouldn't trust them either. Moreover, self-denial is praised in many cultures: we celebrate people who overcome an internal struggle.[17] Seen through that lens, people who sidestep the struggle with commitment devices deserve less credit.

People seem to sense that disapproval—they prefer to use lock boxes and app blockers in private, if possible.[18] The good news is that it is often feasible to do so. The bad news is that the general concern about being judged can make people less likely to use commitment devices, even though they work. Which begs the question: How can we motivate ourselves to make the commitment in the first place?

CONFRONT HYPOCRISY TO CHANGE BEHAVIOR

For Ben, the Screen Time prompt makes him suddenly realize that his smartphone use might be hypocritical. That kind of process has a name: "induced hypocrisy."

We met induced hypocrisy when discussing the trust machine in chapter 2. It's where you ask someone to advocate for a cause or principle and then remind them of the ways that they fall short of it.

Step one: Arushi records a video against distracted driving for a social media campaign. Step two: You make her think about the times when she looked at her phone behind the wheel. Arushi feels unpleasant tension between her advocacy and her actions. She resolves that tension by ignoring her phone while driving.

The tactic of confronting us with our hypocrisy has been used in many ways, from increasing compliance with COVID-19 precautions to getting schoolchildren to disrupt bullying.[19] Overall, it seems to be pretty good at changing behavior in the short term.[20]

But the tactic can also backfire: people often don't like being reminded of their hypocrisy. For example, one set of shoppers in Paris was asked to sign a poster about not using plastic bags. Another set was asked to sign the poster and then asked to remember past times when they *had* used plastic bags. Researchers saw that this second group ended up taking more plastic bags at the checkout.[21]

Here's how to make success more likely. The first step works best if you align the person's views with those other people hold. So first you need to persuade Arushi that most people think distracted driving is bad.[22] Then you should ask her to advocate actively in a way that is both public (the video) and for a purpose (the social media campaign). That part links the behavior to our self-image, while creating a strong signal to others—the more prominent and convincing the advocacy, the stronger the signal.[23]

Using the hypocrisy map can help make the comparisons in the second step more effective. For example, it's best if you can show that the person did not do the *exact* thing that they advocated for—as we saw, the match matters. The inconsistent behavior needs to have taken place *recently*, so people don't just say, "I was a different person then." Ideally, there won't be any extenuating circumstances.

But there's one big difference between the second step and the first step, where the more publicly the person makes their view known the better. That's not true in the second step. You don't want to expose the hypocrisy in public because that will backfire. Confronted by loss of status, people will feel forced to defend themselves. They are more likely to justify their actions and use all the usual tactics to say they weren't really being hypocritical.

Instead, take a gentler approach: have a quiet word with people, be supportive, give them a chance to change without losing face. Induced hypocrisy works when it evokes guilt but backfires when it triggers shame.[24] Technology is your friend here. An Australian study found that delivering a hypocrisy message online (rather than face-to-face) was more effective at reducing smartphone use while driving.[25] It's easier to change when no one is sitting there judging you.

Applying these two steps can be enough to get people to change their behavior—at least in the short term. The impact of time is revealed in a study that showed children in Vietnam a short video about the importance of not eating too much sugar.[26] After the video, they were asked to record a summary of the video's message that would be sent to children in other schools. They then chose either a sweetened or an unsweetened milk drink for themselves.

Compared with children who saw a transport video, the group that saw the sugar video were less likely to choose sweetened milk. But there was one other group—they saw the sugar video but then completed a questionnaire for fifteen minutes before choosing milk. Even that short delay made the video less effective at influencing their choice. More of them chose the sweetened milk.

Sometimes a one-off choice made in the moment is all you need—such as when you're getting people to register to vote or donate an organ. But it might be best to think of induced hypocrisy as creating a *window of opportunity*. Jeff Stone, one of the creators of the induced hypocrisy approach, told me that its value could be as a "teachable moment," when "you might be able to open people up to wanting to solve this problem in a serious way."[27] That's the moment when we can use these tactics to lock in behavior for the long term.

OWN YOUR IMPERFECTIONS THROUGH "HONEST HYPOCRISY"

You're at dinner with friends. People have started talking about ethical shopping. Your friend Monica is making the case for boycotting fast-fashion brands that exploit their workers. She says that we need to pay for what we believe in. People start nodding, carried along by her passion.

You're nodding, too, until you remember the moment last week when you saw Monica stepping out of one of those fast-fashion stores, arms full of bags. You're just about to call out her hypocrisy, when . . .

"I know what you're thinking," she says with a rueful smile. "Where did my jeans come from? I'm not perfect—I don't always live my values. It's hard when things are so easy and cheap. I'm working on it, but I guess I'm a bit of a hypocrite."

The room falls silent. But then Simon speaks. "You all know I've made the moral case against eating meat. The truth is I still can't quite quit bacon. I suppose I can't call myself a vegetarian yet." More admissions follow: a campaigner who hasn't voted, a dentist who doesn't floss.

By putting her inconsistency upfront, Monica dodged an embarrassing exposure. Rather than making others feel bad, she flagged her flaws and triggered a more constructive conversation.

That's the power of being an "honest hypocrite." In the language of the hypocrisy map, you weaken the strength of the signal you send. Sure, you may get less credit to start with, but you take the sting out of any accusations later.[28] Yes, you do come across as hypocritical—how could you not? But you get judged less harshly than hypocrites who build a false front that gets demolished.[29]

Yet honest hypocrisy works only if you admit both that the inconsistency is a *problem* and that you want to do something about it. Otherwise, it looks as if you think that different rules should apply to you: "Yeah, I didn't practice what I'm preaching. So what?" That's a blatant double standard straight out of the world of brazen power plays, and we don't like it.[30] Or you come across as if you're still feeling pretty good about yourself despite the admission. Monica's statement, delivered with a smirk, could come across as a smug ploy. You could revel in your flaws, much as some people felt Boris Johnson cultivated a shambolic image. People want to see your self-image taking a hit as well.[31]

Empty apologies or a flippant "nobody's perfect" attitude will likely backfire. Instead, show how you regret your failings and have suffered for them. People will think you've earned the right to speak, even if your words are inconsistent with your past actions.[32] You've felt bad enough; you've learned your lesson; you've paid a fair price.

Suppose your friend had an affair outside their marriage ten years ago. Now they're advising you not to do the same. If your friend's partner never found out, you'll actually be less likely to listen to them than a friend who never had an affair. But if the affair was discovered, and your friend's life fell to pieces, all this changes. They seem much less of a hypocrite, and you think they have more right to give you advice. Guilt and regret may erase the potential arrogance and hypocrisy of "do as I say, not as I have done."[33]

It can pay off to offer vulnerability and admit that you are a work in progress rather than going for the most credit upfront. It may get you more credibility in the long run because people can see your unprompted admission as a signal that you can be trusted.

Honest hypocrisy matters more than you think. There's a danger that fear of being called a hypocrite leads people to stay silent about things that matter. Take climate change. There are waves of stories that slam climate advocates as hypocrites for doing anything that has any impact on the planet: buying imported fruit, traveling on a plane.[34] As the activist Clover Hogan puts it, "I think one of the biggest barriers to more young people engaging in climate is that they feel that they have to be perfect. . . . But actually talking about our inconsistencies . . . is so so important. Because we're all inconsistent, and we can't let our hypocrisy or our inconsistencies or imperfections prevent us from engaging. You're not going to change the world with ten people doing activism perfectly; you're doing to change it with millions of people doing it imperfectly."[35]

If we think back to the hypocrisy map, maybe we shouldn't be so bothered about this inconsistency on its merits. The outcome is an important one, and there are extenuating circumstances: many societies make carbon emissions hard to avoid. It's plausible that hypocrisy accusations are being used deliberately to undermine advocates of making changes.[36]

And yet . . . there *are* many wealthy people who preach climate activism while making the problem worse. Understandably, what we really hate is their self-satisfied and unjust claims to social status. The honest-hypocrisy approach suggests that if they can confront their flaws and commit to doing better, then they don't have to be perfect in order to support a cause that could benefit us all.

Consider speaking up and owning your imperfections. It might spark a conversation about how you and others can best close the gap between aspirations and reality. You might be surprised at what a little honest hypocrisy can do.

CHALLENGE THE CONSISTENT SELF

Honest hypocrites openly admit that they are inconsistent, but they also say that they are working on fixing that problem. Perhaps we should go even further. Maybe we should question how much consistency it's reasonable to expect—and even why we think consistency is good in the first place.

After all, we certainly dislike inconsistency. When other people are inconsistent, we see them as dishonest, untrustworthy, or unstable.[37] In the words of the famous psychologist Robert Cialdini, "The person whose beliefs, words, and deeds don't match is seen as confused, two-faced, even mentally ill."[38]

We want to claim that our opinions and behaviors make sense together. If they don't, we may seem just like a jumble of half-formed prejudices. We don't want to be a messy collection of impulses shaped by our environment; we want to be cohesive and reasoning beings. If others don't see us this way, we know they will dismiss us and the ideas we hold dear.

In other words, we assume that we can and should have a coherent "self." That self knows what it wants and attempts to get it, knows its beliefs and tries to fulfill them. There is a single overarching "you"; you are a distinct individual.

Since this idea of the self is so integral to Western societies, it can be startling to realize that it hasn't always existed. For example, consider what Eric Havelock saw in Greek civilization before the fourth century BCE: "When confronted with an Achilles, we can say . . . here is a man to whom it has not occurred, and to whom it cannot occur, that he has a personality apart from the pattern of his acts."[39]

In this view, the move away from a purely spoken culture forced the Greek mind to "stop splitting itself up into an endless series of moods" and move to "accepting the premise that there is a 'me,' a 'self,' a 'soul,' a consciousness which is self-governing." Others have also noticed the profound change that seemed to have occurred in this period.[40]

Two other changes like this really affected how we see hypocrisy. In the Enlightenment era of the seventeenth and eighteenth centuries, Western philosophers grappled with the decline of religious certainties. This struggle produced the idea of an independent and consistent self that I just mentioned, one that uses reason to work toward its goals.

The second change was when a different kind of self emerged from the Romantic backlash to the Enlightenment. This self represents a genuine sense of individual spirit and drive in opposition to the oppressive conformism of a society based on reason. Your private, authentic self is the real one—and it's crucial to be true to your passions, not to the roles you are forced to play.[41]

These ideas of the consistent self are different, but both have a hold in Western societies. And hypocrisy offends both.

In terms of the reasoning self, a hypocrite seems to have either a defective mind or a defective character. In the first case, your contradictory opinions make you seem incoherent. In the second one, you must be deliberately deceiving us for your gain. Your words and behaviors are part of a calculated plan because the reasoning self knowingly works toward its goals.[42] A famous quote sums up this view: "Hypocrisy is the most difficult and nerve-racking vice that any man can pursue; it needs an unceasing vigilance and a rare detachment of spirit[;] . . . it is a whole-time job."[43]

In this quote, the *defining* thing about hypocrisy is its unceasing deception. However, I hope this book has convinced you that this is a terrible take on hypocrisy. Hypocrisy is not like being a spy; it's like being funny: sometimes you know you're doing it, sometimes you don't, and, ultimately, others decide anyway.

The inconsistency that the Romantic self focuses on is between your private self and the roles you play in society. These everyday compromises are denials of your true beliefs and instincts. Your acts are out of line with your authentic being, which is the source of your humanity.[44] Much better to be a Romantic hero, strike a pose, and scorn those too scared to do the same. The model is Lord Byron's pirate hero Conrad:

> Lone, wild, and strange, he stood alike exempt
> From all affection and from all contempt . . .
> He knew himself a villain—but he deemed
> The rest no better than the thing he seemed;

And scorned the best as hypocrites who hid
Those deeds the bolder spirit plainly did.[45]

But these ideas of the self can and have been challenged.[46] An alternative idea is that the self is more like a stage character that is formed as it gets performed. We have to play roles all the time in society and, since situations vary, that means inconsistency.

In this view, performing is not a *betrayal* of a true self—it's a process of workshopping a self into being.[47] You get to know your self as you perform it.[48] When someone asks you for directions in the street, the way you respond forms another part of your self rather than being a true or false portrayal of your *real* self.

This concept of the performing self challenges the traditional idea of hypocrisy, which also came from the stage but had the idea that someone was playing a part. There is a true face behind the mask you put on for the performance. The gap between the mask and the true face is what we criticize.

The performing self turns things around completely. There is nothing "behind" the mask of performance; in fact, a better metaphor is that of a chameleon, which changes its appearance to fit its surroundings.[49] For a chameleon, the problem is inconsistency between the appearance and the environment, not between the performance and some hidden, consistent self.

We feel more neutral about chameleons than we do about deceptive actors.[50] Maybe this shows a way forward. Remember how in a world of everyday compromises, we all can gain if someone becomes their performance and fakes it until they make it. Cathy erased the inconsistency by leaning into her role as fundraiser for Diana's nonprofit.

Maybe we should be more sympathetic to people who just want to fit in, even if they have no strong or true opinion or belief "behind" their actions. They are neither consistent nor inconsistent with a real self; they are just acting, in all senses of the word.

Writing in the eighteenth century, Bernard de Mandeville argued that we shouldn't be bothered by these "Fashionable Hypocrites": "Fashionable Hypocrites I call those who, without any motive of religion, or sense of duty, go to church, in imitation of their neighbours; counterfeit devotion, and without any design upon others, comply occasionally with all the rites and ceremonies of public worship, from no other principle than aversion to singularity, and a desire of being in the fashion. . . . [They] are rather beneficial to society, and can only be injurious to themselves."[51]

Mandeville noticed that there's relatively little harm or injustice from this kind of hypocrisy. So why should we be that bothered by it? Well, you can see that there might be risks. If things seem to collapse into a play of surface appearances, suspicion and distrust can thrive; agreeing on a shared view of reality becomes more difficult. We would need to go against the grain of our core assumptions about human nature.

But not all cultures have those assumptions of an independent, consistent, and authentic self. Many in Asia and Latin America, for example, often see the self as *interdependent*: a tapestry of interconnected threads woven into the fabric of relationships and social expectations.[52] The self is made up of different roles you have to play at different times. It's formed by the perceptions of others rather than being an internal essence that you can betray.[53]

Seen through this lens, inconsistency may be a virtue if it means you are being sensitive to the needs of each situation.[54] There are certain faces you must present to certain people—your colleagues, your friends, your family—and they all make up "you."

As you would expect, people from cultures where ideas of the interdependent self are stronger judge hypocrisy less harshly. Experiments show that people from countries such as Indonesia, Japan, and India are more forgiving of not practicing what you preach than are people from the United States.[55] They also feel less discomfort at their own inconsistencies, which means that tactics like induced hypocrisy are likely to have less impact in these places.[56]

Where does the forgiveness come from? In interdependent cultures, people are more likely to assume that hypocrisy arises from prosocial motivations.[57] A guest at a friend's wedding who publicly agrees with an opinion that they reject is more likely to be seen as displaying tact than cowardice. A colleague urging seat-belt use, even though it's known he often doesn't buckle up, could be seen as genuinely wanting to help others despite his failings. In independent cultures, he would probably be judged as a hypocrite who's trying to look better than he is.

People from East Asian cultures are also more likely to accept that sometimes contradictions are just inevitable. Issues can be complex and have conflicting elements. In this situation, Chinese students try to synthesize opposing viewpoints, while US students try to work out which is one is right—so they can reject the other one. In one study, Chinese participants were drawn to proverbs with contradictions, such as "too humble is half proud," while US participants liked those without them, such as "half a loaf is better than no bread."[58]

These views take us closer to the world of everyday compromises. That could be a useful direction for people living in Western democracies, who have the most intolerant views of hypocrisy. Concepts of the performing or networked self, which are so central to many societies, can prompt us to step back from blanket criticisms—and avoid the hypocrisy trap.

If you are skeptical about these cultural ideas of the self, that's OK. Behavioral science offers another route that may change your view. It turns out our minds are biologically wired for inconsistency.

UNDERSTAND WHY WE CAN'T HELP BEING INCONSISTENT

Imagine your brain as a smartphone, with dozens of apps running at once. That's how the behavioral scientist Robert Kurzban sees our minds—as a collection of mental "modules."[59] Each of these modules runs on its own logic, and, crucially, they can run separately from each other without any conflict or friction. That ability allows inconsistency.

Look at the two lines in figure 13.1. The top line looks longer than the bottom one. But if I told you that they are the same length, you'd probably believe me. *Yet we can't help but see them as different.*

Let's pause on what's happening here; it's not just a quirky trick. One part of your mind "knows" that the lines are unequal in length, while another part "knows" they are the same length. These two "apps" in your mental smartphone are running alongside each other, contradicting each other without causing a crisis.

Optical illusions like this make the inconsistency explicit. Yet that's usually not the case: often the operations of one module are sealed off from

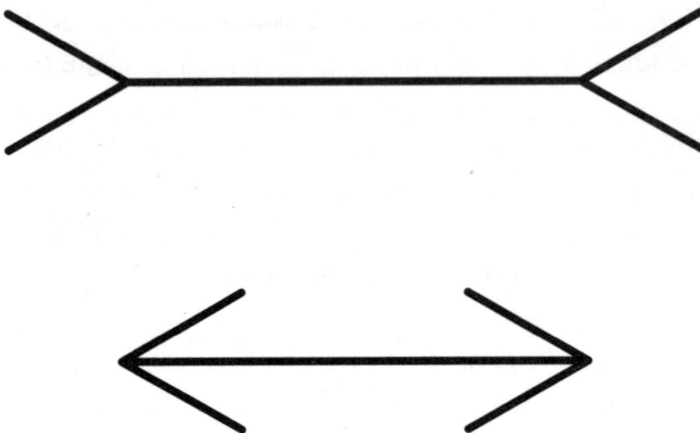

Figure 13.1
The Müller-Lyer illusion.

those of another. They can run alongside each other without you being aware of a contradiction.

Different modules can get switched on or off as we move from context to context. You might count calories at home, but the smell of buttery popcorn in a movie theater means another process takes over instead. That's why our actions can vary so much; that's why we can look hypocritical.

In fact, this view implies that there isn't really a single "you." You are a collection of processes, with no single one consistently in charge. Imagine you are taking a work call while driving. One process might be monitoring for loss of social status on the call, while another one is scanning for objects in front of your car. Someone insults you, and you don't notice the deer stepping out. Or maybe you see the deer but lose track of the conversation.

You might be thinking, "But I feel like a single, consistent me!" Well, that's mainly because we have at least one module that's good at telling stories about why we do things—even to ourselves. But Kurzban suggests we should see this module as like a White House press secretary, who justifies actions and explains events, rather than like a president, who makes decisions.[60]

You are at a party. You've sworn off alcohol for health reasons, but someone pushes a glass of champagne toward your hand and you start drinking. The causes might be instinctive and triggered by the context. But the press secretary will kick into gear and create a narrative that emphasizes consistency because that looks good. "You said that special occasions were OK. And doesn't the evidence suggest one glass is fine?" But it's an improvisation, papering over the gaps on the fly, using whatever materials come to hand. It's not a cover story for some hidden truth; it's just a surface-level performance.[61]

This constant improvisation ends up looking like hypocrisy. The press secretary tries to put our words and deeds into a consistent narrative for ourselves and others. But inconsistency is baked in: our mental processes are trained to respond to varying contexts. Gaps between narrative and action inevitably open up and become harder to explain. Others notice and call them hypocrisy.[62]

So perhaps we need to flip our assumptions. Maybe we need to see inconsistencies as part of our normal state rather than as lapses from a consistent and unified self. Think more about mental functions than moral failings. Making that change will allow us to focus on *what kind* of inconsistencies we should condemn as hypocrisy: the unjust ones that harm us and our societies. That's the way we escape the hypocrisy trap.

14 THE WAY FORWARD

I hope you can see hypocrisy more clearly now. We can be more consistent if we adopt tools and tactics that may seem surprising. We can reduce the chance of accusations by being mindful of what triggers the judgments of others. And we need to change how we make those judgments. If complete consistency is impossible, we need to find the best ways of dealing with our shortcomings.

You now have new tools to recognize the different forms of hypocrisy, understand what drives them, and judge them in a more discerning way. If we relentlessly pursue every inconsistency we don't like, we'll fall into the hypocrisy trap. We'll create a cycle of outrage that feels rewarding but ends up in rigid, inhuman standards or cynical power plays.

Instead, we can use the hypocrisy map to target the cases that are most unjust. That way, we can keep the trust machine running while making the everyday compromises that are needed. We will be able to navigate life's complexities with greater wisdom for the benefit of ourselves and our societies.

So maybe pause before hitting the Like button. Find new ways of designing your workplace to make it easy to be consistent. Be honest about your own hypocrisy when you can. Understand what the politician who makes a big play for authenticity is really doing.

The guide isn't complete, and the task is hard. The solutions may be in tension with each other. Reducing the risk of accusations can be good for you personally while harming society overall. You can protect yourself by invoking your group identity, but that may increase the divisions caused by double-standards hypocrisy. Even though accusations often pay off for us personally, they have a collective cost.

Change will also require disrupting easy, habitual ways of thinking. Blame happens more when it requires little cognitive effort, and our societies offer accusation routines that make blaming very easy indeed.[1] They also reward immediate, simple attacks rather than restrained, nuanced responses. We can't ignore how tough it will be to escape from the hypocrisy trap.

One of the hardest things will be the loss of the clean and simple narratives that we love. Our criticism of hypocrites, which feels so virtuous, may become tinged with guilt that someday our own bill may come due. If compromises are everywhere, we will need to find new ways of holding onto our ideals even if we know we can't always achieve them. We will need to recognize the flaws in ourselves, as well as in others, without falling into cynicism.

And as we change our views of hypocrisy, *we won't be completely consistent.* That means tolerating compromise, incoherence, and maybe even disappointment. Those are the things that loosen the trap's jaws, not neat and simple tricks.

As Sigmund Freud saw, behind all these decisions lies a fundamental choice. It is one that we may not even realize we are making. We need to choose if the hypocrisies that maintain our societies are worth it. Sometimes we may feel so sick of the compromises, so disillusioned at the gap between principle and practice, that we decide they are not.

But I hope that the four worlds I described in this book show that destroying hypocrisy also tears down many things we value. Maybe we would build a better society eventually—yet as it grows, so would a new set of hypocrisies. The real tragedy would be if we shattered our societies in a misguided attempt to save them. In flirting with the edges of the hypocrisy trap, that's exactly what we risk doing. There's still a way out. Let's take it.

Acknowledgments

At MIT Press, I have three editors to thank this time: Bob Prior for suggesting I do another book, Matt Browne for commissioning the project, and Catherine Woods for guiding it over the line. You were an absolute pleasure to work with!

Emily Loose offered an excellent editorial review, and Evan Nesterak provided a set of perceptive comments. Virginia Crossman helped get the book into production. Elspeth Kirkman was kind enough to read the whole book and was as thoughtful and perceptive as always. Nick Down was the first person to read any part of the book, and his reaction encouraged me to keep going. Thea House provided excellent logistical and analytic support for running the online study that I present in part II of the book. Clara Hamer was kind enough to tell me about how hypocrisy is treated in the UK legal system. Dave Nussbaum gave me useful advice in the early stages of this project and sent interesting studies my way. The 2024 MPA students in Princeton University's School of Public and International Affairs patiently listened to me give my first lecture on this material.

Daniel Effron, Jeff Stone, Alison Taylor, and Caroline Webb generously let me interview them, either virtually or in person. Elizabeth Huppert, Jillian Jordan, Ariella Kristal, Sean Laurent, Michael Pasek, and Roseanna Sommers kindly checked that I had represented their work correctly.

Dr. Lee Zhao, Dr. James Borin, and others at NYU Langone Health were good enough to fix my left kidney while I was about halfway through writing this book.

My colleagues, both past and current, provided me with amazing opportunities and a fertile intellectual environment. Thank you!

Finally, and most importantly, I want to thank all those people who helped me personally. Ellen Hallsworth—thank you for twenty incredible years. I couldn't have done any of this without you. My parents, Alan and Marion Hallsworth, listened to the ideas and reviewed the manuscript when I needed an outside perspective. My sister, Ceri Rahman, helped me when times were tough. And my daughter, Alice, not only provided the start of the book but was constantly supportive—and made sure I was up to date with *The Simpsons*. The book is dedicated to her.

Notes

INTRODUCTION

1. Nadeem Badshah, "Video emerges of Conservative HQ Christmas party during Covid," *The Guardian*, June 18, 2023, https://www.theguardian.com/politics/2023/jun/17/video-emerges-of-conservative-hq-christmas-party-during-covid.
2. "Partygate: What's in the Sue Gray report?," BBC, May 25, 2022, https://www.bbc.com/news/uk-politics-60045126.
3. Quoted in Pippa Crerar, "Boris Johnson reportedly joked about being at 'UK's most unsocially distanced party' during lockdown," *The Guardian*, January 11, 2023, https://www.theguardian.com/world/2023/jan/11/boris-johnson-reportedly-joked-he-was-at-most-unsocially-distanced-party-in-uk.
4. "Findings of Second Permanent Secretary's investigation into alleged gatherings on government premises during Covid restrictions," Policy Paper (Prime Minister's Office, May 25, 2022).
5. Daniel Finkelstein, "It's the hypocrisy that will do for Boris Johnson," *The Times*, March 21, 2023, https://www.thetimes.com/uk/politics/article/its-the-hypocrisy-that-will-do-for-boris-johnson-n6mzftnq8.
6. Jemima Kelly, "Why we're all hypocrites in the end," *Financial Times*, August 13, 2020, https://www.ft.com/content/fd3863c8-493c-4c9c-a42b-f3a628dc26fe.
7. Jim Waterson, "How media took nine months to leap on Starmer beer footage," *The Guardian*, May 6, 2022, https://www.theguardian.com/politics/2022/may/06/media-keir-starmer-lockdown-beer-footage.
8. "Ipsos MORI January 2021 Coronavirus polling," January 12–13, 2021, https://www.ipsos.com/sites/default/files/ct/news/documents/2021-01/ipsos_january_2021_coronavirus_polling_tables_150121_public_0.pdf.
9. Judith N. Shklar, *Ordinary Vices* (Harvard University Press, 1984).

10. Catherine Weaver uses the phrase *hypocrisy trap* as the title of a book about the World Bank. However, the term is used only once in the book, in the sense that hypocrisy is "easy to fall into and hard to get out of." Catherine Weaver, *Hypocrisy Trap: The World Bank and the Poverty of Reform* (Princeton University Press, 2008), 8.

11. M. H. Pasek et al., "Misperceptions about out-partisans' democratic values may erode democracy," *Scientific Reports* 12, no. 1 (2022): art. 16284, https://doi.org/10.31234/osf.io/qjy6t.

12. G. Simonovits et al., "Democratic hypocrisy and out-group threat: Explaining citizen support for democratic erosion," *Journal of Politics* 84, no. 3 (2022): 1806–1811.

13. C. Doherty et al., "Public uncertain, divided over America's place in the world," Pew Research Center, May 5, 2016, https://search.issuelab.org/resource/public-uncertain-divided-over-america-s-place-in-the-world-growing-support-for-increased-defense-spending.html.

14. Pasek et al., "Misperceptions about out-partisans' democratic values may erode democracy," 4.

15. E. J. Finkel et al., "Political sectarianism in America," *Science* 370, no. 6516 (2020): 533–536.

16. Pasek et al., "Misperceptions about out-partisans' democratic values may erode democracy."

17. A. Braley et al., "Why voters who value democracy participate in democratic backsliding," *Nature Human Behaviour*, May 22, 2023, 1–12.

18. J. G. Voelkel et al., "Megastudy testing 25 treatments to reduce antidemocratic attitudes and partisan animosity," *Science* 386, no. 6719 (2024): art. eadh4764, https:doi.org/10.1126/science.adh4764; Braley et al., "Why voters who value democracy participate in democratic backsliding."

19. "CO2 emissions per capita," table, Worldometer, accessed January 6, 2025, https://www.worldometers.info/co2-emissions/co2-emissions-per-capita/.

20. Nadja Popovich et al., "The climate impact of your neighborhood, mapped," *New York Times*, December 13, 2022, https://www.nytimes.com/interactive/2022/12/13/climate/climate-footprint-map-neighborhood.html.

CHAPTER 1

1. Matthew 23.

2. Dante Alighieri, *The Divine Comedy*, trans. Clive James (Liveright, 2013), canto 11.

3. Plato, *The Republic*, in *Plato in Twelve Volumes*, vols. 5 and 6, trans. Paul Shorey (Harvard University Press; William Heinemann, 1969), 361.

4. Jean-Jacques Rousseau, "Observations by Jean-Jacques Rousseau on the answer made to his discourse," in *The Discourses and Other Early Political Writings*, ed. and trans. Victor Gourevitch (Cambridge University Press, 2019), 47–48.

5. Hannah Arendt, *On Revolution* (1963) (Penguin, 2006), 94; Judith Shklar, *Ordinary Vices*, 45; J. S. Spiegel, *Hypocrisy: Moral Fraud and Other Vices* (Wipf and Stock, 1999).

6. S. M. Laurent et al., "Punishing hypocrisy: The roles of hypocrisy and moral emotions in deciding culpability and punishment of criminal and civil moral transgressors," *Cognition & Emotion* 28, no. 1 (2014): 59–83; J. J. Jordan et al., "Why do we hate hypocrites? Evidence for a theory of false signaling," *Psychological Science* 28, no. 3 (2017): 356–368.

7. Tennessee Williams, *The Rose Tattoo* (1951) (New Directions, 2010), 118.

8. D. A. Effron et al., "Hypocrisy by association: When organizational membership increases condemnation for wrongdoing," *Organizational Behavior and Human Decision Processes* 130 (2015): 147–159. The study actually tested four combinations: the campaign the candidate worked on was either for safer driving or for underage drinking; the offense was either reckless driving or underage drinking. The results showed that it was the congruence between campaign and offense that drove the results rather than the offense itself.

9. Laurent et al., "Punishing hypocrisy," 73–75.

10. S. L. Grover and M. C. Hasel, "How leaders recover (or not) from publicized sex scandals," *Journal of Business Ethics* 129, no. 1 (2015): 177–194; J. A. Agnew, "The big seducer: Berlusconi's image at home and abroad and the future of Italian politics," *California Italian Studies* 2, no. 1 (2011), https://doi.org/10.5070/C321008943.

11. Edwina Currie, *Diaries 1987–92* (Little, Brown, 2002); Leader, *The Daily Mirror*, September 30, 2002.

12. Shklar, *Ordinary Vices*, 44; David Runciman, *Political Hypocrisy: The Mask of Power, from Hobbes to Orwell and Beyond* (Princeton University Press, 2010), 2; Laurent et al., "Punishing hypocrisy."

13. S. M. Laurent and B. A. Clark, "What makes hypocrisy? Folk definitions, attitude/behavior combinations, attitude strength, and private/public distinctions," *Basic and Applied Social Psychology* 41, no. 2 (2019): 104–121.

14. Mark McLaughlin, "Alister Jack the new Scotland secretary accused of Brexit hypocrisy," *The Times*, July 27, 2019.

15. M. Alicke et al., "Hypocrisy: What counts?," *Philosophical Psychology* 26 no. 5 (2013): 673–701.

16. I. Silver and A. Shaw, "When and why 'staying out of it' backfires in moral and political disagreements," *Journal of Experimental Psychology: General* 151, no. 10 (2022): 2542–2561.

17. Silver and Shaw, "When and why 'staying out of it' backfires in moral and political disagreements."

18. Tiffany Watt Smith, *Schadenfreude: The Joy of Another's Misfortune* (Little, Brown Spark, 2018); C. A. Powell and R. H. Smith, "Schadenfreude caused by the exposure of hypocrisy in others," *Self and Identity* 12, no. 4 (2013): 413–431.

19. John Portmann, *When Bad Things Happen to Other People* (Routledge, 2000); Melvin J. Lerner, "The belief in a just world," in *The Belief in a Just World: A Fundamental Delusion* (Springer, 1980), 9–30; N. T. Feather, "Deservingness and emotions: Applying the structural

model of deservingness to the analysis of affective reactions to outcomes," *European Review of Social Psychology* 17, no. 1 (2006): 38–73; R. H. Smith et al., "Exploring the when and why of schadenfreude," *Social and Personality Psychology Compass* 3, no. 4 (2009): 530–546.

20. Powell and Smith, "Schadenfreude caused by the exposure of hypocrisy in others."

21. Jonathan Haidt, *The Happiness Hypothesis: Finding Modern Truth in Ancient Wisdom* (Basic, 2006).

22. "You can't make this stuff up: Plagiarism guideline paper retracted for . . . plagiarism," Retraction Watch, April 1, 2015, https://retractionwatch.com/2015/04/01/you-cant-make-this-stuff-up-plagiarism-guideline-paper-retracted-for-plagiarism/.

23. M. A. Ferguson and T. E. Ford, "Disparagement humor: A theoretical and empirical review of psychoanalytic, superiority, and social identity theories," *International Journal of Humor Research* 21, no. 3 (2008): 283–312; Thomas Hobbes, *Leviathan* (1651) (Oxford University Press, 1929), 45.

24. C. Anderson et al., "Is the desire for status a fundamental human motive? A review of the empirical literature," *Psychological Bulletin* 141, no. 3 (2015): 574–601; David Dunning, "The relation of self to social perception," in *Handbook of Self and Identity*, ed. Mark R. Leary and June Price Tangney (Guilford Press, 2012), 481–501.

25. Richard H. Smith et al., "Envy and the challenges to good health," in *Envy: Theory and Research*, ed. Richard H. Smith (Oxford University Press, 2008), 290–314; J. A. Minson and B. Monin, "Do-gooder derogation: Disparaging morally motivated minorities to defuse anticipated reproach," *Social Psychological and Personality Science* 3, no. 2 (2012): 200–207.

26. W. W. Van Dijk et al., "The role of self-evaluation and envy in schadenfreude," *European Review of Social Psychology* 26, no. 1 (2015): 247–282; Smith et al., "Exploring the when and why of schadenfreude"; W. W. Van Dijk et al., "Self-esteem, self-affirmation, and schadenfreude," *Emotion* 11, no. 6 (2011): 1445–1449.

27. Timothy P. Collins, *Hypocrisy in American Political Attitudes: A Defense of Attitudinal Incongruence* (Springer, 2017), 289.

28. The experiments employed various ways of determining whether people used the coin—like needing a seal to be broken to access it. C. Daniel Batson and Elizabeth C. Collins, "Moral hypocrisy: A self-enhancement/self-protection motive in the moral domain," in *Handbook of Self-Enhancement and Self-Protection*, ed. Mark D. Alicke and Constantine Sedikides (Guilford Press, 2011), 92–111; S. C. Lin and D. T. Miller, "A dynamic perspective on moral choice: Revisiting moral hypocrisy," *Organizational Behavior and Human Decision Processes* 164 (2021): 203–217.

29. M. Dong et al., "Self-enhancement in moral hypocrisy: Moral superiority and moral identity are about better appearances," *PloS One* 14, no. 7 (2019): art. e0219382, https://doi.org/10.1371/journal.pone.0219382.

30. Dong et al., "Self-enhancement in moral hypocrisy," table 1.

31. David Hume to Colonel Edmoundstone, March 26, 1764, https://www.gutenberg.org/files/42844/42844-h/42844-h.htm#FNanchor_187:2_162; Runciman, *Political hypocrisy*, 1.

32. Sigmund Freud, "Thoughts for the times on war and death" (1915), in *The Standard Edition of the Complete Psychological Works of Sigmund Freud*, vol. 14, *(1914–1916)*, ed. and trans. James Strachey (Hogarth, 1957), 284–285.

33. Béla Szabados and Eldon Soifer, *Hypocrisy: Ethical Investigations* (Broadview Press, 2004), 12.

34. A. M. Mastroianni and D. T. Gilbert, "The illusion of moral decline," *Nature* 618 (2023): 782–789.

35. J. Mewes et al., "Experiences matter: A longitudinal study of individual-level sources of declining social trust in the United States," *Social Science Research* 95 (2021): art. 102537, https://doi.org/10.1016/j.ssresearch.2021.102537.

36. H. E. Brady and T. B. Kent, "Fifty years of declining confidence & increasing polarization in trust in American institutions," *Dædalus* 151, no. 4 (2022): 44.

37. C. Foster and J. Frieden, "Crisis of trust: Socio-economic determinants of Europeans' confidence in government," *European Union Politics* 18, no. 4 (2017): 528.

38. R. J. Lewicki et al., "Trust and distrust: New relationships and realities," *Academy of Management Review* 23, no. 3 (1998): 438–458; A. Weiss et al., "Two-faced morality: Distrust promotes divergent moral standards for the self versus others," *Personality and Social Psychology Bulletin* 44, no. 12 (2018): 1712–1724.

39. Weiss et al., "Two-faced morality."

40. M. Gollwitzer et al., "Victimization experiences and the stabilization of victim sensitivity," *Frontiers in Psychology* 6 (2015): art. 439, https://doi.org/10.3389/fpsyg.2015.00439; Weiss et al., "Two-faced morality."

41. J. Jordan and R. Sommers, "When does moral engagement risk triggering a hypocrite penalty?," *Current Opinion in Psychology* 47 (2022): art. 101404, https://doi.org/10.1016/j.copsyc.2022.101404.

42. K. O'Connor et al., "Moral cleansing as hypocrisy: When private acts of charity make you feel better than you deserve," *Journal of Personality and Social Psychology* 119, no. 3 (2020): 540–559.

43. L. C. Howe and B. Monin, "Healthier than thou? 'Practicing what you preach' backfires by increasing anticipated devaluation," *Journal of Personality and Social Psychology* 112, no. 5 (2017): 718–735.

44. S. N. Bleich et al., "Impact of physician BMI on obesity care and beliefs," *Obesity* 20, no. 5 (2012): 999–1005.

45. Minson and Monin, "Do-gooder derogation."

46. G. Sparkman and S. Z. Attari, "Credibility, communication, and climate change: How lifestyle inconsistency and do-gooder derogation impact decarbonization advocacy," *Energy Research & Social Science* 59 (2020): art. 101290, https://doi.org/10.1016/j.erss.2019.101290.

47. T. A. Kreps and B. Monin, "Core values versus common sense: Consequentialist views appear less rooted in morality," *Personality and Social Psychology Bulletin* 40, no. 11 (2014): 1529–1542; A. B. Van Zant and D. A. Moore, "Leaders' use of moral justifications increases policy support," *Psychological Science* 26, no. 6 (2015): 934–943; J. J. Zlatev, "I may not agree with you, but I trust you: Caring about social issues signals integrity," *Psychological Science* 30, no. 6 (2019): 880–892.

48. E. Huppert et al., "On being honest about dishonesty: The social costs of taking nuanced (but realistic) moral stances," *Journal of Personality and Social Psychology* 125, no. 2 (2023): 259–283.

49. Huppert et al., "On being honest about dishonesty."

50. Alicke et al., "Hypocrisy."

51. Quoted in Michael Specter, "The dangerous philosopher," *New Yorker*, September 6, 1999, https://www.newyorker.com/magazine/1999/09/06/the-dangerous-philosopher.

52. Valerie Elliott, "The animal lab critic, cancer and hypocrisy," *The Times*, August 28, 2004; Nick Bilton, "Steve Jobs was a low-tech parent," *New York Times*, September 11, 2014, https://www.nytimes.com/2014/09/11/fashion/steve-jobs-apple-was-a-low-tech-parent.html; India Knight, "Why we should save the word 'hypocrite' for when it really counts," *The Times*, April 14, 2019, https://www.thetimes.co.uk/article/why-we-should-save-the-word-hypocrite-for-when-it-really-counts-rx6nd00dz.

53. D. A. Effron et al., "From inconsistency to hypocrisy: When does 'saying one thing but doing another' invite condemnation?," *Research in Organizational Behavior* 38 (2018): 61–75; Szabados and Soifer, *Hypocrisy*.

54. "The top-15 valuable Facebook statistics," Zephoria, slides, accessed January 6, 2025, https://zephoria.com/top-15-valuable-facebook-statistics/; Mansoor Iqbal, "YouTube revenue and usage statistics (2024)," Business of Apps, updated November 7, 2024, https://www.businessofapps.com/data/youtube-statistics/.

55. You could argue that these features are building on existing long-term trends. The rise of the written word also provided a record that could highlight people's inconsistencies. It has long been claimed that people are increasingly required to take a public position on issues that used to be considered private matters. See C. Anton, "Technology, hypocrisy and morality: Where, oh where, has all the hypocrisy gone?," *Explorations in Media Ecology* 17, no. 2 (2018): 119–135; M. O'Brien and A. Whelan, "Hypocrisy in politics," *Ergo: An Open Access Journal of Philosophy* 9, no. 63 (2022): 1692–1714.

56. A. E. Schlosser, "Self-disclosure versus self-presentation on social media," *Current Opinion in Psychology* 31 (2020): 1–6.

57. N. Santer et al., "Narratives of the self in polymedia contexts: Authenticity and branding in Generation Z," *Qualitative Psychology* 10, no. 1 (2023): 79–106.

58. Jessica Elgo and Aubrey Allegretti, "Boris Johnson faces fresh outrage over lockdown birthday party," *The Guardian*, January 24, 2022, https://www.theguardian.com/politics/2022/jan/24/boris-johnsons-lockdown-birthday-party-pm-faces-anger-from-mps-and-bereaved.

59. Steven Swinford and Oliver Wright, "Rishi Sunak settles in as Downing St's Captain Sensible," *The Times*, June 20, 2020.

60. Emily Atkinson, "Boris Johnson tells minister there was no cake at lockdown birthday party," *The Independent*, January 27, 2022, https://www.independent.co.uk/politics/boris-johnson-no-cake-birthday-b2002403.html.

61. Shklar, *Ordinary Vices*, 62.

62. "The unselfconscious, righteous hypocrite . . . appears as an antihypocrite. He displays his sense of moral superiority with his willingness to expose the moral failures of others." Ruth W. Grant, *Hypocrisy and Integrity: Machiavelli, Rousseau, and the Ethics of Politics* (University of Chicago Press, 2008), 69. See also Shklar, *Ordinary Vices*; and William Ian Miller, *Faking It* (Cambridge University Press, 2004).

63. Shklar, *Ordinary Vices*, 50.

CHAPTER 2

1. Effron et al., "From inconsistency to hypocrisy."

2. Shklar, *Ordinary Vices*.

3. D. A. Effron and B. A. Helgason, "Moral inconsistency," *Advances in Experimental Social Psychology* 67 (2023): 1–72.

4. Jeff Stone, interview by author, March 31, 2023, Tucson, Arizona.

5. O'Brien and Whelan, "Hypocrisy in politics."

6. David E. Morrison et al., *Media and Values: Intimate Transgressions in a Changing Moral and Cultural Landscape* (Intellect, 2008), 357.

7. Julian Petley, *Media and Public Shaming: Drawing the Boundaries of Disclosure* (Bloomsbury, 2013), 46.

8. M. Walzer, "Just and unjust wars: A moral argument with historical illustrations," *Science and Society* 43, no. 2 (1979): 247–249; Raphael Sassower, *The Specter of Hypocrisy: Testing the Limits of Moral Discourse* (Springer Nature, 2020); Szabados and Soifer, *Hypocrisy*. "Hypocrisy is a parasite, operating by mimicking the attractiveness of virtue, appropriating its rewards." Miller, *Faking It*, 20.

9. J. Isserow and C. Klein, "Hypocrisy and moral authority," *Journal of Ethics and Social Philosophy* 12 (2017): 191–222.

10. Austen Ivereigh, "An interview with Pope Francis," *Commonwealth Magazine*, March 12, 2020, https://www.commonwealmagazine.org/time-great-uncertainty.

11. D. Priolo et al., "Three decades of research on induced hypocrisy: A meta-analysis," *Personality and Social Psychology Bulletin* 45, no. 12 (2019): 1681–1701.

12. Elliot Aronson, "Dissonance, hypocrisy, and the self-concept," in *Cognitive Dissonance: Progress on a Pivotal Theory in Social Psychology*, ed. Eddie Harmon-Jones and Judson Mills (American Psychological Association, 1999), 103–126.

13. However, not all studies of induced hypocrisy have measured or shown cognitive dissonance specifically. See P. K. Durkee et al., "Pride and shame: Key components of a culturally universal status management system," *Evolution and Human Behavior* 40, no. 5 (2019): 470–478; and C. B. Fried and E. Aronson, "Hypocrisy, misattribution, and dissonance reduction," *Personality and Social Psychology Bulletin* 21, no. 9 (1995): 925–933.

14. R. S. Tokunaga, "Following you home from school: A critical review and synthesis of research on cyberbullying victimization," *Computers in Human Behavior* 26, no. 3 (2010): 277–287.

15. Y. Ryoo and W. Kim, "Approach versus avoidance: A self-regulatory perspective on hypocrisy induction in anti-cyberbullying CSR campaigns," *Journal of Business Ethics* 189 (2024): 345–364.

16. J. Stone et al., "Inducing hypocrisy as a means of encouraging young adults to use condoms," *Personality and Social Psychology Bulletin* 20, no. 1 (1994): 116–128; S. J. Kantola et al., "Cognitive dissonance and energy conservation," *Journal of Applied Psychology* 69, no. 3 (1984): 416–421; B. A. Morrongiello and L. Mark, "'Practice what you preach': Induced hypocrisy as an intervention strategy to reduce children's intentions to risk take on playgrounds," *Journal of Pediatric Psychology* 33, no. 10 (2008): 1117–1128.

17. K. Gamma et al., "The double-edged sword of ethical nudges: Does inducing hypocrisy help or hinder the adoption of pro-environmental behaviors?," *Journal of Business Ethics* 161 (2020): 351–373.

18. Concepts adapted from A. McGrath, "Dealing with dissonance: A review of cognitive dissonance reduction," *Social and Personality Psychology Compass* 11, no. 12 (2017): art. e12362, https://doi.org/10.1111/spc3.12362.

19. Priolo et al., "Three decades of research on induced hypocrisy"; J. Stone and N. C. Fernandez, "To practice what we preach: The use of hypocrisy and cognitive dissonance to motivate behavior change," *Social and Personality Psychology Compass* 2, no. 2 (2008): 1024–1051.

20. P. Benn, "What is wrong with hypocrisy?," *International Journal of Moral and Social Studies* 8 (1993): 223–235.

21. Jon Elster, *Reason and Rationality*, trans. Steven Rendall (Princeton University Press, 2009), 51.

22. James Johnson, "Arguing for deliberation: Some skeptical considerations," in *Deliberative Democracy*, ed. Jon Elster (Cambridge University Press, 1998), 161–184.

23. Jon Elster, "Deliberation and constitution making," in *Deliberative Democracy*, ed. Elster, 97–122.

24. Miller, *Faking It.*

25. George Orwell, "Shooting an Elephant," (1936), in *The Collected Essays, Journalism, and Letters of George Orwell,* ed. Sonia Orwell and Ian Angus, vol. 1, *An Age Like This, 1920–1940* (Harcourt, Brace & World, 1968), 265.

26. Timur Kuran, *Private Truths, Public Lies: The Social Consequences of Preference Falsification* (Harvard University Press, 1997).

27. Norma Clair Moruzzi, *Speaking Through the Mask: Hannah Arendt and the Politics of Social Identity* (Cornell University Press, 2000); Sassower, *The Specter of Hypocrisy.*

28. Arendt, *On Revolution*, 94.

29. E. F. Kittay, "On Hypocrisy," *Metaphilosophy* 13, nos. 3–4 (1982): 277–289.

30. Matthew 23:27–28, New International Version.

31. Matthew 6:16–18, New International Version.

32. Miller, *Faking It.*

33. Adam Crafton, "Jordan Henderson's potential Saudi move matters for a lot more reasons than hypocrisy," *The Athletic*, July 14, 2023, https://theathletic.com/4689412/2023/07/14/jordan-henderson-saudi-lgbt/.

34. Rousseau, "Observations by Jean-Jacques Rousseau on the answer made to his discourse," 47.

35. Miguel de Cervantes, *Don Quixote*, trans. John Ormsby (1605/1615; Project Gutenberg, 2004), chap. XXIV, https://www.gutenberg.org/files/5946/old/orig5946-h/p26.htm.

36. Spiegel, *Hypocrisy*; Szabados and Soifer, *Hypocrisy*; R. R. Palmer, "The Twelve Who Ruled (1941)," cited in Arendt, *On Revolution*, 87.

37. Jordan and Sommers, "When does moral engagement risk triggering a hypocrisy penalty?," emphasis added.

38. Effron et al., "From inconsistency to hypocrisy."

39. W. C. Carlos and B. W. Lewis, "Strategic silence: Withholding certification status as a hypocrisy avoidance tactic," *Administrative Science Quarterly* 63, no. 1 (2018): 130–169.

40. S. Hafenbrädl and D. Waeger, "The business case for CSR: A trump card against hypocrisy?," *Journal of Business Research* 129 (2021): 838–848.

41. O'Brien and Whelan, "Hypocrisy in politics."

42. Michael Gerson, "Trump's hypocrisy is good for America," *Washington Post*, November 28, 2016.

43. Angelique Chrisafis, "WikiLeaks cables: 'Nicolas Sarkozy thin-skinned and authoritarian,'" *The Guardian*, November 30, 2010, https://www.theguardian.com/world/2010/nov/30/nicolas-sarkozy-personality-embassy-cables.

44. Slavoj Žižek, *Living in the End Times* (Verso, 2010), 409.

45. Shklar, *Ordinary Vices*, 42.

46. F. X. Chen et al., "Communal narcissism and sadism as predictors of everyday vigilantism," *Personality Science* 4, no. 1 (2023): art. e10523, https://doi.org/10.5964/ps.10523.

47. James Baldwin, "Nobody Knows My Name," (1961), in *Collected Essays*, ed. Toni Morrison (The Library of America, 1998), 277.

48. J. Graham et al., "When values and behavior conflict: Moral pluralism and intrapersonal moral hypocrisy," *Social and Personality Psychology Compass* 9, no. 3 (2015): 166.

49. Arendt, *On Revolution*.

50. Camille Desmoulins, "Revolution Devours Its Own," *Le vieux cordelier*, no. 3 (1793), https://revolution.chnm.org/items/show/419.

51. Arendt, *On Revolution*, 90.

52. Will Storr, *The Status Game: On Human Life and How to Play It* (William Collins, 2021), 188–190.

53. "It was the war upon hypocrisy that transformed Robespierre's dictatorship into the Reign of Terror, and the outstanding characteristic of this period was the self-purging of the rulers." Arendt, *On Revolution*, 89.

54. Kuran, *Private Truths, Public Lies*.

55. A. Gais, "The politics of hypocrisy: Baruch Spinoza and Pierre Bayle on hypocritical conformity," *Political Theory* 48, no. 5 (2020): 588–614.

56. Shklar, *Ordinary Vices*, 69.

57. Armando Iannucci, dir., *In the Loop* (Optimum Releasing, 2009).

58. The author Ambrose Bierce defined politeness as "the most acceptable hypocrisy." Ambrose Bierce, *The Devil's Dictionary* (1911; Project Gutenberg, 2024), https://www.gutenberg.org/cache/epub/972/pg972-images.html.

59. R. Baker, "Let's hear it for hypocrisy," *New York Times*, August 30, 1970; Honoré de Balzac, *The Physiology of Marriage* (1829), trans. J. Walker McSpadden (Avil, 1901), 43.

60. "This kind of hypocrisy is very sociable. It cares greatly what people think, and, for the most part, to be well thought of one must do good deeds. It means having to be reasonably respectful of others, engaging in small acts of civility, cultivating tact, sparing others the pain of too much truth whose only virtue would be to hurt them needlessly and feed your own vanity for being a tough truth teller." Miller, *Faking It*, 27.

61. Miller, *Faking It*.

62. George Gordon Byron, *The Corsair* (1814) (Routledge, 1859), 2:356–357.

63. Jean Kerr, *Finishing Touches* (Dramatists Play Service, 1973), 9. Kerr's character attributes this idea to W. H. Auden. The relevant reference is Auden's foreword to his long poem *The Age of Anxiety* (1947).

64. Emmanuel Kant, *Lectures on Ethics*, trans. Peter Heath (Cambridge University Press, 1997), 217.

65. Friedrich Nietzsche, *Human, All Too Human* (1878), trans. Marion Faber (University of Nebraska Press, 1996), 50–51, emphasis in original.

66. Erving Goffman, *The Presentation of Self in Everyday Life* (Doubleday, 1959).

67. Sassower, *The Specter of Hypocrisy*.

68. This example is taken from Szabados and Soifer, *Hypocrisy*, 50.

69. B. Gert, "To be hypocritical or not to be," *New York Times*, July 15, 1974; Spiegel, *Hypocrisy*.

70. Benn, "What is wrong with hypocrisy?"

71. Miller, *Faking It*, 18.

72. George Orwell, "England, your England," in *The Lion and the Unicorn: Socialism and the English Genius* (1941) (Secker & Warburg, 1954), 202.

73. Orwell, "England, Your England," 202.

74. Steve Rolles, @SteveTransform, tweet, Twitter/X, September 25, 2023, 6:01 a.m., https://x.com/SteveTransform/status/1706247603300561084?s=20. On the prime minister condemning the use of recreational drugs, see *List of Ministers' Interests: November 2024*, https://www.gov.uk/government/publications/list-of-ministers-interests/list-of-ministers-interests-april-2023-html#prime-ministers-office.

75. Mark Forsyth, *A Short History of Drunkenness: How, Why, Where, and When Humankind Has Gotten Merry from the Stone Age to the Present* (Random House, 2017).

76. Grant, *Hypocrisy and Integrity*.

77. Stephen D. Krasner, *Sovereignty: Organized Hypocrisy* (Princeton University Press, 1999); Weaver, *Hypocrisy Trap*.

78. Marco Verweij and Michael Thompson, eds., *Clumsy Solutions for a Complex World: Governance, Politics and Plural Perceptions* (Springer, 2006).

79. In the language of clumsy solutions, the first represents an individualist perspective, the second a hierarchical one. See Mary Douglas, *A History of Grid and Group Cultural Theory* (University of Toronto Press, 2007).

80. R. Crisp and C. Cowton, "Hypocrisy and moral seriousness," *American Philosophical Quarterly* 31, no. 4 (1994): 343–349.

81. Finkel et al., "Political sectarianism in America."

82. George Eliot, *Middlemarch* (1871–1872; Project Gutenberg, 2024), chap. 20, https://www.gutenberg.org/cache/epub/145/pg145-images.html.

83. Shklar, *Ordinary Vices*, 65.

84. Alan Ehrenhalt, "Hypocrisy has its virtues," *New York Times*, February 6, 2001.

85. M. Punch, "Police corruption and its prevention," *European Journal on Criminal Policy and Research* 8, no. 3 (2000): 301–324.

86. O'Brien and Whelan, "Hypocrisy in politics."

87. Joseph N. Cappella and Kathleeen Hall Jamieson, *Spiral of Cynicism: The Press and the Public Good* (Oxford University Press, 1997).

88. Szabados and Soifer, *Hypocrisy.*

89. Shklar, *Ordinary Vices,* 65–67.

90. J. T. Levy, "Hypocrisy isn't the problem: Nihilism is," *Los Angeles Times*, February 8th, 2017.

91. Nate Fischer, @NateAFischer, tweet, Twitter/X, September 15, 2023, 11:17 p.m., https://x.com/NateAFischer/status/1702884339875266993?s=20.

92. Runciman, *Political Hypocrisy.*

93. Sheila Fitzpatrick, *Everyday Stalinism: Ordinary Life in Extraordinary Times: Soviet Russia in the 1930s* (Oxford University Press, 1999); Eugenia Semyonovna Ginzburg, *Journey into the Whirlwind*, trans. Paul Stevenson and Max Hayward (Harcourt Brace Jovanovich, 1967), 36–37.

94. Ben Zimmer, "Cadillac thrives as a figure of speech," *New York Times*, November 8, 2009, https://www.nytimes.com/2009/11/08/magazine/08FOB-onlanguage-t.html.

95. Hannah Arendt, "Totalitarianism," part 3 of *The Origins of Totalitarianism* (1951) (Harcourt, 1968), 80. I have modified the quote from the past to the present tense.

96. George Orwell, *Nineteen Eighty-Four* (1949) (Mariner Books Classics, 2013), 40. On this subject, see also Sassower, *The Specter of Hypocrisy.*

97. On these points, see Runciman, *Political Hypocrisy*, 185–187.

98. Orwell, *Nineteen Eighty-Four*, 17.

99. Orwell, *Nineteen Eighty-Four*, 9.

100. Freud, "Thoughts for the times on war and death," 284–285; B. F. Skinner, *Beyond Freedom and Dignity* (1971) (Hackett, 2002), 215.

101. Freud, "Thoughts for the times on war and death," 284–285.

102. Agatha Christie, *Hercule Poirot's Christmas* (1938) (William Morrow, 2003), 103.

103. Sigmund Freud, *Civilization and Its Discontents* (1931), trans. James Strachey (Penguin, 2005), Kindle loc. 740. See also Sassower, *The Specter of Hypocrisy.*

104. B. Ginzburg, "Hypocrisy as a pathological symptom," *International Journal of Ethics* 32, no. 2 (1922): 160–166.

105. The Riddler, in Matthew Reeves, dir., *The Batman* (Warner Bros., 2022).

106. The Joker, in Christopher Nolan, dir., *The Dark Night* (Warner Bros., 2008).

107. On this subject, see Žižek, *Living in the End Times*, 59.

108. The irony is that the movie ends with yet more layering on of hypocrisy as the heroes decide they need to lie to the city's inhabitants in order to maintain morale and social order.

CHAPTER 3

1. I am exaggerating slightly. The first study of "induced hypocrisy" took place in 1991; the coin-flip experiments that involve assigning an unpleasant task also began in the 1990s; there were a couple of other isolated studies. But, as I discuss later, no academic studies had asked people what they thought about hypocrisy until 2013—and that's a major oversight. For an overview, see Alicke et al., "Hypocrisy."

2. E. F. Kittay, "On hypocrisy," *Metaphilosophy* 13, nos. 3–4 (1982): 277–289; D. Turner, "Hypocrisy," *Metaphilosophy* 21, no. 3 (1990): 262–269.

3. R. Crisp and C. Cowton, "Hypocrisy and moral seriousness," *American Philosophical Quarterly* 31, no. 4 (1994): 343–349; F. Amory, "Whited sepulchres: The semantic history of hypocrisy to the High Middle Ages," *Recherches de théologiè ancienne et médiévale* 53 (1986): 5–39.

4. Szabados and Soifer, *Hypocrisy*.

5. Runciman, *Political Hypocrisy*.

6. *Oxford English Dictionary* (online), s.v. "hypocrisy," accessed February 9, 2025, https://www.oed.com/dictionary/hypocrisy_n?tab=meaning_and_use.

7. Amory, "Whited sepulchres."

8. Béla Szabados and Eldon Soifer state that the word *hanef* means someone with "a crooked or deceptive heart." Szabados and Soifer, *Hypocrisy*, 21.

9. Geoffrey Chaucer, "The Pardoner's Prologue," in *The Canterbury Tales* (c. 1400), trans. Michael Hallsworth, 6, ll. 403–404, https://chaucer.fas.harvard.edu/pages/pardoners-prologue-introduction-and-tale.

10. St. Augustine, *The Lord's Sermon on the Mount* (393 CE), trans. John Jepson (Newman Press, 1948), 129; A. Gais, "The politics of hypocrisy: Baruch Spinoza and Pierre Bayle on hypocritical conformity," *Political Theory* 48, no. 5 (2020): 588–614.

11. Joseph Pérez, *The Spanish Inquisition: A History* (Yale University Press, 2005).

12. Charles Dickens, *David Copperfield* (1850; Project Gutenberg, 2024), chap. 52, https://www.gutenberg.org/cache/epub/766/pg766-images.html.

13. Cited in Michael K. Kellogg, *The Wisdom of the Enlightenment* (2022) (Rowman & Littlefield, 2022), 58.

14. Szabados and Soifer, *Hypocrisy*; Joseph Butler, "Upon Self-Deceit" (1749), in Joseph Butler, *Fifteen Sermons and Other Writings on Ethics*, ed. David McNaughton (Oxford University Press, 2017), 84–92.

15. Sassower, *The Specter of Hypocrisy*.

16. Laurent and Clark, "What makes hypocrisy?"

17. Benoît Monin and Anna Merritt, "Moral hypocrisy, moral inconsistency, and the struggle for moral integrity," in *The Social Psychology of Morality: Exploring the Causes of Good and Evil*, ed. Mario Milkulincer and Phillip R. Shaver (American Psychological Association, 2012), 168; Spiegel, *Hypocrisy*, 118; C. McKinnon, "Hypocrisy, with a note on integrity," *American Philosophical Quarterly* 28, no. 4 (1991), 323, emphasis in original.

18. "The existing literature on hypocrisy is sparse." W. J. Hale Jr. and D. R. Pillow, "Asymmetries in perceptions of self and others' hypocrisy: Rethinking the meaning and perception of the construct," *European Journal of Social Psychology* 45, no. 1 (2015): 1. "Little research has examined factors that influence the extent of perceived hypocrisy." Laurent and Clark, "What makes hypocrisy?," 117.

19. Szabados and Soifer, *Hypocrisy*, 48; J. Lott, *In Defense of Hypocrisy: Picking Sides in the War on Virtue* (Thomas Nelson, 2006), Kindle loc. 847. Jessica Isserow and Colin Klein note that "it is far from obvious just what the hypocrite's distinctive failure *is*." J. Isserow and C. Klein, "Hypocrisy and moral authority," *Journal of Ethics and Social Philosophy* 12 (2017): 192, emphasis in original.

20. Alicke et al., "Hypocrisy."

21. Alicke et al., "Hypocrisy."

22. Laurent and Clark, "What makes hypocrisy?," 109.

CHAPTER 4

1. In creating this framework, I am indebted to the excellent work done by scholars such as Daniel Effron, Jillian Jordan, Roseanna Sommers, and Kieran O'Connor.

2. Effron et al., "From inconsistency to hypocrisy." Effron and colleagues write about "undeserved moral benefits" (68), but I do not think that the benefits have to be related to morality.

3. Lerner, "The belief in a just world"; Michael Ross and Dale T. Miller, eds., *The Justice Motive in Everyday Life* (Cambridge University Press, 2002).

4. Effron et al., "From inconsistency to hypocrisy."

5. M. Walzer, "Political action: The problem of dirty hands," *Philosophy and Public Affairs* 2, no. 2 (1973): 160–180.

6. Eliot, *Middlemarch*, chap. 61.

7. B. A. Helgason and D. A. Effron, "From critical to hypocritical: Counterfactual thinking increases partisan disagreement about media hypocrisy," *Journal of Experimental Social Psychology* 101 (2022): art. 104308, https://doi.org/10.1016/j.jesp.2022.104308.

8. A. H. Hastorf and H. Cantril, "They saw a game; a case study," *Journal of Abnormal and Social Psychology* 49, no. 1 (1954): 129–134.

9. John Bisognano, "What they're saying in Washington about the Supreme Court nomination," May 5, 2016, Obama White House Archives, https://obamawhitehouse.archives.gov/blog/2016/05/05/what-theyre-saying-washington-about-supreme-court-nomination.

10. Grace Segers, "McConnell says Trump's nominee to replace Ruth Bader Ginsburg 'will receive a vote on the floor' of Senate," CBS News, September 19, 2020, https://www.cbsnews.com/news/mcconnell-trump-supreme-court-nominee-senate-ruth-bader-ginsburg/.

CHAPTER 5

1. Laurent and Clark, "What makes hypocrisy?," 119; Alicke et al., "Hypocrisy."

2. Laurent and Clark, "What makes hypocrisy?," 109.

3. I thank Thea House and the Behavioural Insights Team for their cooperation and support in carrying out this study. The mean age of respondents was forty-five years old; 50.3 percent identified as male, 49.2 percent as female, and 0.5 percent as other.

4. This study was well powered. Corrections for multiple comparisons were made using the Benjamini-Hochberg procedure. Rather than giving a full statistical analysis, I can provide a basic guide to reading these estimates: any difference between groups of more than around 0.2 points was statistically significant at the $p < 0.01$ level, even after corrections for multiple comparisons.

5. Jordan et al., "Why do we hate hypocrites?" There are a few reasons why this happens. We are continually monitoring where we stand in the social pecking order. If others clearly seem to be bragging in order to get ahead, we are quick to knock them down. The statement given in the text could seem less like overt self-promotion and therefore come across as more persuasive. Certainly, it is seen as communicating information about our future behavior. See I. Scopelliti et al., "You call it 'self-exuberance'; I call it 'bragging': Miscalibrated predictions of emotional responses to self-promotion," *Psychological Science* 26, no. 6 (2015): 903–914; and R. A. Gordon, "Impact of ingratiation on judgments and evaluations: A meta-analytic investigation," *Journal of Personality and Social Psychology* 71, no. 1 (1996): 54–70.

6. The differences are not statistically significant.

7. See, for example, Laurent and Clark, "What makes hypocrisy?"; J. Jordan and R. Sommers, "False signaling and personal moral failings: Two distinct pathways to hypocrisy with unequal moral weight," working paper (Harvard Business School, January 2021), https://www.hbs.edu/faculty/Pages/item.aspx?num=59490.

8. Alicke et al., "Hypocrisy."

9. Laurent and Clark, "What makes hypocrisy?"

10. "Hypocrisy involves deceiving others with regard to one's true motivations." Elster, *Reason and Rationality*, 51.

11. Jordan and Sommers, "False signaling and personal moral failings."

12. Laurent and Clark, "What makes hypocrisy?"

13. The difference between hypocrisy and wrongness ratings for these groups is statistically significant at the $p < 0.0001$ level.

14. The ratings are low compared to those of the other groups, but you could also argue that the absolute levels of these ratings are not as low as you'd expect. This scenario was constructed to be as consistent and unhypocritical as possible. Yet the ratings are still around 3 on a 7-point scale. One explanation is that respondents gravitate toward the middle of response scales. Another is that people have a tendency to see hypocrisy everywhere. A final explanation is that people do not like others prescribing standards of behavior for them even if they can live up to those standards.

15. T. Simons et al., "Revisiting behavioral integrity: Progress and new directions after 20 years," *Annual Review of Organizational Psychology and Organizational Behavior* 9 (2022): 365–389.

16. The difference between round 1 and round 2 is significant at the $p < 0.001$ level for both groups; the comparison between groups for hypocrisy and wrongness in round 2 is significant at the $p < 0.0001$ level.

17. *Gatley on Libel and Slander*, 13th ed. (Sweet & Maxwell, 2022), 838.

18. "*Itchy & Scratchy* & Marge," season 2, episode 9, *The Simpsons*, dir. J. Reardon, Fox, December 20, 1990.

19. "Inconsistency is graded and scalable, and any information that suggests greater inconsistency will suggest greater hypocrisy." Laurent and Clark, "What makes hypocrisy?," 119.

20. Alicke et al., "Hypocrisy," 683.

21. Powell and Smith, "Schadenfreude caused by the exposure of hypocrisy in others, self and identity"; J. Stone et al., "When exemplification fails: Hypocrisy and the motive for self-integrity," *Journal of Personality and Social Psychology* 72, no. 1 (1997): 54–65; Smith et al., "Exploring the when and why of schadenfreude."

22. J. J. Ganney and S. Gove, "Reputation and corporate social responsibility aberrations, trends, and hypocrisy: Reactions to firm choices in the stock option backdating scandal," *Journal of Management Studies* 48, no. 7 (2011): 1562–1585.

23. There have been some attempts to distinguish between "direct" and "indirect" or "narrow" and "broad" kinds of inconsistency, but I don't think they tell us much. So this is my attempt to go further. See Hale and Pillow, "Asymmetries in perceptions of self and others' hypocrisy"; and Szabados and Soifer, *Hypocrisy*.

24. Fiona Harvey et al., "Rishi Sunak accused of hypocrisy after backing phase-out of fossil fuels at Cop28," *The Guardian*, December 2, 2023.

25. See, for example, "Oath of Modern Hippocrates," College of Medicine, Pennsylvania State, accessed January 7, 2025, https://students.med.psu.edu/md-students/oath/. You could argue that this is an imperfect example because the terms in these oaths are often open to interpretation. The vow "I shall do by my patients as I would be done by" could be used to justify many different actions.

26. Carl Campanile, "NYC Councilwoman Vickie Paladino forced to explain unregistered Aston Martin with paper tags in driveway," *New York Post,* July 24, 2023, https://nypost.com/2023/07/24/nyc-councilwoman-vickie-paladino-forced-to-explain-unregistered-aston-martin-with-paper-tags-in-driveway/.

27. Effron et al., "Hypocrisy by association."

28. Effron et al., "From inconsistency to hypocrisy."

29. J. Barden et al., "'Saying one thing and doing another': Examining the impact of event order on hypocrisy judgments of others," *Personality and Social Psychology Bulletin* 31, no. 11 (2005): 1463–1474.

30. Laurent and Clark, "What makes hypocrisy?" As Jamie Barden and colleagues point out, this is known as "asymmetric conjunction." Barden et al., "'Saying one thing and doing another,'" 1464. See also Susan F. Schmerling, "Asymmetric conjunction and rules of conversation," in *Syntax and Semantics*, vol. 3, *Speech Acts*, ed. Peter Cole and Jerry L. Morgan (Academic Press, 1975), 211–231.

31. Tim Stobierski, "15 eye-opening corporate social responsibility statistics," *Harvard Business School Online*, June 15, 2021, https://online.hbs.edu/blog/post/corporate-social-responsibility-statistics.

32. Volkswagen, "External environment awards," accessed January 7, 2025, https://annualreport2014.volkswagenag.com/group-management-report/sustainable-value-enhancement/environmental-management/environmental-awards.html; "Volkswagen game day commercial," Superbowl 2014, YouTube, January 29, 2014, https://www.youtube.com/watch?v=S8x7NFYHtm8.

33. Arindra Mishra, "Volkswagen corporate social responsibility," *Management Weekly*, November 21, 2020, https://managementweekly.org/volkswagen-corporate-social-responsibility/.

34. Kalyeena Makortoff, "Volkswagen cut from top sustainability index," CNBC, September 29, 2015, https://www.cnbc.com/2015/09/29/volkswagen-cut-from-dow-jones-sustainability-ranking.html; "Volkswagen says diesel scandal has cost it 31.3 billion euros," Reuters, March 17, 2020, https://www.reuters.com/article/idUSKBN2141JA/.

35. D. Landes, "Ericsson in child labour scandal," *The Local*, May 14, 2008, https://www.thelocal.se/20080514/11762; C. D. Ditlev-Simonsen, "Are non-financial (CSR) reports trustworthy? A study of the extent to which non-financial reports reflect the media's perception of the company's behavior," *Issues in Social and Environmental Accounting* 8, no. 2 (2014): 116–133; *Ericsson Corporate Responsibility and Sustainability Report 2008: Vision, Voice and Value* (Ericsson, 2008), 14.

36. T. Wagner et al., "Corporate hypocrisy: Overcoming the threat of inconsistent corporate social responsibility perceptions," *Journal of Marketing* 73, no. 6 (2009): 77–91.

37. Effron et al., "From inconsistency to hypocrisy."

38. C. Coyle, "Barrett denies hypocrisy over divorce U-turn," *Sunday Times*, May 7, 2017, https://www.thetimes.co.uk/article/barrett-denies-hypocrisy-over-divorce-u-turn-ppqh60lgf.

39. Don't worry: I checked that my mother is fine with my sharing these stories about her.
40. Effron et al., "From inconsistency to hypocrisy."
41. Neil Levy, "Not so hypocritical after all: Belief revision is adaptive and often unnoticed," in *Empirically Engaged Evolutionary Ethics*, ed. Johan De Smet and Helena De Cruz (Springer International, 2021), 41–61.
42. B. Helgason and J. Z. Berman, "Reflecting on identity change facilitates confession of past misdeeds," *Journal of Experimental Psychology: General* 151, no. 9 (2022): 2259–2264.
43. Daniel Effron, interview by author, May 24, 2024, by phone.

CHAPTER 6

1. Lerner, "The belief in a just world"; Ross and Miller, eds., *The Justice Motive in Everyday Life.*
2. J. Stacy Adams, "Inequity in social exchange," in *Advances in Experimental Social Psychology*, vol. 2, ed. Leonard Berkowitz (Academic Press, 1965), 267–299.
3. E. Allan Lind, "Fairness judgments as cognitions," in *The Justice Motive in Everyday Life*, ed. Ross and Miller, 416–431.
4. Effron et al., "From inconsistency to hypocrisy."
5. L. Cosmides and J. Tooby, "Evolutionary psychology: New perspectives on cognition and motivation," *Annual Review of Psychology* 64 (2013): 201–229.
6. "Hypocrisy is, in its most abstract sense, no different from other kinds of competition." Robert O. Kurzban, *Why Everyone (Else) Is a Hypocrite: Evolution and the Modular Mind* (Princeton University Press, 2010).
7. Matthew 7:1–12, New International Version.
8. T. E. Pettys, "Judging hypocrisy," *Emory Law Journal* 70 (2020): 270. Also, "[Hypocrisy] offends against the commitment to the equality of persons that is constitutive of moral relations in the first place." R. J. Wallace, "Hypocrisy, moral address, and the equal standing of persons," *Philosophy and Public Affairs* 38, no. 4 (2010): 308.
9. Darrin M. McMahon, *Equality: The History of an Elusive Idea* (Basic, 2024).
10. J. Rawls, "Fairness to goodness," *Philosophical Review* 84, no. 4 (1975): 536–554.
11. S. Gershman, "Alexis de Tocqueville and slavery," *French Historical Studies* 9, no. 3 (1976): 467–483.
12. Alexis de Tocqueville, *Democracy in America* (1835–1840), trans. Arthur Goldhammer (Library of America, 2004), 2.
13. "By 1791, the geographer Jedidiah Morse could describe New England as a place 'where every man thinks himself at least as good as his neighbours, and believes that all mankind have, or ought to possess, equal rights.'" Alain De Botton, *Status Anxiety* (Vintage, 2008), 31.
14. Tocqueville, *Democracy in America*, 520.

15. Francis Bacon, "Of envy," in *The Essays or Counsels, Civil and Moral* (1597), ed. M. Kiernan (Oxford University Press, 2000), 29.

16. N. Van de Ven and M. Zeelenberg, "The counterfactual nature of envy: 'It could have been me,'" *Cognition and Emotion* 29 (2015): 954–971.

17. Tocqueville, *Democracy in America*, 226.

18. Tocqueville, *Democracy in America*, 626.

19. Baron de Montesquieu, *The Spirit of Laws: Complete Edition*, trans. T. Nugent (Cosimo Classics, 2011), bk. 5, chap. 5.

20. "When we make a moral argument against [hypocrisy], we are making an equality-focused plea for something akin to the rule of law in our interpersonal relations." Pettys, "Judging hypocrisy," 274.

21. E. A. Smith et al., "Wealth transmission and inequality among hunter-gatherers," *Current Anthropology* 51, no. 1 (2010): 2; Storr, *The Status Game*, 13.

22. Christopher Boehm, *Hierarchy in the Forest: The Evolution of Egalitarian Behavior* (Harvard University Press, 2009); Polly Wiessner, "Leveling the hunter: Constraints on the status quest in foraging societies," in *Food and the Status Quest: An Interdisciplinary Perspective*, ed. Polly Weissner and Wulf Schiefenhövel (Berghahn, 1996), 171–192.

23. Quoted in R. B. Lee, *The !Kung San: Men, Women and Work in a Foraging Society* (Cambridge University Press, 1979), 457.

24. Christopher Boehm recounts an episode where a hunter quietly cheated by positioning his net so that he was more likely to catch an animal and get the credit. His cheating was noticed, and he was publicly shamed by the group. Christopher Boehm, *Moral Origins: The Evolution of Virtue, Altruism, and Shame* (Basic, 2012), 38.

25. C. von Rueden, "Making and unmaking egalitarianism in small-scale human societies," *Current Opinion in Psychology* 33 (2020): 167–171.

26. Lee, *The !Kung San*, 458.

27. Richard Wrangham, *The Goodness Paradox: The Strange Relationship Between Virtue and Violence in Human Evolution* (Vintage, 2019); R. L. Trivers, "The evolution of reciprocal altruism," *Quarterly Review of Biology* 46, no. 1 (1971): 35–57.

28. Trivers, "The evolution of reciprocal altruism."

29. M. Gurven et al., "'It's a wonderful life': Signaling generosity among the Ache of Paraguay," *Evolution and Human Behavior* 21, no. 4 (2000): 263–282. "Pre-historically humans began to make use of social control so intensively that individuals who were better at inhibiting their own antisocial tendencies, either through fear of punishment or through absorbing and identifying with their group's rules, gained superior fitness. By learning to internalize rules, humankind acquired a conscience, and initially this stemmed from the punitive type of social selection I mentioned previously, which also had the effect of strongly suppressing free riders." Boehm, *Moral Origins*, 16.

30. Charles Darwin, *The Descent of Man* (1871) (Appleton & Co., 1872), 101–102.

31. D. P. Fry, "Reciprocity: The foundation stone of morality," in *Handbook of Moral Development*, ed. Melanie Killen and Judith G. Smetana (Lawrence Erlbaum Associates, 2005), 399–422.

32. For example, Frederich Nietzsche and Georg Wilhem Fredrich Hegel had this view.

33. M. A. Nowak et al., "Fairness versus reason in the ultimatum game," *Science* 289, no. 5485 (2000): 1773–1775.

34. J. Tooby et al., "Cognitive adaptations for n-person exchange: The evolutionary roots of organizational behavior," *Managerial and Decision Economics* 27, nos. 2–3 (2006): 126.

35. E. M. Zitek and L. Z. Tiedens, "The fluency of social hierarchy: The ease with which hierarchical relationships are seen, remembered, learned, and liked," *Journal of Personality and Social Psychology* 102, no. 1 (2012): 98–115.

36. Von Rueden, "Making and unmaking egalitarianism in small-scale human societies." The existence of the U-shaped curve has been debated; some argue for a "Z-curve" that incorporates constitutional democracies. But what seems to be agreed is that "if a tendency to hierarchy lurks in our DNA, so, too, on the other hand, does an inclination to resist it." McMahon, *Equality*, 33.

37. D. M. Buss et al., "Human status criteria: Sex differences and similarities across 14 nations," *Journal of Personality and Social Psychology* 119, no. 5 (2020): 979–998; von Rueden, "Making and unmaking egalitarianism in small-scale human societies."

38. J. Z. Berman and I. Silver, "Prosocial behavior and reputation: When does doing good lead to looking good?," *Current Opinion in Psychology* 43 (2022): 102–107.

39. Alicke et al., "Hypocrisy," 687.

40. D. A. Effron and B. Monin, "Letting people off the hook: When do good deeds excuse transgressions?," *Personality and Social Psychology Bulletin* 36, no. 12 (2010): 1624.

41. I. Blanken et al., "A meta-analytic review of moral licensing," *Personality and Social Psychology Bulletin* 41, no. 4 (2015): 540–558.

42. This scenario and the results are adapted from Jordan and Sommers, "False signaling and personal moral failings."

43. Kuran, *Private Truths, Public Lies.*

44. Vittorio De Sica, dir., *Bicycle Thieves* (Ente Nazionale Industrie Cinematografiche, 1948).

45. Spiegel, *Hypocrisy.*

46. Alicke et al., "Hypocrisy"; Jordan and Sommers, "False signaling and personal moral failings."

47. B. Rossi, "The commitment account of hypocrisy," *Ethical Theory and Moral Practice* 21, no. 3 (2018): 553–567.

48. Richard Linklater, dir., *School of Rock* (Scott Rudin, 2003).

49. Alicke et al., "Hypocrisy," 686.

50. Alicke et al., "Hypocrisy."

51. E. E. Levine, "Community standards of deception: Deception is perceived to be ethical when it prevents unnecessary harm," *Journal of Experimental Psychology: General* 151, no. 2 (2022): 410–436.

52. K. Bocian and B. Wojciszke, "Self-interest bias in moral judgments of others' actions," *Personality and Social Psychology Bulletin* 40, no. 7 (2014): 898–909; A. B. Mueller and L. J. Skitka, "Liars, damned liars, and zealots: The effect of moral mandates on transgressive advocacy acceptance," *Social Psychological and Personality Science* 9, no. 6 (2018): 711–718.

53. T. A. Kreps et al., "Hypocritical flip-flop, or courageous evolution? When leaders change their moral minds," *Journal of Personality and Social Psychology* 113, no. 5 (2017): 730–752.

54. J. Graham et al., "When values and behavior conflict: Moral pluralism and intrapersonal moral hypocrisy," *Social and Personality Psychology Compass* 9, no. 3 (2015): 158–170.

55. A. Waytz et al., "The whistleblower's dilemma and the fairness–loyalty tradeoff," *Journal of Experimental Social Psychology* 49, no. 6 (2013): 1027–1033.

56. Tina Nguyen, "Conservatives charge liberals with social-distancing hypocrisy," *Politico*, June 6, 2020, https://www.politico.com/news/2020/06/06/conservatives-charge-liberals-with-social-distancing-hypocrisy-304435; Dan Diamond, "Suddenly, public health officials say social justice matters more than social distance," *Politico*, June 4, 2020, https://www.politico.com/news/magazine/2020/06/04/public-health-protests-301534.

CHAPTER 7

1. His full name is Giovanni Battista Fidanza, with *fidanza* meaning "trust."

2. Joseph Conrad, *Nostromo* (1904; Project Gutenberg, 2021), chap. 8, https://www.gutenberg.org/cache/epub/2021/pg2021-images.html.

3. R. F. Cochran Jr., "Honor as a deficient aspiration for the honorable profession: The lawyer as Nostromo," *Fordham Law Revue* 69 (2000), https://ir.lawnet.fordham.edu/cgi/viewcontent.cgi?article=3679&context=flr.

4. Conrad, *Nostromo*, chap. 12.

5. T. Seeley, "Conrad's modernist romance: *Lord Jim*," *ELH* 59, no. 2 (1992): 495–511.

6. Joseph Conrad, *Lord Jim* (1900; Project Gutenberg, 2022), chaps. 1, 3, https://www.gutenberg.org/cache/epub/5658/pg5658-images.html.

7. Conrad, *Lord Jim*, chap. 3.

8. Anderson et al., "Is the desire for status a fundamental human motive?"; C. Anderson et al., "The local-ladder effect: Social status and subjective well-being," *Psychological Science* 23, no. 7 (2012): 764–771; Robert H. Frank, *Choosing the Right Pond: Human Behavior and the Quest for Status* (Oxford University Press, 1985); E. J. Jones et al., "Subjective social status

and longitudinal changes in systemic inflammation," *Annals of Behavioral Medicine* 57, no. 11 (2023): 951–964.

9. M. Wilson and M. Daly, "Competitiveness, risk taking, and violence: The young male syndrome," *Ethology and Sociobiology* 6 (1985): 59–73; Roger V. Gould, *Collision of Wills: How Ambiguity About Social Rank Breeds Conflict* (University of Chicago Press, 2003).

10. V. Griskevicius et al., "Aggress to impress: Hostility as an evolved context-dependent strategy," *Journal of Personality and Social Psychology* 96, no. 5 (2009): 980–994.

11. Anderson et al., "Is the desire for status a fundamental human motive?"; Durkee et al., "Pride and shame"; C. M. Pick et al., "Fundamental social motives measured across forty-two cultures in two waves," *Scientific Data* 9, no. 1 (2022): 499.

12. W. David Marx, *Status and Culture: How Our Desire for Social Rank Creates Taste, Identity, Art, Fashion, and Constant Change* (Penguin, 2022).

13. Storr, *The Status Game*, 11.

14. Buss et al., "Human status criteria."

15. P. K. Durkee et al., "Psychological foundations of human status allocation," *Proceedings of the National Academy of Sciences* 117, no. 35 (2020): 21235–21241.

16. Anderson et al., "Is the desire for status a fundamental human motive?"; Joseph Henrich, *The Secret of Our Success: How Culture Is Driving Human Evolution, Domesticating Our Species, and Making Us Smarter* (Princeton University Press, 2016).

17. Storr, *The Status Game*.

18. "Status enactment is always a plea, a petition, for status is given, never taken." Hugh Dalziel Duncan, *Communications and Social Order* (Bedminster Press, 1962), quoted in Marx, *Status and Culture*, Kindle loc. 1,135. "Status is inherently a social exchange. People will voluntarily confer status to someone only if there is the possibility of gaining something in return." Anderson et al., "Is the desire for status a fundamental human motive?," 2. "Human status is acquired within the context of a social exchange contract of service-for-prestige, which stipulates that group members will allocate greater status to individuals to the extent that they generate benefits for the community and its members." Durkee et al., "Pride and shame," 471.

19. Mark R. Leary et al., "The pursuit of status: A self-presentational perspective on the quest for social value," in *The Psychology of Social Status*, ed. Joey T. Cheng et al. (Springer, 2014), 159–178.

20. Marx, *Status and Culture*.

21. Benn, "What is wrong with hypocrisy?"

22. The idea comes from many disciplines, including economics, biology, and sociology. See, for example, B. Spence, "Job market signaling," *Quarterly Journal of Economics* 87, no. 3 (1973): 355–374; R. Bliege Bird and E. A. Smith, "Signaling theory, strategic interaction, and symbolic capital," *Current Anthropology* 46, no. 2 (2005): 221–248; E. Funkhouser, "Beliefs as

signals: A new function for belief," *Philosophical Psychology* 30, no. 6 (2017): 809–831; Bryan Caplan, *The Case Against Education: Why the Education System Is a Waste of Time and Money* (Princeton University Press, 2018); S. T. Certo, "Influencing initial public offering investors with prestige: Signaling with board structures," *Academy of Management Review* 28, no. 3 (2003): 432–446.

23. Jordan et al., "Why do we hate hypocrites?," 7, emphasis added.

24. V. Griskevicius et al., "Going green to be seen: Status, reputation, and conspicuous conservation," *Journal of Personality and Social Psychology* 98, no. 3 (2010): 392–404; Irenäus Eibl-Eibesfeldt, *Human Ethology* (Routledge, 1989), 308, 354.

25. De Botton, *Status Anxiety*.

26. R. Tallis, "Art world prattlers are now revealed as hypocrites," *The Times*, April 6, 2013, https://www.thetimes.co.uk/article/art-world-prattlers-are-now-revealed-as-hypocrites-g58gwwp88w3.

27. Barden et al., "'Saying one thing and doing another.'"

28. "Some lies are simply lies—telling an untruth does not necessarily involve putting on an act, because an act involves the attempt to convey an impression that extends beyond the instant of the lie itself. A lie creates the immediate impression that one believes something that happens to be false, but that does not mean that one is not what one seems (indeed, people who have a well-deserved reputation for lying may by telling a lie be confirming exactly who they are). Hypocrisy turns on questions of character rather than simple coincidence with the truth." Runciman, *Political Hypocrisy*, 9.

29. The other difference between lying and a false signal is that you may not intend to send a false signal. That's another reason why hypocrisy is not just about deception. You may truly believe you always display the qualities you are signaling. Or you may not be aware of the signals that your haircut and your clothes are sending to others. Either possibility could actually bring you more advantages than deliberate signaling.

30. "The more convincing the hypocrisy the more we blame the unmasked hypocrite." Szabados and Soifer, *Hypocrisy*, 21.

31. T. I. Vaughan-Johnston, "Hypocrisy judgements are affected by target attitude strength and attitude moralization," *European Journal of Social Psychology* 54, no. 2 (2024): 397–414.

32. T. A. Kreps et al., "Hypocritical flip-flop, or courageous evolution? When leaders change their moral minds," *Journal of Personality and Social Psychology* 113, no. 5 (2017): 730–752.

33. Huppert et al., "On being honest about dishonesty."

34. Laurent and Clark, "What makes hypocrisy?"; H. Yu et al., "Neural and cognitive signatures of guilt predict hypocritical blame," *Psychological Science* 33, no. 11 (2022): 1909–1927; Isserow and Klein, "Hypocrisy and moral authority."

35. D. A. Yudkin et al., "A large-scale investigation of everyday moral dilemmas," July 2023, https://doi.org/10.31234/osf.io/5pcew.

36. Laurent and Clark, "What makes hypocrisy?," 109.

37. "In the same way, the person who relates a juicy piece of gossip claims status by indicating that he or she understands what the rules are in the context of the anecdote." R. F. Baumeister et al., "Gossip as cultural learning," *Review of General Psychology* 8, no. 2 (2004): 117.

38. Jordan et al., "Why do we hate hypocrites?," supplementary material.

39. Jordan et al., "Why do we hate hypocrites?"

40. Trivers, "The evolution of reciprocal altruism," 50–51.

41. Z. K. Rothschild and L. A. Keefer, "A cleansing fire: Moral outrage alleviates guilt and buffers threats to one's moral identity," *Motivation and Emotion* 41 (2017): 209–229.

42. "We also find that communicators who make absolute proclamations are perceived as feeling guiltier when they lie, consistent with the inference that absolute proclamations are seen as communicating one's underlying commitment to honesty and general tendency to behave honestly." Huppert et al., "On being honest about dishonesty," 5.

43. Yu et al., "Neural and cognitive signatures of guilt predict hypocritical blame."

44. R. F. Baumeister et al., "Does high self-esteem cause better performance, interpersonal success, happiness, or healthier lifestyles?," *Psychological Science in the Public Interest* 4, no. 1 (2003): 1–44; C. Sedikides et al., "Pancultural self-enhancement," *Journal of Personality and Social Psychology* 84, no. 1 (2003): 60–79; M. Dufner et al., "Self-enhancement and psychological adjustment: A meta-analytic review," *Personality and Social Psychology Review* 23, no. 1 (2019): 48–72.

45. Benoît Monin and Alexander H. Jordan, "The dynamic moral self: A social psychological perspective," in *Personality, Identity, and Character: Explorations in Moral Psychology*, ed. Darcia Narvaez and Daniel K. Lapsley (Cambridge University Press, 2009), 341–354; C. L. Guenther et al., "The authentic self is the self-enhancing self: A self-enhancement framework of authenticity," *Personality and Social Psychology Bulletin* 50, no. 6 (2023): art. 01461672231160653, https://doi.org/10.1177/01461672231160653.

46. E. Zell et al., "The better-than-average effect in comparative self-evaluation: A comprehensive review and meta-analysis," *Psychological Bulletin* 146, no. 2 (2020): 118–149.

47. Alicke et al., "Hypocrisy?," 685.

48. Effron et al., "From inconsistency to hypocrisy." As noted earlier, this paper talks about "undeserved moral benefits" from hypocrisy, but we have just seen that the benefits do not have to be related to morality.

49. Some doubts have been raised over how important or real these "licensing" or "moral-cleansing" effects are. In a sense, this issue does not matter for my point as long as people *think* that some kind of justification along these lines is happening. See A. Rotella and P. Barclay, "Failure to replicate moral licensing and moral cleansing in an online experiment," *Personality and Individual Differences* 161, no. 4 (2020): art. 109967, https://doi.org/10.1016/j.paid.2020.109967; I. Blanken et al., "Three attempts to replicate the moral licensing effect,"

Social Psychology 45, no. 3 (2014): 232–238; N. Kuper and A. Bott, "Has the evidence for moral licensing been inflated by publication bias?," *Meta-Psychology* 3 (2019), https://doi.org/10.15626/MP.2018.878.

50. Scenario adapted from O'Connor et al., "Moral cleansing as hypocrisy," 544.

51. Adapted from study 5 in O'Connor et al., "Moral cleansing as hypocrisy."

52. Oscar Wilde, *The Picture of Dorian Gray* (1890; Project Gutenberg, 2024), chap. XX, https://www.gutenberg.org/cache/epub/174/pg174-images.html.

53. Carol Reed, dir., *Oliver!* (Columbia Pictures, 1968).

54. James Baldwin, *Go Tell It on the Mountain* (1953) (Vintage, 2013), 216.

55. D. Statman, "Hypocrisy and self-deception," *Philosophical Psychology* 10, no. 1 (1997): 57–75.

56. Alicke et al., "Hypocrisy."

57. Z. Chance and M. I. Norton, "The what and why of self-deception," *Current Opinion in Psychology* 6 (2015): 104–107.

58. M. von Grundherr et al., "To condemn is not to punish: An experiment on hypocrisy," *Games* 12, no. 2 (2021): 38; O'Connor et al., "Moral cleansing as hypocrisy."

59. Jordan and Sommers, "False signaling and personal moral failings"; von Grundherr et al., "To condemn is not to punish."

60. Statman, "Hypocrisy and self-deception."

61. Jordan and Sommers, "False signaling and personal moral failings." The private hypocrite is rated higher on the "weakness of will" measure.

62. L. S. Newman et al., "A new look at defensive projection: Thought suppression, accessibility, and biased person perception," *Journal of Personality and Social Psychology* 72, no. 5 (1997): 980–1001.

63. "Two Girls for Every Boyd," *Cheers*, season 8, episode 10, dir. James Burrows.

64. M. M. Gervais and D. M. Fessler, "On the deep structure of social affect: Attitudes, emotions, sentiments, and the case of 'contempt,'" *Behavioral and Brain Sciences* 40 (2017): art. e225, https://doi.org/10.1017/S0140525X16000352; A. K. Steele and I. J. Roseman, "Appraisals associated with interpersonal negative emotions: What distinguishes anger, contempt, dislike, and hatred?," *Psychology and Developing Societies* 34, no. 2 (2022): 175–199; C. A. Martínez et al., "Hate: Toward understanding its distinctive features across interpersonal and intergroup targets," *Emotion* 22, no. 1 (2022): 46–63.

65. If it is helpful, you could contrast this scenario with a self-deceived hypocrite who has power and who therefore elicits hate, not contempt. Think of a dictator who boasts that his people love him unconditionally despite the fact that they are starving and thinking of revolution.

66. P. Schwardmann and J. Van der Weele, "Deception and self-deception," *Nature Human Behaviour* 3, no. 10 (2019): 1055–1061; C. Anderson et al., "A status-enhancement

account of overconfidence," *Journal of Personality and Social Psychology* 103, no. 4 (2012): 718–735.

67. Statman, "Hypocrisy and self-deception." The theory of "self-signaling" suggests that the audience you are trying to deceive through self-deception may be yourself. Self-signaling is "the attempt to convince ourselves that we possess some desired underlying characteristic or trait." Suppose you have two processes going on in your mind, but they are not accessible to each other. Your behavior may then act as an external signal to one of your internal processes about what kind of person you are: "I gave money to that charity; therefore, I must have charitable impulses." R. McKay, D. Mijović-Prelec, and D. Prelec, "Protesting too much: Self-deception and self-signaling," *Behavioral and Brain Sciences*, 34, no.1 (2011): 34–35; D. Mijović-Prelec and D. Prelec, "Self-deception as self-signalling: A model and experimental evidence," *Philosophical Transactions of the Royal Society B: Biological Sciences* 365, no. 1538 (2010): 227–240.

68. W. Von Hippel and R. Trivers, "The evolution and psychology of self-deception," *Behavioral and Brain Sciences* 34, no. 1 (2011): 1–16.

69. B. M. DePaulo et al., "Cues to deception," *Psychological Bulletin* 129, no. 1 (2003): 74–118; A. Vrij et al., "Detecting deception by manipulating cognitive load," *Trends in Cognitive Sciences* 10, no. 4 (2006): 141–142.

70. H. Lu and L. Chang, "Deceiving yourself to better deceive high-status compared to equal-status others," *Evolutionary Psychology* 12, no. 3 (2014): 635–654.

CHAPTER 8

1. This may be a case of "sour grapes," as in the fable about the fox who can't reach some grapes and decides that he didn't want them anyway. The sociologist Jon Elster calls this type of response "adaptive preference formation." Jon Elster, *Sour Grapes* (Cambridge University Press, 1983), 111.

2. That may be because I had never expressed these thoughts to anyone (until now), and so I didn't fear punishment. See J. T. Tedeschi et al., "Cognitive dissonance: Private ratiocination or public spectacle?," *American Psychologist* 26, no. 8 (1971): 685–695.

3. Adam Smith, *The Theory of Moral Sentiments* (1759; Project Gutenberg, 2024), chap. II, https://www.gutenberg.org/cache/epub/67363/pg67363-images.html.

4. Kurzban, *Why Everyone (Else) Is a Hypocrite.*

5. K. P. Mark et al., "Infidelity in heterosexual couples: Demographic, interpersonal, and personality-related predictors of extradyadic sex," *Archives of Sexual Behavior* 40 (2011): 971.

6. A. E. Thompson and L. F. O'Sullivan, "Drawing the line: The development of a comprehensive assessment of infidelity judgments," *Journal of Sex Research* 53, no. 8 (2016): 910–926; G. Brewer et al., "'But it wasn't really cheating': Dark triad traits and perceptions of infidelity," *Personality and Individual Differences* 202 (2023): art. 111987, https://doi.org/10.1016/j.paid.2022.11198.

7. B. F. Malle et al., "Actor-observer asymmetries in explanations of behavior: New answers to an old question," *Journal of Personality and Social Psychology* 93, no. 4 (2007): 491–514; B. F. Malle, "The actor-observer asymmetry in attribution: A (surprising) meta-analysis," *Psychological Bulletin* 132, no. 6 (2006): 895–919; F. D. Fincham and R. W. May, "Infidelity in romantic relationships," *Current Opinion in Psychology* 13 (2017): 70–74.

8. Adapted from A. E. Thompson and L. F. O'Sullivan, "I can but you can't: Inconsistencies in judgments of and experiences with infidelity," *Journal of Relationships Research* 7 (2016): art. e3, https://doi.org/10.1017/jrr.2016.1.

9. Hale and Pillow, "Asymmetries in perceptions of self and others' hypocrisy," 11.

10. K. Wilson et al., "The gray area: Exploring attitudes toward infidelity and the development of the Perceptions of Dating Infidelity Scale," *Journal of Social Psychology* 151, no. 1 (2011): 63–86.

11. G. N. Sande et al., "Perceiving one's own traits and others': The multifaceted self," *Journal of Personality and Social Psychology* 54, no. 1 (1988): 13–20; A. Aron et al., "Self-expansion motivation and inclusion of others in self: An updated review," *Journal of Social and Personal Relationships* 39, no. 12 (2022): 3821–3852.

12. Note that this effect appears only for negative events. The reverse is not true for positive events. See Malle, "The actor-observer asymmetry in attribution."

13. Malle et al., "Actor-observer asymmetries in explanations of behavior."

14. P. H. Kim et al., "A theory of ethical accounting and its implications for hypocrisy in organizations," *Academy of Management Review* 46, no. 1 (2021): 172–191.

15. M. M. Abeele et al., "Phubbing behavior in conversations and its relation to perceived conversation intimacy and distraction: An exploratory observation study," *Computers in Human Behavior* 100 (2019): 35.

16. T. T. Thomas et al., "Phubbing in romantic relationships and retaliation: A daily diary study," *Computers in Human Behavior* 137, no. C (2022): art. 107398, https://doi.org/10.1016/j.chb.2022.107398; C. J. Beukeboom and M. Pollmann, "Partner phubbing: Why using your phone during interactions with your partner can be detrimental for your relationship," *Computers in Human Behavior* 124, no. 1 (2021): art. 106932, https://doi.org/10.1016/j.chb.2021.106932.

17. E. M. Barrick et al., "The unexpected social consequences of diverting attention to our phones," *Journal of Experimental Social Psychology* 101 (2022): art. 104344, https://doi.org/10.31234/osf.io/7mjax.

18. Barrick et al., "The unexpected social consequences of diverting attention to our phones."

19. J. Kruger and T. Gilovich, "Actions, intentions, and self-assessment: The road to self-enhancement is paved with good intentions," *Personality and Social Psychology Bulletin* 30, no. 3 (2004): 328–339.

20. Mueller and Skitka, "Liars, damned liars, and zealots."

21. E. Pronin and L. Hazel, "Humans' bias blind spot and its societal significance," *Current Directions in Psychological Science* 32, no. 5 (2023): 402–409.

22. O. Thomas and O. Reimann, "The bias blind spot among HR employees in hiring decisions," *German Journal of Human Resource Management* 37, no. 1 (2023): 5–22.

23. E. Pronin and M. B. Kugler, "Valuing thoughts, ignoring behavior: The introspection illusion as a source of the bias blind spot," *Journal of Experimental Social Psychology* 43, no. 4 (2007): 565–578.

24. Smith et al., "Exploring the when and why of schadenfreude," 532.

25. V. Iacoviello et al., "A normative perspective of discrimination in the minimal group paradigm: Does it apply to both ingroup love and outgroup hate?," *Journal of Experimental Social Psychology* 109 (2023): 1–11.

26. D. Abrams et al., "A double standard when group members behave badly: Transgression credit to ingroup leaders," *Journal of Personality and Social Psychology* 105, no. 5 (2013): 799–815.

27. Rob Henderson, "What is social status? Understanding dominance, prestige, and power," *Rob Henderson's Newsletter*, June 4, 2023, https://www.robkhenderson.com/p/what-is-social-status; Wrangham, *The Goodness Paradox*.

28. On status, see M. Foschi, "Double standards for competence: Theory and research," *Annual Review of Sociology* 26, no. 1 (2000): 21–42; on tax-filing errors, see N. Raaphorst and S. Groeneveld, "Double standards in frontline decision making: A theoretical and empirical exploration," *Administration & Society* 50, no. 8 (2018): 1175–1201; on men and sexual behavior, see J. J. Endendijk et al., "He is a stud, she is a slut! A meta-analysis on the continued existence of sexual double standards," *Personality and Social Psychology Review* 24, no. 2 (2020): 163–190; on hiring and race, see D. Neumark, "Experimental research on labor market discrimination," *Journal of Economic Literature* 56, no. 3 (2018): 799–866.

29. Shklar, *Ordinary Vices*, 77.

30. Alicke et al., "Hypocrisy."

31. J. Henrich and F. J. Gil-White, "The evolution of prestige: Freely conferred deference as a mechanism for enhancing the benefits of cultural transmission," *Evolution and Human Behavior* 22, no. 3 (2001): 165–196.

32. J. K. Maner, "Dominance and prestige: A tale of two hierarchies," *Current Directions in Psychological Science* 26, no. 6 (2017): 526–531.

33. Joey T. Cheng and Jessica L. Tracy, "Toward a unified science of hierarchy: Dominance and prestige are two fundamental pathways to human social rank," in *The Psychology of Social Status*, ed. Joey T. Cheng et al. (Springer, 2014), 3–27.

34. William Golding, *Lord of the Flies* (1954) (Perigree, 2006), 102.

35. The term *antinomianism* is complicated and has sometimes been used in an inconsistent and pejorative way—that is, as a means of labeling a group negatively.

36. P. Cary, "Sola fide: Luther and Calvin," *Concordia Theological Quarterly* 71, nos. 3–4 (2007): 265–281.

37. John Calvin, *Institutes of the Christian Religion*, chap. 21, accessed January 7, 2025, https://www.ccel.org/ccel/calvin/institutes.v.xxii.html#v.xxii-p19.

38. Daniel Defoe, *Dictionarium sacrum seu religiosum: A Dictionary of All Religions* (James Knapton, 1704), https://archive.org/details/dictionariumsacr00unkn/page/n5/mode/2up.

39. As I mentioned earlier, religious and moral status forms one part of prestige status. Clearly, there are aspects of common-standards hypocrisy here as well—the amoral person dressed as a superior moral being. There's both false signaling and self-image benefits. But I think the double-standards element is the most distinctive.

40. James Hogg, *The Private Memoirs and Confessions of a Justified Sinner* (1824; Project Gutenberg, 2020), https://www.gutenberg.org/cache/epub/2276/pg2276-images.html.

41. Brian Leiter, *The Routledge Philosophy Guidebook to Nietzsche on Morality* (Routledge, 2003).

42. Weiss et al., "Two-faced morality."

CHAPTER 9

1. Jordan et al., "Why do we hate hypocrites?"

2. Szabados and Soifer, *Hypocrisy*. "Slight changes in scenarios could make a huge difference to whether or not they could be characterized as cases of hypocrisy" (340).

3. Jordan and Sommers, "When does moral engagement risk triggering a hypocrite penalty?"

CHAPTER 10

1. J. G. Frazer, ed. and trans., *Apollodorus, The Library, with an English Translation* (Putnam, 1921), sec. 2.5.2.

2. Shklar, *Ordinary Vices*, 66.

3. I'm not suggesting at this point that we become more consistent by simply lowering our aims and making them easier to reach. But that's also an option.

4. Jordan and Sommers, "When does moral engagement risk triggering a hypocrite penalty?"

5. Isserow and Klein, "Hypocrisy and moral authority," 216.

6. D. Sanderson, "Interview on *This Morning* triggered hypocrite Clifford's downfall," *The Times*, April 29, 2014; Max Clifford and Angela Levin, *Max Clifford: Read All About It* (Ebury, 2005), 150.

7. Sanderson, "Interview on *This Morning* triggered hypocrite Clifford's downfall."

CHAPTER 11

1. Gerson, "Trump's hypocrisy is good for America"; Dennis F. Thompson, "Hypocrisy and democracy," in *Liberalism Without Illusions: Essays on Liberal Theory and the Political Vision of Judith Shklar*, ed. Bernard Yack (Chicago: Chicago University Press, 1996), 173–190.
2. Runciman, *Political Hypocrisy*, 3.
3. Zach, "How hypocrisy works," *The Vim* (blog), December 24, 2017, https://thevimblog.com/2017/12/24/hypocrisy/.
4. Shklar, *Ordinary Vices*, 81.
5. C. von Sikorski and C. Herbst, "Not practicing what they preached! Exploring negative spillover effects of news about ex-politicians' hypocrisy on party attitudes, voting intentions, and political trust," *Media Psychology* 23, no. 3 (2020): 436–460.
6. Sassower, *The Specter of Hypocrisy*.
7. Brad Wilcox et al., "Do two parents matter more than ever?," Institute for Family Studies, September 20, 2023, https://ifstudies.org/blog/do-two-parents-matter-more-than-ever; Brad Wilcox, "The awfulness of elite hypocrisy on marriage," *The Atlantic*, February 13, 2024; Eli J. Finkel, "Educated Americans paved the way for divorce—then embraced marriage," *The Atlantic*, January 8, 2019.
8. I used word-deed inconsistency here, but it would also work for word-word inconsistency.
9. Jonathan Haidt, *The Righteous Mind: Why Good People Are Divided by Politics and Religion* (Penguin, 2012), 4, 112. Haidt claims that this dumbfounding happens if the person does not acknowledge that morality has other foundations apart from whether harm occurs—such as whether disgust or degradation is present.
10. M. Baekgaard and S. Serritzlew, "Interpreting performance information: Motivated reasoning or unbiased comprehension," *Public Administration Review* 76, no. 1 (2016): 73–82; M. Baekgaard et al., "The role of evidence in politics: Motivated reasoning and persuasion among politicians," *British Journal of Political Science* 49, no. 3 (2019): 1117–1140.
11. Lee Ross and Andrew Ward, "Naive realism in everyday life: Implications for social conflict and misunderstanding," in *Values and Knowledge*, ed. Lee Ross and Andrew Ward (Lawrence Erlbaum Associates, 1996), 103–135.
12. G. Sammut et al., "The spiral of conflict: Naïve realism and the black sheep effect in attributions of knowledge and ignorance," *Peace and Conflict: Journal of Peace Psychology* 21, no. 2 (2015): 289–294.
13. See, for example, D. J. Hopkins et al., "The muted consequences of correct information about immigration," *Journal of Politics* 81, no. 1 (2019): 315–320.
14. G. Pennycook and D. G. Rand, "Lazy, not biased: Susceptibility to partisan fake news is better explained by lack of reasoning than by motivated reasoning," *Cognition* 188 (2019): 39–50;

G. Pennycook et al., "Shifting attention to accuracy can reduce misinformation online," *Nature* 592, no. 7855 (2021): 590–595.

15. P. Lorenz-Spreen et al., "How behavioural sciences can promote truth, autonomy and democratic discourse online," *Nature Human Behaviour* 4, no. 11 (2020): 1102–1109.

16. Karissa Bell, "Retweets are back to normal as Twitter ends its quote tweet experiment," Engadgit, updated December 16, 2020, https://www.engadget.com/twitter-ends-quote-tweet-experiment-retweets-003202686.html; P. de Freitas Melo et al., "Can WhatsApp counter misinformation by limiting message forwarding?," in *Complex Networks and Their Applications VIII*, vol. 1, *Proceedings of the Eighth International Conference on Complex Networks and Their Applications COMPLEX NETWORKS 2019* (Springer International, 2020), 372–384; Miranda Bryant, "Instagrams anti-bullying AI asks users: 'Are you sure you want to post this?,'" *The Guardian*, July 9, 2019, https://www.theguardian.com/technology/2019/jul/09/instagram-bullying-new-feature-do-you-want-to-post-this.

17. H. Lin et al., "Reducing misinformation sharing at scale using digital accuracy prompt ads," working paper (MIT, last edited March 22, 2024), https://doi.org/10.31234/osf.io/u8anb.

18. L. Jahn et al., "Friction interventions to curb the spread of misinformation on social media," preprint, arXiv, July 21, 2023, https://doi.org/10.48550/arXiv.2307.11498.

19. Braley et al., "Why voters who value democracy participate in democratic backsliding," 1285.

20. K. Ruggeri et al., "The general fault in our fault lines," *Nature Human Behaviour* 5, no. 10 (2021): 1369–1380.

21. J. Voelkel et al., "Megastudy testing 25 treatments to reduce antidemocratic attitudes and partisan animosity," *Science* 386, no. 6719 (2024): art. eadh4764, https://www.science.org/doi/10.1126/science.adh4764.

22. "Tempered expectations and hardened divisions a year into the Biden presidency," Bright Line Watch, survey, November 2021, https://brightlinewatch.org/tempered-expectations-and-hardened-divisions-a-year-into-the-biden-presidency; J. N. Druckman, "Correcting misperceptions of the other political party does not robustly reduce support for undemocratic practices or partisan violence," *Proceedings of the National Academy of Sciences* 120, no. 37 (2023): art. e2308938120, https://www.pnas.org/doi/10.1073/pnas.2308938120.

23. O'Brien and Whelan, "Hypocrisy in politics."

24. See Aristotle's *Rhetoric*, bk. 1, chaps. 4–8.

25. O'Brien and Whelan, "Hypocrisy in politics."

26. Shklar, *Ordinary Vices*, 75.

27. Runciman, *Political Hypocrisy*; A. Rawnsley, *The End of the Party* (Penguin, 2010); Gunn S. Enli, *Mediated Authenticity: How the Media Constructs Reality* (Peter Lang, 2015).

28. Loulla-May Eleftheriou-Smith, "Jeremy Corbyn becomes favourite to win Labour leadership race in latest Ladbrokes odds," *The Independent*, July 29, 2015, https://www

.independent.co.uk/news/uk/politics/jeremy-corbyn-becomes-favourite-to-win-labour-leadership-race-in-latest-ladbrokes-odds-10424088.html.

29. "Jeremy Corbyn wins Labour leadership contest and vows 'fightback,'" BBC News, September 12, 2015, https://www.bbc.com/news/uk-politics-34223157; Rachel Shabi, "Corbynmania isn't dangerous–there's irony in those chants," *The Guardian*, July 20, 2017, https://www.theguardian.com/commentisfree/2017/jul/20/jeremy-corbyn-corbynmania-dangerous-supporters-young-people-labour.

30. Sonia Sodha, "Why Jeremy Corbyn seems like the real deal," *The Observer*, August 1, 2016; T. Peck, "Jeremy Corbyn set out to be a political failure. Now he stands on the brink of success," *The Independent*, September 28, 2017; Editorial, *The Observer*, September 12, 2015; M. Iszatt-White et al., "The 'Corbyn phenomenon': Media representations of authentic leadership and the discourse of ethics versus effectiveness," *Journal of Business Ethics* 159 (2019): 535–549.

31. Iszatt-White et al., "The 'Corbyn phenomenon'"; P. Kidd, "Corbyn on the ropes at end of final round," *The Times*, September 4, 2015.

32. A. Whittle, "Making sense of the rise and fall of Jeremy Corbyn: Towards an ambiguity-centred perspective on authentic leadership," *Leadership* 17, no. 4 (2021): 441–463.

33. John Crace, "The making of the Maybot: A year of mindless slogans, U-turns and denials," *The Guardian*, July 10, 2017.

34. J. Bloodworth and B. Friedman, "A cold fish relishing his red hot moment," *Sunday Times*, August 16, 2015.

35. Shelley Phelps, "Can Jeremy Corbyn crack the whip?," BBC News, October 21, 2015, https://www.bbc.com/news/uk-politics-34554670.

36. Whittle, "Making sense of the rise and fall of Jeremy Corbyn."

37. S. L. Jensen et al., "Lying is sometimes ethical, but honesty is the best policy: The desire to avoid harmful lies leads to moral preferences for unconditional honesty," *Journal of Experimental Psychology: General* 153, no. 1 (2024): 122–144.

38. As I discussed earlier, antihypocrisy is more like a protest movement than a basis for government.

39. B. Cammaerts et al., "Journalistic transgressions in the representation of Jeremy Corbyn: From watchdog to attackdog," *Journalism* 21, no. 2 (2020): 191–208.

40. There is much evidence that Johnson's behavior was an act. See Rhodes Murphy, "John Oliver breaks down Boris Johnson's 'carefully calibrated' buffoonery," *Slate*, July 29, 2019, https://slate.com/culture/2019/07/john-oliver-last-week-tonight-boris-johnson-buffoonery.html.

41. Jennifer Szalai, "What makes a politician 'authentic'?," *New York Times*, July 10, 2016, https://www.nytimes.com/2016/07/10/magazine/what-makes-a-politician-authentic.html.

42. J. Rubin, "Hillary breaking the hypocrisy meter," *Washington Post*, April 15, 2015.

43. Jim Zarroli, "Emails reveal Clinton's mixed relationship with Wall Street," National Public Radio, October 8, 2016; Amy Chozick and Nicholas Confessore, "Hacked transcripts reveal a genial Hillary Clinton at Goldman Sachs events," *New York Times*, October 15, 2016; Dana Milbank, "Hillary Clinton's hypocrisy," *Washington Post*, May 19, 2015.

44. Jonathan Rauch, "Why Hillary Clinton needs to be two-faced," *New York Times*, October 22, 2016.

45. Whittle, "Making sense of the rise and fall of Jeremy Corbyn"; Szalai, "What makes a politician 'authentic'?"; Justin Talbot-Zorn and Leigh Marz, "Donald Trump is not 'authentic' just because he says the bad things in his head," *Time*, October 10, 2016, https://time.com/4519851/2016-election-authenticity/.

46. Jasmine C. Lee and Kevin Quealy, "The 598 people, places and things Donald Trump has insulted on Twitter: A complete list," *New York Times*, May 24, 2019, https://www.nytimes.com/interactive/2016/01/28/upshot/donald-trump-twitter-insults.html; Liz Spayd, "Not 'she said, he said.' Mockery, plain and simple," *New York Times*, January 10, 2017.

47. Kelly, "Why we're all hypocrites in the end."

48. Jacob T. Levy, "Op-ed: Hypocrisy isn't the problem. Nihilism is," *New York Times*, February 8, 2017, https://www.latimes.com/opinion/op-ed/la-oe-levy-hyocrisy-nihilism-20170208-story.html.

49. Salena Zito, "Taking Trump seriously, not literally," *The Atlantic*, September 23, 2016.

50. Although this view is common, the reality may be more complex. See James M. Poterba, "Is the gasoline tax regressive?," in *Distributional Effects of Environmental and Energy Policy*, ed. Don Fullerton (Routledge, 2017), 31–50.

51. R. S. Tol, "The economic impacts of climate change," *Journal of Economic Perspectives* 23, no. 2 (2018): 29–51; R. S. Tol, "The distributional impact of climate change," *Annals of the New York Academy of Sciences* 1504, no. 1 (2021): 63–75.

52. A. Ledgerwood et al., "Flexibility now, consistency later: Psychological distance and construal shape evaluative responding," *Journal of Personality and Social Psychology* 99, no. 1 (2010): 32–51.

53. S. Alper, "Explaining the complex effect of construal level on moral and political attitudes," *Current Directions in Psychological Science* 29, no. 2 (2020): 115–120; S. Alper, "An abstract mind is a principled one: Abstract mindset increases consistency in responses to political attitude scales," *Journal of Experimental Social Psychology* 77 (2018): 89–101.

54. Constitution of Brazil, 1988, art. 196, translation from M. Teixeira, "Health care as a human right: Reflections on Brazil's 1988 Constitution during a pandemic," Center for History and Economics, Harvard University, 2024, https://histecon.fas.harvard.edu/climate-loss/brazil/index.html.

55. Mark Britnell, *In Search of the Perfect Health System* (Bloomsbury, 2015).

56. David Runciman, "Institutional hypocrisy," *London Review of Books*, April 21, 2005.

57. L. Bahia and M. Scheffer, "O SUS e o setor privado assistencial: Interpretações e fatos," *Saúde em debate* 42, no. 3 (2018): 158–171, https://doi.org/10.1590/0103-11042018S312.

58. L. Lavinas, "How social developmentalism reframed social policy in Brazil," *New Political Economy* 22, no. 6 (2017): 640.

59. Bra. Const., title VIII, chap. II, sec. II, art. 199.

60. C. V. Machado and G. A. E. Silva, "Political struggles for a universal health system in Brazil: Successes and limits in the reduction of inequalities," *Globalization and Health* 15 (2019): 1–12; A. Massuda et al., "The Brazilian health system at crossroads: Progress, crisis and resilience," *BMJ Global Health* 3, no. 4 (2018): art. e000829, https://gh.bmj.com/content/3/4/e000829; M. Jansen Ferreira, "Health financialization in Brazil: Some evidence in the hospital sector," *Économie et institutions* 30–31 (2022), https://doi.org/10.4000/ei.7512; V. Junqueira and Á. N. Mendes, "The Brazilian public health in contemporary capitalism," *International Journal of Health Services* 48, no. 4 (2018): 760–775.

61. Sheryl Gay Stolberg and Robert Pear, "Obama signs health care overhaul bill, with a flourish," *New York Times*, March 23, 2010.

62. Office of the Assistant Secretary for Planning and Evaluation (ASPE), US Department of Health and Human Services, "Health coverage under the Affordable Care Act: Current enrollment trends and state estimates," March 23, 2023, https://aspe.hhs.gov/reports/current-health-coverage-under-affordable-care-act; ASPE, US Department of Health and Human Services, "Health insurance coverage for Americans with pre-existing conditions: The impact of the Affordable Care Act," January 5, 2017, https://aspe.hhs.gov/sites/default/files/private/pdf/255396/Pre-ExistingConditions.pdf; "KFF health tracking poll: The public's views on the ACA," KFF, May 15, 2024, https://www.kff.org/interactive/kff-health-tracking-poll-the-publics-views-on-the-aca.

63. Jonathan Cohn, *The Ten Year War: Obamacare and the Unfinished Crusade for Universal Coverage* (St. Martin's Press, 2021), 62.

64. Angie Drobnic Holan, "Obama has praised single-payer plans in the past," Politifact, August 12, 2009, https://www.politifact.com/factchecks/2009/aug/12/barack-obama/obama-has-praised-single-payer-plans-past/.

65. Zaid Jilani, "FLASHBACK: Obama repeatedly touted public option before refusing to push for it in the final hours," Think Progress, December 22, 2009, https://archive.thinkprogress.org/flashback-obama-repeatedly-touted-public-option-before-refusing-to-push-for-it-in-the-final-hours-380cbf31b6e0/; Scott Wilson, "Obama lists financial rescue as 'most important thing' of his first year," *Washington Post*, December 23, 2009, https://www.washingtonpost.com/wp-dyn/content/article/2009/12/22/AR2009122202101.html?hpid=topnews; Chris Frates, "Obama tries to distance himself from the public option," *Politico Live Pulse*, December 22, 2009, https://www.politico.com/livepulse/1209/Obama_tries_to_distance_himself_from_the_public_option.html#.

66. Barack Obama, *A Promised Land* (Penguin, 2021), 377.

67. Cohn, *The Ten Year War*, 72; Drobnic Holan, "Obama has praised single-payer plans in the past."

68. Quoted in Marie Corrigan, "Obama adopts universal health care as policy theme," *New York Times*, January 25, 2007.

69. "Trade-offs were everywhere." Cohn, *The Ten Year War*, 136.

70. White House, Office of the Press Secretary, "Remarks by the president on the Affordable Care Act," Miami Dade College, Miami, October 20, 2016, https://obamawhitehouse.archives.gov/the-press-office/2016/10/20/remarks-president-affordable-care-act.

71. Runciman, *Political Hypocrisy*, 220.

72. Huppert et al., "On being honest about dishonesty."

73. Huppert et al., "On being honest about dishonesty," 4.

74. Elizabeth Huppert, personal communication, September 2, 2024.

75. Shklar, *Ordinary Vices*, 67.

76. Laura Wagner, "It's not about hypocrisy," *Defector*, March 7, 2023, https://defector.com/its-not-about-hypocrisy; Wallace, "Hypocrisy, moral address, and the equal standing of persons." "An ethic of anti-hypocrisy can for this reason be trivializing, detracting attention away from the much more serious (if sometimes controversial) forms of wrongdoing" (307).

77. Ehrenhalt, "Hypocrisy has its virtues."

78. Grant, *Hypocrisy and Integrity*.

79. Runciman, *Political Hypocrisy*.

80. James Ponsoldt, dir., *The Circle* (STXfilms, 2017).

81. Dave Eggers, *The Circle* (Vintage, 2014), 124, 134, 135.

82. David Runciman, "Shklar on hypocrisy," *Talking Politics: History of Ideas*, series 2, podcast, April 20, 2021, https://shows.acast.com/history-of-ideas/episodes/shklaronhypocrisy.

83. Huppert et al., "On being honest about dishonesty."

84. Levine, "Community standards of deception."

85. David Runciman calls this a "tricky double act. They need to be familiar enough so that we let them rule us, but not so familiar that we cease to regard what they do as rule." Runciman, *Political Hypocrisy*, 43.

86. Runciman makes this argument at length in his book on political hypocrisy. He calls the first kind "first-order hypocrisy" and the second kind "second-order hypocrisy." Runciman, *Political Hypocrisy*, 53.

87. It's possible that these kinds of hypocrites know what they are doing, but it's more likely that they are self-deceived and believe their own narrative. Both situations are problematic in different ways. See Stephen K. Medvic, *In Defense of Politicians: The Expectations Trap and Its Threat to Democracy* (Routledge, 2013).

88. Grant, *Hypocrisy and Integrity*. "Prudence, judgment, and the art of politics coexist in perpetual tension with formal, theoretically grounded, abstract principles" (3).

89. Medvic, *In Defense of Politicians*.

90. Medvic, *In Defense of Politicians*.

91. Runciman, *Political Hypocrisy*, 205.

92. "Prudential flexibility remains compatible with integrity as long as political compromise flows from judgment of the circumstances and not from the corrupting pressures of dependence." Grant, *Hypocrisy and Integrity*, 17.

93. Christopher Beam, "Code Black: Of course Obama talks differently to different groups. So do most politicians," *Slate*, January 11, 2010, https://slate.com/news-and-politics/2010/01/of-course-barack-obama-talks-differently-to-different-groups-so-do-most-politicians.html.

94. E. Zell et al., "It's their fault: Partisan attribution bias and its association with voting intentions," *Group Processes & Intergroup Relations* 25, no. 4 (2022): 1139–1156; M. Priedols et al., "Political trust and the ultimate attribution error in explaining successful and failed policy initiatives," *SAGE Open* 12, no. 2 (2022): art. 21582440221102427, https://doi.org/10.1177/21582440221102427; J. Tilley and S. B. Hobolt, "Is the government to blame? An experimental test of how partisanship shapes perceptions of performance and responsibility," *Journal of Politics* 73, no. 2 (2011): 316–330.

95. D. P. Redlawsk, "Hot cognition or cool consideration? Testing the effects of motivated reasoning on political decision making," *Journal of Politics* 64, no. 4 (2002): 1021–1044.

96. D. Westen et al., "Neural bases of motivated reasoning: An fMRI study of emotional constraints on partisan political judgment in the 2004 US presidential election," *Journal of Cognitive Neuroscience* 18, no. 11 (2006): 1947–1958.

97. M. Kneuer, "Unravelling democratic erosion: Who drives the slow death of democracy, and how?," *Democratization* 28, no. 8 (2021): 1442–1462.

98. V. A. Boese et al., "State of the world 2021: Autocratization changing its nature?," *Democratization* 29, no. 6 (2022): 983–1013.

CHAPTER 12

1. M. Plitt et al., "Are corporations people too? The neural correlates of moral judgments about companies and individuals," *Social Neuroscience* 10, no. 2 (2015): 113–125.

2. L. T. Harris and S. T. Fiske, "Dehumanizing the lowest of the low: Neuroimaging responses to extreme out-groups," *Psychological Science* 17, no. 10 (2006): 847–853.

3. J. Jauernig et al., "The ethics of corporate hypocrisy: An experimental approach," *Futures* 131 (2021): art. 102757, https://doi.org/10.1016/j.futures.2021.102757; Effron et al., "From inconsistency to hypocrisy."

4. Alison Taylor, interview by author, May 3, 2024, by phone.

5. Plitt et al., "Are corporations people too?"

6. I. Baghi and P. Antonetti, "The higher they climb, the harder they fall: The role of self-brand connectedness in consumer responses to corporate social responsibility hypocrisy," *Corporate Social Responsibility and Environmental Management* 28, no. 4 (2021): 1216–1230; J. L. Aaker, "Dimensions of brand personality," *Journal of Marketing Research* 34, no. 3 (1997): 347–356; A. Golossenko et al., "Seeing brands as humans: Development and validation of a brand anthropomorphism scale," *International Journal of Research in Marketing* 37, no. 4 (2020): 737–755.

7. Alison Taylor, *Higher Ground: How Business Can Do the Right Thing in a Turbulent World* (Harvard Business School Press, 2024).

8. Pilita Clark, "Employers face a rising climate conundrum," *Financial Times*, June 1, 2024. These demands make sense from a selfish perspective. Remember that people can use your job against you—if there's a mismatch between your company's values and your own behavior. See Effron et al., "Hypocrisy by association."

9. Bain and Company, "Consumers say their environmental concerns are increasing due to extreme weather; study shows they're willing to change behavior, pay 12% more for sustainable products," November 13, 2023, https://www.bain.com/about/media-center/press-releases/2023/consumers-say-their-environmental-concerns-are-increasing-due-to-extreme-weather-study-shows-theyre-willing-to-change-behavior-pay-12-more-for-sustainable-products/.

10. Cindy Boren, "Nike ad sends serious message about equality, opportunity and discrimination," *Washington Post*, February 12, 2017, https://www.washingtonpost.com/news/early-lead/wp/2017/02/12/nike-ad-sends-serious-message-about-equality-opportunity-and-discrimination/; Coca-Cola Company, "Our Purpose," accessed January 8, 2025, https://investors.coca-colacompany.com/about/our-purpose; Chanel, "Our Sustainability Ambition," accessed January 8, 2025, https://www.chanel.com/us/sustainability/.

11. J. Jauernig and V. Valentinov, "CSR as hypocrisy avoidance: A conceptual framework," *Sustainability Accounting, Management and Policy Journal* 10, no. 1 (2019): 2–25.

12. L. T. Christensen et al., "Timely hypocrisy? Hypocrisy temporalities in CSR communication," *Journal of Business Research* 114 (2020): 327–335.

13. "Whatever happened to Tom's Shoes?," *Bloomberg*, April 6, 2021, https://www.businessoffashion.com/news/retail/what-ever-happened-to-toms-shoes/.

14. N. Nemes et al., "An integrated framework to assess greenwashing," *Sustainability* 14, no. 8 (2022): art. 4431, https://doi.org/10.3390/su14084431.

15. A. C. Baker et al., "Diversity washing," *Journal of Accounting Research* 62, no. 5 (2024): 1677.

16. "Don't buy this jacket, Black Friday and the *New York Times*," Patagonia, November 25, 2011, https://www.patagonia.com/stories/dont-buy-this-jacket-black-friday-and-the-new-york-times/story-18615.html.

17. "Good on you: How ethical is Patagonia?," Patagonia, March 29, 2023, https://goodonyou.eco/how-ethical-is-patagonia/; "1% for the planet," Patagonia, accessed January 8, 2025, https://www.patagonia.com/one-percent-for-the-planet.html; David Gelles, "Billionaire no more: Patagonia founder gives the company away to fight climate change," *New York Times*, September 14, 2022, https://www.nytimes.com/2022/09/14/climate/patagonia-climate-philanthropy-chouinard.html.

18. Emy Demkes, "The more Patagonia rejects consumerism, the more the brand sells," *The Correspondent*, April 28, 2020, https://thecorrespondent.com/424/the-more-patagonia-rejects-consumerism-the-more-the-brand-sells.

19. C. Hwang et al., "'Don't buy this jacket': Consumer reaction toward anti-consumption apparel advertisement," *Journal of Fashion Marketing and Management* 20, no. 4 (2016): 436.

20. Joan Voight, "Patagonia is taking on a provocative 'anti-growth' position: Is it all just a marketing ploy?," *Adweek*, September 29, 2013, https://www.adweek.com/brand-marketing/patagonia-taking-provocative-anti-growth-position-152782/.

21. "Don't buy this jacket, Black Friday and the *New York Times*."

22. Demkes, "The more Patagonia rejects consumerism, the more the brand sells."

23. Brayden G. King and Mary-Hunter McDonnell, "Good firms, good targets: The relationship among corporate social responsibility, reputation, and activist targeting," in *Corporate Social Responsibility in a Globalizing World*, ed. Kiyoteru Tsutsui and Alwyn Lim (Cambridge University Press, 2015), 430–454; D. J. Vogel, "Is there a market for virtue? The business case for corporate social responsibility," *California Management Review* 47, no. 4 (2005): 19–45.

24. N. Nguyen et al., "CSR-related consumer scepticism: A review of the literature and future research directions," *Journal of Business Research* 169 (2023): art. 114294, https://doi.org/10.1016/j.jbusres.2023.114294.

25. Wagner et al., "Corporate hypocrisy"; F. Moreno and J. Kang, "How to alleviate consumer skepticism concerning corporate responsibility: The role of content and delivery in CSR communications," *Corporate Social Responsibility and Environmental Management* 27, no. 6 (2020): 2477–2490.

26. S. Scheidler et al., "Scrooge posing as Mother Teresa: How hypocritical social responsibility strategies hurt employees and firms," *Journal of Business Ethics* 157 (2019): 339–358.

27. N. C. Hoffmann et al., "Chain of blame: A multi-country study of consumer reactions towards supplier hypocrisy in global supply chains," *Management International Review* 60, no. 2 (2020): 247–286.

28. "Confidence in institutions," Gallup poll, accessed January 8, 2025, https://news.gallup.com/poll/1597/confidence-institutions.aspx.

29. D. Smith and E. Rhiney, "CSR commitments, perceptions of hypocrisy, and recovery," *International Journal of Corporate Social Responsibility* 5 (2020): 1–12; A. Guèvremont and B. Grohmann, "Does brand authenticity alleviate the effect of brand scandals?," *Journal of Brand*

Management 25 (2018): 322–336; I. Silver et al., "Inauthenticity aversion: Moral reactance toward tainted actors, actions, and objects," *Consumer Psychology Review* 4, no. 1 (2021): 70–82; Scheidler et al., "Scrooge posing as Mother Teresa."

30. C. M. Jung and W. M. Hur, "How does corporate hypocrisy reduce customer co-creation behaviors? Moderated mediation analysis of corporate reputation and self-brand connection," *International Journal of Bank Marketing* 42, no. 2 (2024): 205–225.

31. Baghi and Antonetti, "The higher they climb, the harder they fall."

32. I. Lenz et al., "Can doing good lead to doing poorly? Firm value implications of CSR in the face of CSI," *Journal of the Academy of Marketing Science* 45 (2017): 677–697; K. Walker and F. Wan, "The harm of symbolic actions and green-washing: Corporate actions and communications on environmental performance and their financial implications," *Journal of Business Ethics* 109 (2012): 227–242.

33. Gabriela Salinas and Jeeva Somasundaram, "Business school teaching case study: Unilever chief signals rethink on ESG," *Financial Times*, May 23, 2024.

34. Beth Kowitt, "Get ready bosses: Today's protesters are tomorrow's workers," *Bloomberg Opinion*, May 16, 2024, https://www.bloomberg.com/opinion/articles/2024-05-16/college-gaza-protestors-are-tomorrow-s-workers.

35. S. Baskentli et al., "Consumer reactions to corporate social responsibility: The role of CSR domains," *Journal of Business Research* 95 (2019): 502–513; D. A. Jones et al., "Why are job seekers attracted by corporate social performance? Experimental and field tests of three signal-based mechanisms," *Academy of Management Journal* 57, no. 2 (2014): 383–404.

36. Hafenbrädl and Waeger, "The business case for CSR."

37. Chelsea Ritschel, "Woman claims Coach intentionally destroys 'unwanted merchandise' so 'no one can use it,'" *The Independent*, October 11, 2021, https://www.independent.co.uk/life-style/tiktok-coach-purse-destroyed-sustainability-b1936218.html.

38. Coach, "We have now ceased destroying in-store returns," Instagram post, October 11, 2021, https://www.instagram.com/p/CU6FY_DgZft/?img_index=2.

39. Alana Semuels, "Group has axe to grind with Unilever," *Los Angeles Times*, October 10, 2007; Silver et al., "Inauthenticity aversion."

40. Thomas Buckley and Matthew Campbell, "If Unilever can't make feel-good capitalism work, who can?," *Bloomberg Businessweek*, August 31, 2017.

41. E. Love et al., "Do well, do good, and know your audience: The double-edged sword of values-based CSR communication," *Journal of Brand Management* 29, no. 6 (2022): 598–614; Sophie Perryer, "Sustainability pioneer Paul Polman to step down as Unilever CEO," EuropeanCEO, accessed January 8, 2025, https://www.europeanceo.com/business-and-management/sustainability-pioneer-paul-polman-to-step-down-as-unilever-ceo/; GlobeScan, "About the 2022 Sustainability Leaders Survey," June 23, 2022, https://globescan.com/2022/06/23/2022-sustainability-leaders-report/.

42. Unilever, "Defining a new era for sustainability leadership," April 19, 2024, https://www.unilever.com/news/news-search/2024/defining-a-new-era-for-sustainability-leadership/; Salinas and Somasundaram, "Business school teaching case study"; Steven Downes, "Is Unilever's ESG rethink good business or green betrayal?," *Sustainability Magazine*, April 24, 2024, https://sustainabilitymag.com/articles/is-unilevers-esg-rethink-good-business-or-green-betrayal.

43. Boren, "Nike ad sends serious message about equality, opportunity and discrimination."

44. Gareth Davies and Liam Quinn, "'Hypocritical' Nike is slammed for politically correct ad which promotes diversity despite claims that the firm mistreats its workers in poor countries," *Daily Mail*, February 13, 2017, https://www.dailymail.co.uk/news/article-4220316/Nike-slammed-hypocritical-equality-ad.html; Christensen et al., "Timely hypocrisy?"

45. Walmart, *2013 Global Responsibility Report* (Walmart, 2013), https://corporate.walmart.com/content/dam/corporate/documents/purpose/environmental-social-and-governance-report-archive/updated-2013-global-responsibility-report_130113953638624649%20(1).pdf; Scheidler et al., "Scrooge posing as Mother Teresa"; Karen McVeigh, "Walmart workers protest over minimum wage in 15 US cities," *The Guardian*, September 5, 2013, https://www.theguardian.com/business/2013/sep/05/walmart-workers-strike-us-thursday; Aaron Davis and Michael A. Fletcher, "Hundreds protest against Wal-Mart in 15 cities, demanding higher wages," *Washington Post*, September 5, 2013.

46. Scheidler et al., "Scrooge posing as Mother Teresa."

47. S. Saccardo and M. Serra-Garcia, "Enabling or limiting cognitive flexibility? Evidence of demand for moral commitment," *American Economic Review* 113, no. 2 (2023): 396–429.

48. M. Hallsworth, "A manifesto for applying behavioural science," *Nature Human Behaviour* 7, no. 3 (2023): 310–322.

49. "Starbucks strawless lids now available across US and Canada," *Tea&Coffee*, September 14, 2020, https://www.teaandcoffee.net/news/25387/starbucks-strawless-lids-now-available-across-us-and-canada/; Michael Ko, "New, more sustainable Starbucks cold cups are made with up to 20 percent less plastic," Starbucks, April 18, 2024, https://stories.starbucks.com/stories/2024/new-more-sustainable-starbucks-cold-cups-are-made-with-up-to-20-percent-less-plastic/.

50. P. S. Ellen et al., "Building corporate associations: Consumer attributions for corporate socially responsible programs," *Journal of the Academy of Marketing Science* 34, no. 2 (2006): 147–157; M. R. Foreh and S. Grier, "When is honesty the best policy? The effect of stated company intent on consumer skepticism," *Journal of Consumer Psychology* 13, no. 3 (2003): 349–356.

51. However, I have some concerns about the quality of the studies that make this claim. See, for example, Hafenbrädl and Waeger, "The business case for CSR"; G. De Vries et al., "Sustainability or profitability? How communicated motives for environmental policy affect public perceptions of corporate greenwashing," *Corporate Social Responsibility and Environmental Management* 22, no. 3 (2015): 142–154; and M. Bae, "Overcoming skepticism toward

cause-related marketing claims: The role of consumers' attributions and a temporary state of skepticism," *Journal of Consumer Marketing* 35, no. 2 (2018): 194–207.

52. Y. Yoon et al., "The effect of corporate social responsibility (CSR) activities on companies with bad reputations," *Journal of Consumer Psychology* 16, no. 4 (2006): 377–390.

53. "Starbucks invests in next generation of Colombian coffee farmers," Starbucks, July 10, 2017, https://historias.starbucks.com/en-es/stories/2017/starbucks-invests-in-next-generation-of-colombian-coffee-farmers/; "Starbucks to eliminate plastic straws globally by 2020," Starbucks, July 9, 2018, https://stories.starbucks.com/asia/stories/2018/starbucks-to-eliminate-plastic-straws-globally-by-2020.

54. Taylor, *Higher Ground.*

55. D. Yoo and J. Lee, "The effects of corporate social responsibility (CSR) fit and CSR consistency on company evaluation: The role of CSR support," *Sustainability* 10, no. 8 (2018): art. 2956, https://doi.org/10.3390/su10082956; Love et al., "Do well, do good, and know your audience."

56. M. Hogan, "Kendall Jenner ad uproar 'shows how far Pepsi has fallen,' marketing exec says," CNBC, April 5, 2017, https://www.cnbc.com/2017/04/05/kendall-jenner-ad-uproar-shows-how-far-pepsi-has-fallen-marketer.html.

57. A. Landman et al., "Tobacco industry youth smoking prevention programs: Protecting the industry and hurting tobacco control," *American Journal of Public Health* 92, no. 6 (2002): 917–930.

58. E. Y. Kang and L. Atkinson, "Effects of message objectivity and focus on green CSR communication: The strategy development for a hotel's green CSR message," *Journal of Marketing Communications* 27, no. 3 (2021): 229–249.

59. D. C. Orazi and E. Y. Chan, "'They did not walk the green talk!' How information specificity influences consumer evaluations of disconfirmed environmental claims," *Journal of Business Ethics* 163 (2020): 107–123; T. Wagner et al., "Deconstructing corporate hypocrisy: A delineation of its behavioral, moral, and attributional facets," *Journal of Business Research* 114 (2020): 385–394.

60. Elizabeth Segran, "H&M, Zara, and other fashion brands are tricking shoppers with vague sustainability claims," Fast Company, August 7, 2019, https://www.fastcompany.com/90385370/hm-zara-and-other-fashion-brands-are-tricking-consumers-with-vague-sustainability-claims.

61. S. Kim and M. A. T. Ferguson, "Dimensions of effective CSR communication based on public expectations," *Journal of Marketing Communications* 24, no. 6 (2018): 549–567; Moreno and Kang, "How to alleviate consumer skepticism concerning corporate responsibility"; N. Babu et al., "Hypocritical organizations: Implications for employee social responsibility," *Journal of Business Research* 114 (2020): 376–384; A. Samuel et al., "Unpacking the authenticity gap in corporate social responsibility: Lessons learned from Levi's 'Go Forth Braddock' campaign," *Journal of Brand Management* 25 (2018): 53–67.

62. S. Du and E. T. Vieira, "Striving for legitimacy through corporate social responsibility: Insights from oil companies," *Journal of Business Ethics* 110 (2012): 413–427.

63. T. P. Lyon and A. W. Montgomery, "Tweetjacked: The impact of social media on corporate greenwash," *Journal of Business Ethics* 118 (2013): 747–757.

64. C. Higgins et al., "On managing hypocrisy: The transparency of sustainability reports," *Journal of Business Research* 114 (2020): 395–407.

65. Sassower, *The Specter of Hypocrisy.*

66. Nils Brunsson, *The Consequences of Decision-Making* (Oxford University Press, 2007); Higgins et al., "On managing hypocrisy."

67. L. T. Christensen et al., "CSR as aspirational talk," *Organization* 20, no. 3 (2013): 372–393.

68. Brad Smith, "Microsoft will be carbon negative by 2030," Microsoft, January 16, 2020, https://blogs.microsoft.com/blog/2020/01/16/microsoft-will-be-carbon-negative-by-2030/.

69. Christensen et al., "CSR as aspirational talk," 380.

70. Eric Abrahamson and Philippe Baumard, "What lies behind organizational façades and how organizational façades lie: An untold story of organizational decision making," in *The Oxford Handbook of Organizational Decision Making*, ed. Gerard P. Hodgkinson and William H. Starbuck (Oxford University Press, 2008), 437–453; D. Schoeneborn et al., "Formative perspectives on the relation between CSR communication and CSR practices: Pathways for walking, talking, and t(w)alking," *Business & Society* 59, no. 1 (2020): 5–33.

71. Quoted in P. Winkler et al., "Vicious and virtuous circles of aspirational talk: From self-persuasive to agonistic CSR rhetoric," *Business & Society* 59, no. 1 (2020): 107.

72. N. Brunsson, "Ideas and actions: Justification and hypocrisy as alternatives to control," *Accounting, Organizations and Society* 18, no. 6 (1993): 489–506; M. J. Carrington et al., "Lost in translation: Exploring the ethical consumer intention–behavior gap," *Journal of Business Research* 67, no. 1 (2014): 2759–2767; Rothschild and Keefer, "A cleansing fire."

73. F. Luthans and B. J. Avolio, "Authentic leadership development," *Positive Organizational Scholarship* 241, no. 258 (2003): 1–26; Effron et al., "Hypocrisy by association"; B. R. Dineen et al., "Supervisory guidance and behavioral integrity: Relationships with employee citizenship and deviant behavior," *Journal of Applied Psychology* 91, no. 3 (2006): 622–635.

74. Caroline Webb, interview by author, May 16, 2024, by phone.

75. D. Nyberg and S. Sveningsson, "Paradoxes of authentic leadership: Leader identity struggles," *Leadership* 10, no. 4 (2014): 437–455.

76. R. Oldenkamp et al., "Valuing the human health damage caused by the fraud of Volkswagen," *Environmental Pollution* 212 (2016): 121–127; D. Alexander and H. Schwandt, "The impact of car pollution on infant and child health: Evidence from emissions cheating," *Review of Economic Studies* 89, no. 6 (2022): 2872–2910.

77. N. K. Kougiannou and M. O. Wallis, "'Chimneys don't belch out carnations!' The (in)tolerance of corporate hypocrisy: A case study of trust and community engagement strategies," *Journal of Business Research* 114 (2020): 348–362.

CHAPTER 13

1. A. Gennara et al., "When more is less: Self-control strategies are seen as less indicative of self-control than just willpower," *Journal of Experimental Social Psychology* 106 (2023): art. 104457, https://doi.org/10.1016/j.jesp.2023.104457.

2. M. Inzlicht and M. Friese, "Willpower is overrated," *Behavioral and Brain Sciences* 44 (2021): art. e42, https://doi.org/10.1017/S0140525X20000795.

3. W. Hofmann et al., "Everyday temptations: An experience sampling study of desire, conflict, and self-control," *Journal of Personality and Social Psychology* 102, no. 6 (2012): 1318–1335.

4. D. T. D. de Ridder et al., "Taking stock of self-control: A meta-analysis of how trait self-control relates to a wide range of behaviors," *Personality and Social Psychology Review* 16, no. 1 (2012): 76–99.

5. Katy Milkman, *How to Change: The Science of Getting from Where You Are to Where You Want to Be* (Penguin, 2021). The basic distinction of hard/soft commitment is from G. Bryan et al., "Commitment devices," *Annual Review of Economics* 2, no. 1 (2010): 671–698.

6. J. Burke et al., "Soft versus hard commitments: A test on savings behaviors," *Journal of Consumer Affairs* 52, no. 3 (2018): 733–745.

7. Of course, not every failed pledge seems hypocritical to us. If someone says they will try to do something and fails, that seems like a straightforward case of weakness of will. We start seeing hypocrisy if the person is making a wider claim of consistency, or they judge others, or they get some other kind of benefit from the claim—all the factors in the hypocrisy map.

8. P. M. Gollwitzer, "Implementation intentions: Strong effects of simple plans," *American Psychologist* 54, no. 7 (1999): 493–503.

9. In the psychological literature, these are formally known as "implementation intentions." See P. M. Gollwitzer and P. Sheeran, "Implementation intentions and goal achievement: A meta-analysis of effects and processes," *Advances in Experimental Social Psychology* 38 (2006): 69–119.

10. B. J. Fogg, *Tiny Habits: The Small Changes That Change Everything* (Eamon Dolan, 2019).

11. F. I. Rahmillah et al., "Evaluating the effectiveness of apps designed to reduce mobile phone use and prevent maladaptive mobile phone use: Multimethod study," *Journal of Medical Internet Research* 25 (2023): art. e42541, https://doi.org/10.2196/42541.

12. R. Hoong, "Self control and smartphone use: An experimental study of soft commitment devices," *European Economic Review* 140, no. 3 (2021): art. 103924, https://doi.org/10.1016/j.euroecorev.2021.103924.

13. Arnold Lobel, *Frog and Toad Together* (Harper and Row, 1972), 34–41.

14. James Brains, "This time-locking safe helps me manage bad phone habits—and it's a 'Shark Tank' favorite," *Business Insider*, updated December 27, 2023, https://www.businessinsider.com/guides/home/ksafe-review.

15. A. S. Kristal and J. J. Zlatev, "Going beyond the 'self' in self-control: Interpersonal consequences of commitment strategies," *Journal of Personality and Social Psychology* 126, no. 5 (2024): 804–817.

16. Kristal and Zlatev, "Going beyond the 'self' in self-control."

17. J. Z. Berman and D. A. Small, "Discipline and desire: On the relative importance of willpower and purity in signaling virtue," *Journal of Experimental Social Psychology* 76 (2018): 220–230; A. Furnham, "The Protestant work ethic: A review of the psychological literature," *European Journal of Social Psychology* 14, no. 1 (1984): 87–104; F. Ma et al., "Delay of gratification as reputation management," *Psychological Science* 31, no. 9 (2020): 1174–1182.

18. Kristal and Zlatev, "Going beyond the 'self' in self-control."

19. L. Pearce and J. Cooper, "Fostering COVID-19 safe behaviors using cognitive dissonance," *Basic and Applied Social Psychology* 43, no. 5 (2021): 267–282; M. Mauduy et al., "Fostering victim-defending behaviors among school bullying witnesses: A longitudinal and experimental test of two new strategies for changing behavior," *Social Psychology of Education* 26, no. 1 (2023): 263–274.

20. Priolo, "Three decades of research on induced hypocrisy."

21. L. Rubens et al., "Being a hypocrite or committed while I am shopping? A comparison of the impact of two interventions on environmentally friendly behavior," *Environment and Behavior* 47, no. 1 (2015): 3–16.

22. M. Mauduy et al., "Does the first step of the induced-hypocrisy paradigm really matter? An initial investigation using a meta-analytic approach," *Social Psychological and Personality Science* 15, no. 5 (2024): 529–539; M. Mauduy et al., "When combining injunctive and descriptive norms strengthens the hypocrisy effect: A test in the field of discrimination," *Frontiers in Psychology* 13 (2022): art. 989599, https://doi.org/10.3389/fpsyg.2022.989599.

23. Stone and Fernandez, "To practice what we preach."

24. Ryoo and Kim, "Approach versus avoidance."

25. C. Gauld et al., "An exploration of the effectiveness of in-person and online versions of the induced hypocrisy paradigm to reduce smartphone use among young drivers," *Transportation Research Part F: Traffic Psychology and Behaviour* 82 (2021): 462–474.

26. T. Nguyen et al., "Sweet or not: Using information and cognitive dissonance to nudge children toward healthier food choices," *Economics & Human Biology* 47 (2022): art. 101185, https://doi.org/10.2499/p15738coll2.134565.

27. Jeff Stone, interview by author, March 31, 2023, Tucson, Arizona.

28. Jordan and Sommers, "When does moral engagement risk triggering a hypocrite penalty?"

29. Jordan et al., "Why do we hate hypocrites?"

30. Laurent and Clark, "What makes hypocrisy?"

31. Jordan and Sommers, "When does moral engagement risk triggering a hypocrite penalty?"

32. O'Connor et al., "Moral cleansing as hypocrisy."

33. D. A. Effron and D. T. Miller, "Do as I say, not as I've done: Suffering for a misdeed reduces the hypocrisy of advising others against it," *Organizational Behavior and Human Decision Processes* 131 (2015): 16–32.

34. Jack Malvern, "Extinction Rebellion founder 'a hypocrite' for buying imported fruit and driving diesel car," *The Times*, April 21, 2023; Adam Sage, "Jet-setting Marion Cotillard a 'hypocrite' for criticising Macron's ban of eco group," *The Times*, June 23, 2023.

35. Clover Hogan, "Clover Hogan's post," LinkedIn, video, accessed January 8, 2025, https://www.linkedin.com/posts/cloverhogan_climateanxiety-climatecrisis-climateemergency-activity-7026248940756848640-l4_1?utm_source=share&utm_medium=member_desktop.

36. V. Beck, "Climate hypocrisy and environmental integrity," *Journal of Social Philosophy*, May 18, 2023, https://doi.org/10.1111/josp.12522.

37. Monin and Merritt, "Moral hypocrisy, moral inconsistency, and the struggle for moral integrity."

38. Robert B. Cialdini, *Influence: Science and Practice*, 4th ed. (Allyn & Bacon, 2000), 54.

39. Eric A. Havelock, *Preface to Plato*, vol. 1 (Harvard University Press, 1963), 199–200.

40. Havelock, *Preface to Plato*, 199–200. Some startling claims have been made to explain the change. Julian Jaynes says it marks the breakdown of the preexisting "bicameral mind," in which a speaking part of the brain gave instructions to the listening part, which hallucinated the statements as coming from gods external to themselves. Although this claim seems bizarre and unprovable, Jaynes offers some evidence in support of it. Such a mind is a stark illustration of a divided and inconsistent existence. See A. E. Cavanna et al., "The 'bicameral mind' 30 years on: A critical reappraisal of Julian Jaynes' hypothesis," *Functional Neurology* 22, no. 1 (2007): 11–15.

41. Timothy C. Blanning, *The Romantic Revolution: A History* (Modern Library, 2010).

42. McKinnon, "Hypocrisy, with a note on integrity."

43. W. Somerset Maugham, *Cakes and Ale, or The Skeleton in the Cupboard* (William Heinemann, 1930).

44. Shklar, *Ordinary Vices*, 74–78.

45. Byron, *The Corsair*, 1:265–272.

46. For example, David Hume (a major figure of the Enlightenment) saw the self as a loose collection of impressions and traits. See David Hume, *A Treatise of Human Nature: Being an Attempt to Introduce the Experimental Method of Reasoning into Moral Subjects* (1840).

47. "[The self] is a dramatic effect arising diffusely from a scene that is presented, and the characteristic issue, the crucial concern, is whether it will be credited or discredited." Erving Goffman, *The Presentation of the Self in Everyday Life* (Anchor, 1959), 252–253.

48. Sassower, *The Specter of Hypocrisy.*

49. Sassower, *The Specter of Hypocrisy.*

50. However, some people will be suspicious because chameleons benefit through their adaptiveness. Robert Burton complained about how "a man turn[s] himself into all shapes like a chameleon . . . to act twenty parts and persons at once, for his advantage." Robert Burton, *The Anatomy of Melancholy* (1621; Project Gutenberg, 2024), https://www.gutenberg.org/cache/epub/10800/pg10800-images.html.

51. Bernard de Mandeville, *An Enquiry into the Origin of Honour, and the Usefulness of Christianity in War* (1732) (Frank Cass, 1971), 201–202. I have modernized the capitalization and spelling and inserted paragraph breaks for clarity.

52. Hazel Rose Markus and Alana Conner, *Clash! How to Thrive in a Multicultural World* (Penguin, 2014).

53. D. A. Effron et al., "Hypocrisy and culture: Failing to practice what you preach receives harsher interpersonal reactions in independent (vs. interdependent) cultures," *Journal of Experimental Social Psychology* 76 (2018): 371–384.

54. Richard Nisbett, *The Geography of Thought: How Asians and Westerners Think Differently . . . and Why* (Simon and Schuster, 2004).

55. Effron et al., "Hypocrisy and culture"; Huppert et al., "On being honest about dishonesty"; R. Friedman et al., "The impact of culture on reactions to promise breaches: Differences between East and West in behavioral integrity perceptions," *Group & Organization Management* 43, no. 2 (2018): 273–315.

56. E. Hoshino-Browne et al., "On the cultural guises of cognitive dissonance: The case of easterners and westerners," *Journal of Personality and Social Psychology* 89, no. 3 (2005): 294–310.

57. Effron et al., "Hypocrisy and culture."

58. Iain McGilchrist, *The Master and His Emissary: The Divided Brain and the Making of the Western World* (Yale University Press, 2009), 455.

59. Kurzban, *Why Everyone (Else) Is a Hypocrite*. See page 16 for his discussion of the Müller-Lyer illusion.

60. Kurzban, *Why Everyone (Else) Is a Hypocrite*, 57.

61. Nick Chater, *The Mind Is Flat: The Illusion of Mental Depth and the Improvised Mind* (Penguin UK, 2018).

62. Kurzban, *Why Everyone (Else) Is a Hypocrite.*

CHAPTER 14

1. V. Bambrah et al., “Outrage fatigue? Cognitive costs and decisions to blame,” *Motivation and Emotion* 46, no. 2 (2022): 171–196.

Index

Page numbers followed by "f" refer to figures.